AMBIVALENCE

AMBIVALENCE
CROSSING THE ISRAEL/PALESTINE DIVIDE
JONATHAN GARFINKEL

VIKING
CANADA

VIKING CANADA

Published by the Penguin Group

Penguin Group (Canada), 90 Eglinton Avenue East, Suite 700, Toronto, Ontario, Canada
M4P 2Y3 (a division of Pearson Canada Inc.)

Penguin Group (USA) Inc., 375 Hudson Street, New York, New York 10014, U.S.A.
Penguin Books Ltd, 80 Strand, London WC2R 0RL, England
Penguin Ireland, 25 St Stephen's Green, Dublin 2, Ireland (a division of Penguin Books Ltd)
Penguin Group (Australia), 250 Camberwell Road, Camberwell, Victoria 3124, Australia
(a division of Pearson Australia Group Pty Ltd)
Penguin Books India Pvt Ltd, 11 Community Centre, Panchsheel Park, New Delhi – 110 017, India
Penguin Group (NZ), 67 Apollo Drive, Rosedale, North Shore 0632, Auckland, New Zealand
(a division of Pearson New Zealand Ltd)
Penguin Books (South Africa) (Pty) Ltd, 24 Sturdee Avenue, Rosebank, Johannesburg 2196, South
Africa

Penguin Books Ltd, Registered Offices: 80 Strand, London WC2R 0RL, England

First published 2007

1 2 3 4 5 6 7 8 9 10   (RRD)

Manufactured in the U.S.A.

ISBN-13: 978-0-670-06677-3
ISBN-10: 0-670-06677-X

Library and Archives Canada Cataloguing in Publication data available upon request.

Visit the Penguin Group (Canada) website at **www.penguin.ca**

Special and corporate bulk purchase rates available; please see
www.penguin.ca/corporatesales or call 1-800-810-3104, ext. 477 or 474

For my parents,
Paul and Dorothy

"Sing to me, dear bird,
of miracles far away.
Tell me, is there much evil there, and pain too
in that land of warmth and beauty?"
—C.N. BIALIK, "TO THE BIRD"

Prologue

"What's your father's name?"

I mumble something.

"Open your bag, sir."

The security official rifles through my stuff. I don't know why I don't say my father's real name. I don't tell them my religion, if I pray, what I believe in. Don't say a thing.

"What's the purpose of your trip?"

"Tourist."

Clothes are removed from my suitcase. Empty notebooks. A letter from my dead grandfather, folded three times. A yellow Duo-Tang. The cover is a pasted-on magazine photo of the Dome of the Rock, golden skin shining beneath the fluorescent lights of Ben-Gurion Airport, Tel Aviv. On thin yellow cardboard, thick Hebrew letters: *Yerushalayim.* Jerusalem. A place I've never set foot in.

The security official thumbs through the notebook. The pages are written in Hebrew.

"Why didn't you just say so?" she asks.

I shrug my shoulders. Think: I'd like to enter this place without tribe, history, identity. The idea is ridiculous. I mean, look where I am.

"Now's not the best time to be visiting, you know," she says.

"Isn't it always a good time to visit the Holy Land?"

DEPARTURES

"I have to return to the witness that I am.
And first of all, to the Jew that I was."

—JEAN DANIEL, *THE JEWISH PRISON*

CHAPTER 1

Several years earlier
Kensington Market, Toronto

From the wooden benches we rise, shuffling, dutifully turning 180 degrees to face the back wall of the synagogue. Normally we face east toward Jerusalem, but for this verse we're praying west. Like a drunken geriatric choir we welcome the Sabbath Bride.

Lecha dodi, likrat kala
P'nai Shabbat nekabla

Come my beloved to meet the bride,
let us welcome the Sabbath

There are only fourteen men here tonight, but we belt out the song anyway.

There's Yakov on the bimah leading the way. He's a dentist by day and folksinger by night. He's gone grey and mid-life, talks bitter, a sarcastic jab to the ribs, but when he sings it's gold and you can glimpse an inkling of his soul.

Old Yankl, he's a lion with a mane of white hair, dry and saint-like. He has pale, pockmarked skin. Standing next to me with his open prayer book, his thin blue cat-eyes stare at the red-stained glass above the women's section. He watches the shadow of a pigeon on the landing behind the window. Yankl likes to pray, drink Alberta rye and play the track. Rumour has it he lives in the Waverly Hotel, has since Milton Acorn days.

Next to Yankl is his best friend, the Engineer, droning out something that resembles a bass line. He used to be a whiz of a physicist at the University of Chicago. No one knows where he lives or what he does now; the story goes he lives on the streets. Sometimes I see him in the Lillian Smith Library scribbling in his notebook. He's working on his magnum opus, a book about the relation between quantum mechanics and aged cheddar cheese. The guy's splitting a green suit three sizes too small. The sleeves come up to his elbows, the pants to his shins, and his large belly hangs over a cardboard belt. "I look like a shlump," I once heard the Engineer say, "because that's what the world does to the poor: turns them into shlumps. And, shlump to shlump, you may notice that this once-beautiful Harry Rosen silk suit—which I purposefully washed in the washing machine to get it wrinkly and small—is the suit of Satan."

Behind me to the right is G., a real pretty choirboy's tenor. He used to be a woman. After a year's supply of testosterone pills and OHIP-assisted surgery, G. joined the men's section at the Anshei Minsk. He wears thick black glasses and has a black beard I envy. I don't think that anybody at the synagogue knows G. was born a woman except for me. He confided this to me one Yom Kippur.

"Jonathan," he said in a voice that cracked at the "Jona" and found itself again at the "thin," "I used to be a lesbian." He brushed his beard with his hand as though it were a lint brush and his beard an expensive jacket.

I thought he was joking, using that tiresome pickup line I'd heard once at a college frat party. But G. is no frat boy (although he has confessed his attraction to their barbaric, tribalistic rituals). As we sat on the park bench next to the Al Waxman statue in Kensington

Market, G. showed me an old Ontario driver's licence. Her name was Alexis Wallace. She had angel black hair and Emily Watson eyes.

"You used to be a shiksa," I said. He didn't find that funny.

"It's not my fault my mother didn't tell me she was Jewish until four years ago," he said.

"G.," I said, realizing what he needed was a friend, confidant, brother, *"mazel tov."*

He was talking to me because of my ambivalent relationship to Judaism. Like G., I both love and reject my faith. I simultaneously crave the postmodern and worship the ancient.

G. and I sat on the bench while pigeons landed and shat on Al Waxman's head. A couple of teenagers stoned on mouthwash and nutmeg played "ding the empty beer" with stones. I surreptitiously examined the package between G.'s legs to glean just how good the operation was. Fasting does strange things to the head. Did he have a bris? Was his mother there with bowls of chopped liver and pickled herring? It is, after all, an occasion of joy when a Jewish male is welcomed into the fold. When I was at my brother Joseph's bris (I was six) I could not take my eyes off the mohel's steady hand, stared at the towel dipped in wine to sedate my baby brother. The curious precision of the mohel who wore not hospital white but a lovely navy-blue pinstripe suit. In two deft snips, my brother's covenant was sealed. Then we moved to the dining room, to stuff our faces with chopped egg, poppy seed bagels, cheese blintzes and lox.

I TURN TO MY prayer book and join the other men in song.

Lecha dodi, lecha dodi likrat kala
P'nai Shabbat nekabla ...

When I sing Lecha Dodi, I think maybe it's easier this way, not to fight what I was given, the world I was handed on day eight of my life with a *snip snip* of the *tip tip*. But Lecha Dodi is more than inheritance and duty. The music makes me feel cleaner. I sing it and lose all skepticism, stupidity, desire for the outside raciness of things. That is, until I look at the translation.

They say the mystic Shlomo Halevi wrote the lyrics in Safad, sixteenth-century Palestine. Halevi and his disciples would wander out into the fields singing this song as night fell, greeting the Sabbath Bride with these words:

> *May your oppressors be downtrodden,*
> *And may those who devoured you be cast far off.*

In other words: *May God kick the shit out of our enemies.*

The rest of the song isn't like this. But I stumble over this verse. Why are Halevi and his cohort encouraging vengeance on the day of rest? Why this eye for an eye rhetoric on the holiest day of the week? I imagine Halevi and nine of his buddies in white *kittels*, holding hands, gently swaying in a field in Galilee. I can see two Arabs on their way home from a hard day's work. It's evening, and they hear the ten men chanting, *"And may those who devoured you be cast far off."*

ARAB #1: Good God. What are those crazy Jews doing now?
ARAB #2: Dancing like idiots.
ARAB #1: They're singing to the friggin' wheat.
ARAB #2: Morons.
ARAB #1: Wheat needs tending to, not prayer.

THEY SAY THE JEWS FROM MINSK, Belarus, came to Canada and built this shul in Kensington Market, 1930. Brick by brick, the design is identical to the synagogue they left behind to flame and smoke, blessed be its memory.

See the white chandelier hanging like a crown over the men in this room. And the silver Torah crowns that take in that light. And the paintings on the wall: to be strong like a lion, fast like a deer, words of encouragement in Hebrew. And more: paintings of trombones, clarinets and violins, sounds of my musical ancestors. *Praised be this klezmer, how I wish we could carry a tune.*

And the smell, wafting up from downstairs: Sarah's chicken soup, stale herring, the dust from fluorescent lights.

And the smell of men: sweet and rancid, sweat and mould, meat gone bad before the maggots.

Outside these thirty-foot-high wood doors linger the ghosts of Kensington: old Jewish, turn-of-the-nineteenth-century neighbourhood. Once there were synagogues on nearly every corner. On Chanukah, they say there wasn't a window or storefront on Augusta Avenue or Baldwin Street that didn't glow with festival candles. Gone are the kosher butchers, the Jewish tailors; gone to richer, suburban lives in Forest Hill, North York, Thornhill. Anywhere but this *shmutsik* ghetto that stinks of you-know-where, may those rotten shtetls only be remembered in Shalom Aleichem books. Now the windows of Kensington are sticky with sweet and sour pork, Café Kim cheap beer. And inside the Minsk, these fourteen men. Our lame out-of-time, out-of-tune prayer. Praying for the Sabbath Bride and a free meal, compliments of Perl's kosher foods.

Rabbi Spero is imported from Cleveland. He comes over to shake my hand. A smile on his face, a chuckle that says, "Good to see you, where the hell you been, you schmuck?" He wishes I were a better Jew. Who can blame him? I haven't been here in months. That's how it is with me, one month I believe, the next I don't. And yet in spite of my long absences the rabbi's black eyes are warm with forgiveness. His handshake is firm in a way that makes me feel solid, secure.

Spero's young for a rabbi, forty-two, has five kids and a beautiful wife we simply call *Rebbetzen*. His face as you'd expect: skin Elmer's Glue white and his beard thick from learning. What's surprising is the guy's in pretty good shape, has decent biceps. While two of his children hang on to his shoulders screaming for attention, he continues to pray. They're like monkeys, the two kids, climbing up his belly, his back, hanging from his neck. But the rabbi doesn't get upset or angry. Focused, he bends at the knees, bows his head and chants. How does he do it?

Sometimes I imagine the rabbi in his basement, shirtless but for his tallis, black moons of hair swirling his chest. Surrounded by candles he lies on the dank, cement floor and starts bench-pressing Torahs, five, six, seven, eight of them at once, precariously balanced one on top of the other.

"One more, Rebbetzen," he shouts to his wife. "Throw another Torah on top. This is how strong my faith is!"

I'M LOOKING FOR SOMETHING to make me believe. It doesn't have to be rabbi-level conviction—half a Spero would do. It would be nice to stumble upon a burning bush, a parting of the sea. Even a neon sign that says, "This way to revelation, idiot." Of course, what I'd do with a miracle—if and when confronted by one—is a whole other matter.

I've witnessed one miracle in my life. It happened six years ago in Winnipeg with my Baba Jesse not long before she died. She was in her eighties and couldn't speak on account of a stroke that had frozen the right side of her face. Her smile was a half-smile. Half of her alive, the other half numb to the world.

It had been three years since Baba had uttered an intelligible word. I was visiting with Laura, my girlfriend at the time. We were hitchhiking across Canada that spring and we stopped in Winnipeg to spend some time with my grandparents. It was a warm spring day. Baba wanted to go outside, so I helped her struggle to the door with the walker. Laura was fixing lunch in the kitchen. In the hallway I could hear my grandfather's continuous scribble. Behind a pile of papers—pyramids of drafts, bills and documents—Zaida

Ben worked at the dining-room table composing letters to Boris Yeltsin and Bill Clinton urging radical environmental reform. Earlier in the week he'd ordered vast quantities of canned tomato soup (the day Laura and I arrived we stacked 144 cans of the stuff next to the piano). An environmental chemist, he anticipated one global catastrophe after another; that week it was thermonuclear holocaust.

I helped Baba down the front four steps of the house to the walkway. She inched her way forward, feet stuttering on asphalt. Fifteen metres took five minutes. The lawns of Winnipeg's south end were smiling, winter over at last. While Baba worked with the walker, I read to her the day's news: market reports from Taiwan, financial goals in Australia, long-term predictions for Hong Kong. She loved when I read her the Business section, something I thought odd given her communist sympathies.

We stopped by the sidewalk to sit on lawn chairs. The sun felt good on the skin. Baba stared at me, and her gaze made me uncomfortable. She looked at me as though I were a foreign country. Tried to read me, a language she couldn't understand.

"Is she Jewish?" she asked.

"What?"

"Is she Jewish?" Baba repeated herself, as though to show this was no accident.

"Do you mean Laura?"

"IS. SHE. JEWISH?"

I saw two roads ahead of me.

One road was the truth: Laura was from an aristocratic family in equestrian country, New Jersey. Her ancestors came to America on the *Mayflower*. She celebrated Christmas, waxed nostalgic for Bing Crosby, used lard in her pies and bacon in her sandwiches.

The other road was the lie. I can't say I like lying too much. But I'm aware that lying is also a kind of longing. It's willing the right answer, wishing my grandmother a small measure of happiness in her final days. A gift.

I did my best to meet Baba Jesse's gaze. "Yes, she's Jewish."

"Good," she said, closing her eyes.

This was the last time my grandmother would ever speak.

THERE'S A WOMAN up in the balcony who looks a lot like my mother. I know my mother would never set foot in this synagogue unless there was a wedding or bris. She's uncomfortable with downtown Jews, the messiness of the Market, the lack of elegance in this eclectic hodge-podge of congregants. While I have nostalgia for all things Eastern European, my mother goes to the Narayever, the hippie shul a little farther north in The Annex. My mother has zero hippie in her, but the Narayever is modern, egalitarian and clean. Like her mother, Baba Jesse, she's irritated by the idea of women being confined to three narrow rows on the second-floor balcony. "Women closer to heaven, my foot," my mother would likely say. "Jonathan, this isn't the Dark Ages. Don't you think it's time for members of the female sex to be allowed to touch a Torah?"

Three years ago my mother returned from a vacation in Europe to find my father gone—packed up and moved out. After thirty-three years of marriage, three sons, weekly Shabbos dinners, kvetching, brises, brisket, bar mitzvahs, weddings, shivas, Seders, sukkahs, chametz, Hebrew, tears, latkes, guilt, the Marx Brothers, Baba's pickles, Zaida's mustard, it's no wonder I had dreams the basement in the house of my childhood had flooded. The news swamped the foundations: My father had abandoned ship.

I don't know if my parents were wildly in love when I was a child. By the end, they patiently endured each other. They managed to sweep every disagreeable sentence, emotion and argument under the rug. Everyone was happy, happy, happy. In the eyes of our neighbours and friends, we were perfect—my parents known as the Ward and June Cleaveritches of Forest Hill. We were Conservative with a dash of modern Orthodox. On Saturdays we went to a synagogue with separate seating for men and women, and we had two sets of dishes, milk and meat. My mother spent her days in the kitchen riffing on tradition. Her hand-made potato things tasted more *gnocchi* than *knish*, and her mandelbroit like the finest *cantucci* in Tuscany. Her gefilte fish was famous the street over, as was her cure-all chicken-carrot-ginger-mushroom soup (hers was a nouvelle-Yiddish cuisine, *herbes de Provence* meet the shit-streams of The Pale). My father went to work every day with a humble brown briefcase, drove a humble brown Ford, and attended to ballet dancers and *Playboy* centrefold models with eating disorders at the Clarke Institute. Each morning he went to listen to the problems of the anorexic, the bulimic, the nearly dead.

After my father left my mother, the Jewishness in my family, as I knew it, came to an end. We tried to continue in splintered-off versions. A Passover Seder, the odd Friday-night dinner. But nothing was the same. Judaism is about ethics, Torah and prayer. But more than anything, it's family. And ever since mine has broken apart, I've been left wondering what remains of the religion I've inherited. This is partly why in the last three years I've started to go to shul again for the first time as an adult. I need to touch a fragment of my faith.

Four months after my parents' separation, my grandmother died. With her death in 2000, Baba's "Is she Jewish?" quotient appeared to be in grave danger. My brothers are now both engaged, to a Catholic and an agnostic. My father's living with a Presbyterian. My mother, who wouldn't let my ex-girlfriend Laura stay over in our house five years ago, is heading out on a date this week with a Presbyterian. Jewish Garfinkel blood is now on the endangered species list.

My mother hasn't dated anyone since she was eighteen years old. She called me yesterday evening for some advice. Our conversation went something like this:

MOTHER: What does he want from me?

ME: He wants to take you on a date.

MOTHER: But I just want to go to the opera.

ME: That's perfect. You have a free ticket.

MOTHER: How long does a date last?

ME: Say you have to be home by midnight. You have work the next day.

MOTHER: Midnight? Does it have to go so late?

WE SING THE ALEINU. I bend at my knees and bow my head, belt out the song by rote. I've sung it thousands of times in my life. It's as natural as breathing.

I'm thinking of you, Baba, the miracle of your speech. I'm wondering: Why does the communist who hates synagogue and rejects religion still care if my girlfriend is Jewish? What is this instinct that survives Marxism and the freezing of the left hemisphere of the brain?

Sometimes I imagine my Baba standing here with me in the synagogue. It sounds strange, especially given her secular leanings (and that she's of the female persuasion). But I would've wanted her to meet Judith.

"So you got rid of Laura and got a new girlfriend," Baba would say to me.

"Her name is Judith. And we've been together three years."

I'd point her out, sitting in the second row of the women's section in the balcony.

"Nice eyes. A real Jewess, that Yehudit. What she do for a living?"

"She's a theatre director."

"An artist? Not very secure, but nourishing nonetheless. You're going to have to be the man."

I wouldn't tell Baba that Judith and I have broken up two times already. Wouldn't tell her that our relationship is barely holding itself together, and when the weave is at its thinnest we seem to cling tighter to each other.

"So when's the wedding?" Baba Jesse would most certainly ask.

I TRY TO MAKE EYES at Judith. I want to catch her attention but she's engrossed in her siddur. I make a sour-cat face, cock my head to the side, but I know she won't look. Tonight I want something to overwhelm us. A prayer: *May the confusion of the heart scatter from its chambers.* For a moment it seems to work. Judith becomes beautiful again, the way I knew her when I first met her. Can you see her long black skirt, her river of black hair tied back in a ponytail, blue eyes at prayer?

In spite of our eternal road of bumpy patches, Friday is our night. We come to synagogue to feel clean again. Shabbat is the holiest day of the week for Jews—and lovers. For it is deemed sacred, a mitzvah, when a man and woman make love on this night. Life becomes simpler in the synagogue, connects us to the ancient.

IN THE BEGINNING Judith's hands were doves, two birds Noah sent into the world in search of land. To bring back an olive leaf, a resting place, a sign of peace.

When we fell in love Judith would place her head in my neck and coo-coo me with long fingers. She'd give her analysis of a Bruno Schulz short story while S-curving my back—delightful. She sang "Falling in Love Again" in a deep tenor's voice, read Heine and Goethe to me in German. Judith showed me how to read her palm, and we read each other's lives, the maps of ourselves, love, life, fate. I held her, kissed her thin aerodynamic ears (I often imagined her jumping out of an airplane and breaking all kinds of skydiving records). Once she pressed her hands against my ears saying, "Don't listen to the world outside. Go on, go in."

When Judith was my age she toured Europe as a street actor, studied theatre directing in Berlin. She's inspired me to write with passion, love with appetite, drink slivovitz straight from the freezer. And her dead Romanian father courses through her when she dances to gypsy music, late night over the wooden floors of the bakery we live above in Kensington Market.

I watch her read the English translation of prayers, following carefully with her index finger. She reads the words in her prayer book with the kind of awe someone has when first falling in love. Judith was not brought up with religion. Her mother, a Holocaust survivor, despised all things Jewish when Judith was a kid. It was only a few years before we met that Judith came to embrace her past. Now she wants to know more, learn the heritage she was refused.

She loves that I can speak Hebrew, is amazed by the fact I went to Bialik, a Labour Zionist day school in Toronto. From ages five to thirteen I studied everything that has been denied Judith: Jewish history and Israeli literature, Tanakh and Hebrew grammar. She constantly asks me questions. How can one be a Zionist but not be religious? Why do we face west when we sing the second-to-last stanza of Lecha Dodi? What is the Balfour Declaration? Why the shattered glass at a wedding?

We fell in love when I was twenty-six, lying on the purple dyed cotton of her Romanian grandmother's *plapuma*, sewn silver to reflect the light. We spent the first winter unemployed, reading to each other from a book whose name we did not know. *Madrigals*, we named it, an obscure surrealist novella by a writer whose name and title were torn off the cover (we found the book at a garage sale). Our voices became the words of that unknown author. She read me the story of the watchmaker who took his grandson to a beach in Tel Aviv. The grandson wanted to learn how to fly. The grandfather stared out at the horizon of sea, his grey eyes stained silver. Led by three balloons in his hand, the grandson suddenly left the earth and drifted over the Mediterranean.

"We create the reality we desire," announced the watchmaker, following the arc of his grandson's flight.

When I fell asleep I found myself flying too, so I wasn't sure if it was the book I was hearing or Judith I was following. I'd never dreamt of flight, not even as a child. But there I was, between waking and dreaming, the soft cadences of Judith's voice and the unknown passages of the book, soaring over a country I'd never been to, had only seen in films and textbooks.

That winter she proposed we travel. "We could go to Jerusalem." And the idea of the city glistened.

In the minds of lovers, boundaries break down, the walled-in thoughts seep under doors and a dream may be shared. The night she proposed the journey, we fell asleep reading *Madrigals* to each other, dreaming the same dream. The two of us, walking hand in hand, through the ancient walled city of David. Neither of us had ever been before.

WE'RE GETTING TOWARD the end of the service. The men are hungry, the smell of chicken almost overdone. Two women descend into the basement to make sure all is in order in the kitchen. Judith covers her mouth with her prayer book as though she were kissing its pages, looks at me from the corner of her eyes behind black-rimmed glasses. When I catch her, she turns away, pretends to concentrate on the book.

She's pissed at me. Four weeks ago I received a phone call from a theatre director in Israel who said that if I could come up with a good-enough proposal, he'd land me a playwright residency for a Tel Aviv theatre. *If* the proposal is good enough. The board wants something Jewish, Barak (the director) wants something with a broader universal appeal. "The catch," Barak explained to me over the telephone in his thick Israeli accent, "is to get it past the shit-for-brains board, while keeping me intrigued."

When I told Judith about the offer, she was thrilled, thinking we could fulfill the original dream. But she heard something wrong in my voice.

"Do you not want me to come with?" she asked.

I said nothing. Felt only confusion.

Aside from the fact I have yet to come up with a proposal Barak likes, there's another question that nags at me. Do I want to go to Israel? I've managed to avoid the place for thirty years and don't feel I've been lacking for it. I do not pine for Israel the way the rabbi longs for it as a place of study and spiritual revelation. Friends of mine have travelled there for free on "birthright" trips. Others have fought in the army, become Orthodox, thought they were messiahs. I have done nothing of the sort.

Bialik taught me the borders of Israel as understood by its former citizens—my teachers. For nine years I drew one map of the country after another each day in class: for Bible studies, geography, literature and history. I can draw the country by heart. As a child the maps I drew had borders that never varied—they were learned by rote as the teacher outlined the country on the blackboard, and we were expected to draw the same maps in our books. The eastern border was always the Jordan River.

I had dreams of these illustrations, my ballpoint pen tracing the lines, borders, cities, rivers, ink transforming itself magically into landscape. In my mind, I've already been to Israel.

Of course I knew I'd go to Israel at some point in my life. A Jew in the Diaspora grows up with this assumption: One must visit, *eventually*. Three years ago Judith proposed a new Jerusalem. It was a city different from the one I'd been taught as a child and this appealed to me—I could see Israel on my terms as an adult. But the promise of travel became the unwritten covenant of Judith and me: our destiny bound to Jerusalem. Whether or not we made it to Israel became the standard by which we measured our relationship's success. I certainly never intended it that way. I only wanted to visit the damn place.

Judith still talks about Israel as though it were some kind of holy mission, a life or death pilgrimage. She wants us to get married by the Kotel, the Western Wall in Jerusalem. Me? When she mentions the word *Israel*, I want to run, tear through a forest, bury my head in the ground. Forget the place even exists.

JUDITH PRAYS, the rabbi prays, Yankl picks his teeth. G. adjusts his crotch. Yitzhak, a black-and-white photographer who likes to capture people when they're sleeping, is himself asleep on the back wooden bench, snoring. What a gang we are. Often the rabbi brings in guest speakers to try to attract fresh blood to the withered downtown Jewish community. Today the rabbi introduces a guest speaker from the such-and-such settlement, West Bank. His name is Yosef and he wears thick glasses. His voice is unwavering, New Jersey solid.

"Ladies and gentlemen, I will keep my sermon brief. I know you are all hungry and ready for the Shabbos meal downstairs, and *Baruch Hashem*, I am told some great gefilte fish awaits us. Jews of Toronto, we need your support. Prime Minister Sharon, once a great prophet who believed in building the land of Israel, now talks about pulling out of Gaza. But to pull out now is a message that says, 'Terror, you have won. Fear, you're stronger than our faith.'"

I'm not sure why he's speaking to this congregation. As a kid I used to walk up and down Ava Road in Forest Hill, keeping an inventory of luxury cars in the Holy Blossom parking lot on Yom Kippur. One September I counted fifty-two Mercedes, thirty-four Jaguars and twenty-nine BMWs. Needless to say, if Yosef were giving this same speech at Holy B., he'd be guaranteed an audience that could generate at least a few grand. Easy. Farther north, at Bathurst and Wilson—known among some Toronto Jews as "The Gaza Strip"—thousands of Orthodox types would gladly offer their support, financially, politically and otherwise. Here in the downtown shul? Yitzhak adjusts the cap on his head. The Engineer farts. Yosef continues to speak.

"Remember the land of the Book! When I drive through Samaria and Judea, it brings me great joy to know that Abraham had a vision here, that Jacob had a dream there, and Sampson slaughtered Philistines in the name of our merciful Lord. We've waited two thousand years. We've suffered and continue to suffer for our beliefs. Do not forget Israel: our heart, our soul and our blood."

"Amen!" shouts the rabbi.

"Amen!" says everyone else.

Yitzhak continues to snore.

"I'm not asking for money. What I want is your faith. God can tell when you waver! God can tell when you are uncertain! Let's pray with conviction. Hashem, protect us from the anti-Semites in Europe and the anti-Semites in the Middle East."

The men's responses come out scattered, out of sync. "Yeshekoach. Ah-men."

"This Sunday afternoon, we'll be praying outside the Minsk at three," announces Yosef. "Join us in solidarity."

"'Adon Olam,'" announces the rabbi. "Everyone sing."

Yitzhak awakes in time to join us for a rousing "Adon Olam." On the way downstairs, the Engineer flips through a pile of leaflets for the solidarity prayer. I glance at the leaflet, feign interest and continue on my way.

WE ANTICIPATE greasy chicken soup bombarded with heavy dill pickles. And more: *lokshn, schmalz,* kidney beans drowned in vinegar, coleslaw with enough sugar to kill a pancreas. Yankl walks around the tables, doling out shots of whisky and vodka.

"Schnapps?" he asks. I comply. Yankl leans over and whispers into my ear, "You know, it's been a long time since we've had a wedding here." He smells like he lives in an aquarium of whisky.

"I know."

"I'll pay for it."

"I'll think about it."

"The problem with you poets is you don't know how to think. Take Milton Acorn. Every morning he said he was checking out of the Waverly. Every night he paid for his room. For ten years he pays a nightly rate. Why are poets such morons?"

"Shabbat shalom," Judith says, sitting beside me. Yankl continues serving the rest of the table. There are more people here to eat than there were to pray.

"Gut Shabbos," I reply. We can't kiss. We can't even shake hands because we're in public and we're not married.

"How was it?" I ask.

"Good," she says. "I enjoyed praying tonight. I got into it."

She likes synagogue, wants us to be coming more often.

"How'd you enjoy it?"

"Fifty-fifty," I say, which is fairly honest.

"Fifty-fifty? What do you mean?"

"I like it when I sing, but I don't like it when I look at what the words mean."

"What's wrong with the words?"

"I don't want to get into it right now."

Yosef sits next to me at the table. I nod to him, "Gut Shabbos." I don't know what to make of his speech. For all of Judith's awe for my education, my knowledge is locked in a time capsule. Since the age of fourteen I've avoided reading much of anything about Israel. When I see an article in the paper, a picture of a bus bombing, a teenage boy with a stone in his hand, my eyes glaze over. "Oh, that again," I say to myself. The Eternal Mess.

Of course I'm aware of Israel on some level. Israel is a given: It was given to me. But I'd rather not think about it too much. I never choose to bring it up in conversation. It's too volatile. If it comes up at a family dinner, I try to excuse myself from the table; I once hid in the bathroom for twenty minutes until a heated discussion blew over. Certain friendships have become impossible simply because of this issue. Also, it's assumed you have an opinion on the subject— everyone's an expert. I admit it, I find Israel endlessly confusing. Do I agree with Yosef's speech? I have no idea what to think, and I don't know enough to say. Besides, tonight I have to put any negative thoughts out of my head. It's the Shabbat, a night for celebration, not criticism. And who am I to criticize? I don't live in Israel. I haven't even been there.

My father and I rarely talked about Israel when I was a kid. During High Holidays the synagogue president, Eddie Kreplachsky, would stand in front of our small congregation, Beit Haminyan, and deliver a sermon on the need to buy Israeli bonds. We were there for Kol Nidre, to pray for our souls to be inscribed in the Book of Life. Before the davening began, little navy and royal-blue cardboard cards were passed out. Numbers inscribed in small, separate ridges at the top looked like the candles of a menorah. Each flame had a figure to fold over—100, 250, 500 or 1000. "Times are tough over there," Kreplachsky would say. The men's section would nod their heads, and the women's section, seated on the opposite side of the gym (we were a wandering, nomadic shul) would nod too, almost in unison, so the congregants' heads were a kind of song, man and woman, a choir of consent. "Times are tough over there," Kreplachsky would intone again, and the task of donating money was as important as praying to God. My father would let me fold over one of the flames—I wanted to do a thousand, he insisted on a more modest amount. Neither he nor I longed to be *over there*. He sent me to Bialik, not with the hopes of me moving to Israel, but simply so I could receive a Jewish education. We were perfectly content with our lives in Canada. Yet he always gave money, and I believed in that giving. What would Jews be without the State of Israel? And should times in the Diaspora ever turn bad—for a Jew is never completely safe—there was always Israel to go to. Yerushalayim, our safety net, eternal refuge. In the meantime, to know it was there, to help, this was enough. Our Zionist prayer.

THE RABBI HOLDS two challahs in the air. He hoists them like an athlete holds a trophy to the sky. He closes his eyes, recites the blessing and rubs one loaf against the other. The rabbi proceeds to tear the delicate braided bread into giant clumps. Each piece is dipped in salt to remind us of our tears when we lost the temple, our constant exile. Like a Little League batting coach, the rabbi whips pieces of bread at all those seated at the table. A piece falls onto Yitzhak's plate, another pelts Yankl's face, grazes my left hand, lands on Judith's lap. This is a distinctly Minsker tradition.

"Barak called," says Judith after she's taken a bite of the bread. "Says he needs to talk to you."

"Thanks," I say, "I'll give him a call."

"What's up?"

"He emailed me yesterday. He didn't like the proposal."

"Why not?"

"Too North American. Too easy or too obvious. I can't remember the words he used."

"You know I could come and live in Tel Aviv for a few months."

"What would you do?"

"I could study Hebrew. Maybe even take some Bible classes." Judith plays with the plastic cutlery—a fork. She starts to bend it.

Yosef leans in to our conversation and says in a strong New Jersey accent, "Did I hear someone say Tel Aviv?"

"We're thinking of going," Judith says.

"Wonderful," says Yosef.

"First I have to come up with an idea that's going to get me there. Then we can talk about Tel Aviv," I say.

Yosef asks, "What sort of idea?"

I rub my eyes as though I had glasses. Judith does the talking. "Jonathan's a playwright. He might work in Israel at a theatre if he comes up with a good-enough concept."

"That's a big *if*," I say.

"How about a play about the Gaza withdrawal?" Yosef scratches a zit on the end of his nose.

"Right," I say sarcastically. "A musical."

"Why not?" says Yosef. "A Jew can do anything." He leans closer toward me. "Isn't it strange—the number of Nobel Prize winners— how many of them are Jews? Just take a look at history. Freud. Einstein. Even Jesus was a Jew." Yosef puts his hand on my shoulder. "You worry too much. Don't. I have a good feeling about you. Israel is going to make you into a great playwright." He takes back a shot of schnapps and turns to Judith. "You two should come in spring. It's the nicest time of year. You can stay at my house for Pesach."

"Thanks," I say.

"It's a pebble in the ocean compared to the generosity of Hashem."

Judith: "Neither of us has ever been."

"*Oy gevalt.* Never to the Holy Land?"

"It hasn't been the right time," I say.

Judith breaks the fork in two. She holds a part in each hand. One is smaller than the other.

Yosef shoos my words away with his hands. "It's always the right time." He takes back another shot of rye; he's made friends with the ten-year-old bottle of Crown Royal Yankl left at our end of the table. "We have great programs for first-timers. You can come and work in the Negev, plant trees for the JNF."

"Thank you," I say. "We'll be sure to look into it."

Yosef shrugs his shoulders and dips a piece of challah into his soup. "When I stand in a field and look down into a valley, I think, this is the land God has chosen for us. If not for His mercy, if not for His election, what would we be?" Yosef waits for Judith or me to reply. Judith takes a sip of vodka, and I indulge in some rye. "We wouldn't be chosen. We'd be like all the other nations of the earth."

Judith nods. I look down at my feet. Yosef opens up the ArtScroll Siddur to show us that oft-repeated prayer, the Aleinu. The English translation reads:

It is our duty to praise the master of all
To ascribe greatness to the Molder of primeval creation
For He has not made us like the nations of the lands
And has not emplaced us like the families of the earth

Yosef says, "In other words, Dear God, thanks for not making us like those stupid goys." He cackles, takes back another Crown Royal.

I always liked that prayer. How one bows at the knees exactly when the words command, concluding the service with a gesture of humility. Yosef goes on to tell us about Palestine before the Jews: a land full of disease and disorder when we weren't at its helm. Now the Negev flourishes. Imagine, a nation that grows fruit in the desert, turns salt water into fresh! Who but the Jewish people? I look at the English translation again. One shouldn't put too much stock in the meaning of words.

CHAPTER 2

I'm six years old and I'm one of the chosen people. So my mother tells me.

MOTHER: You've been chosen by God.

SHALOM: What does God want me to do?

MOTHER: He wants you to be a good Jew.

SHALOM: Why does God care about me?

MOTHER: This is the miracle of the nameless Almighty. He cares about little pishers like Shalom Garfinkel.

SHALOM: Do you think God would mind if I'm a cosmonaut?

MOTHER: It depends on whether you're a good Jew or not.

SHALOM: Laika isn't a Jew.

MOTHER: Who's Laika?

SHALOM: Laika is a dog. The Russians sent her to outer space in her own private space ship.

MOTHER: You're not a dog, Shalom. Consider yourself lucky.

SHALOM: I'm not lucky. Laika is still in outer space. I'm stuck here!

MOTHER: Well you're going to an even more special place than Laika. Because you've been accepted. *Chosen.*

I eye my mother mistrustfully. Like God in the Torah, my mother has a very specific notion of what a special place is, one that likely differs from my notions of paradise. Heaven for me is to live in outer space like Laika the Moscavite Mutt who was sent up in the Sputnik II rocket. They say she never returned because the Russian engineers hadn't figured out a way to make spaceships come back to earth. I have my doubts. I think the Russian scientists actually had a way to get Laika to return, but she simply didn't want to. Laika *chose* to leave the orbit of this planet to seek better, sunnier destinations. "Hello, Laika!" I sometimes wave from my bedroom window. "Can you see me down here? How blue is the world? How blurry are the stars? And how is the orange Tang?"

I think about God, and I think about Laika. At least Laika has a name I can say. I even have a picture of her. That's more than I can say for the Nameless Whatever.

If I can't live in outer space, my second-best paradise would be to become the starting centre-fielder for the St. Louis Cardinals. I've never been to St. Louis, but my dad says it's got good stadium grass, and that's what's important. "You need good grass," he once explained, "for preservation of the knees, a true hop of the ball."

I look at my mother's sesame-brown eyes and curly brown hair. She may as well be God herself. After all, she's created the heavens and the earth, named all the plants and the animals. Now she's chosen where I'm to spend the next nine years of my life.

MOTHER: Bialik Hebrew Day School.
SHALOM: Is this where I'm going to study to be a cosmonaut?
MOTHER: You can be whatever you want, Shalom. As long as it's
         Jewish.

I cling to my mother's tough, fleshy palm. The sight of the school—its sallow brick and concrete, the parking lot they call a playground—burrows a hole in my stomach. This is not the Jewish space station I had imagined.

The building's only three storeys high but it's massive—like an entire country, foreign and hostile. The windows are narrow, long and filthy. Here, no one is allowed to watch things. "Thou shalt not lose thine eyes in worldly events!" say those windows.

Zionism, I think the building says.

I have no idea what the word means.

My mother taught me to ride a bicycle this past summer—guiding then pushing then letting go. I did not notice her absence as I careened south down Vesta Drive, rows of maple and pine flashing beside my eyes like the movie trailer of my life. Today I'm not letting go of her. There's no hope for speed, no death-defying balance to achieve. We walk toward the front doors of the school. Rain pitter-patters in small puddles beneath my rubber boots. The red and white flag of Canada and the blue and white flag of Israel stand wrapped together, soggy from the morning's rain.

Three times my mother tries to let go of my hand.

"You're strong," she says, "when you want to be."

I close my eyes and make two prayers.

1. May these hallways be decked with astrolabs and rare and exciting views of the cosmos.
2. If prayer #1 is beyond the means of the school, I'll settle for God instead.

(That is, if I can't meet Laika, I'd like to meet The Big Guy.)

I let go of my mother's hand.

Your mission, Shalom Garfinkel, should you choose to accept it, lies within these walls. I turn on my imaginary walkie-talkie and listen to its static. *Chhhh, Bialik,* I say to my right hand clenched in a fist. Nothing happens. *Bialik,* I utter to my thumb, pointing it like an antenna to the sky. The word is foreign but not alien. *Bialik,* I say, one more time. And a metal-framed glass door swings open.

"Come inside," sings the voice of a woman holding open the door.

An enormous mole marks her chin. The mole makes me think of my great-grandmother's tombstone in Winnipeg—black and terrible and impossible not to look at. A long red hair grows out of it and I have the urge to pull it out.

"My child, you don't want to get sick now, do you?"

She continues to hold the door open. It rains harder and we're both getting wet. She wears a creamy white blouse. I can see her missile-like breasts pointing at me thanks to generous splashes of rain. Is she God?

"Get inside!" she commands.

I enter quickly, the sound of glass and metal banging behind me. I walk toward the yellow walls and fluorescent lights, guided by the smell of Mrs. Blintzkrieg's rose-perfumed sweat.

CHAPTER 3

I'm on my way to the Cumberland Cinema. It's a warm September day, midway through the Toronto International Film Festival. I don't normally go to films at the fest. At twenty bucks a pop, it's become an exclusive affair. But this film caught my eye and it's gotten a lot of press. *Divine Intervention,* made by a Palestinian director. I figure: I'm thinking to go to Israel to write. I should at least try to educate myself. Why not start with a movie?

On my way to the film I pass by the Minsk. I'm supposed to meet with the rabbi for some "spiritual counselling," but I want to change our appointment until after the film. Yankl and the Engineer are sitting outside on the steps.

"You joining us for prayers?" the Engineer asks. He's spooning chopped egg from a small zip-lock onto matzo.

"On a Thursday?" I say.

Yankl says, "What's wrong with Thursday?" He's sipping vodka from a Styrofoam cup. It isn't yet eleven.

"Jews pray every day," the Engineer says.

"Three times," says Yankl.

"Well, I'm heading to a movie," I say.

Yankl: "He's heading to a movie." He's a bit tipsy, rough in the tongue.

"Pisher doesn't have time for his people anymore. He's a big shot. He goes to the House of Cinema instead of the House of Prayer."

"So what you seeing?" asks the Engineer. He chomps on a piece of matzo. Egg falls over the sides of his grimy hands.

I pause, don't know how to respond. I could tell them. After all, the film won the Jury Prize at Cannes. On the other hand, it's supposed to be controversial. I don't want to offend them. I imagine the conversation.

THE ENGINEER: You know it's made by a Palestinian.

ME: I know.

THE ENGINEER: While that in itself is not enough to call it a terrible film, I have substantial evidence that proves it's propaganda.

He pulls from his briefcase a report entitled Divine Intervention and the Next Holocaust.

ME: But it won first prize in Cannes.

THE ENGINEER: Exactly. France. Land of good wine and virulent anti-Semitism.

YANKL: So you gave twenty bucks to a lying Palestinian?

ME: I haven't bought the ticket yet. And besides, it's not like the money goes to the director.

YANKL: It's full of lies.

ME: Have you two even seen it?

YANKL: We don't need to.

THE ENGINEER: Look. *They* want to drive *us* into the *Sea*. Their armies couldn't do it. Now they're going to use a movie instead. Propaganda disguised as high art. Lessons from Goebbels.

In reality, the two men say nothing. Yankl feeds crumbs of matzo to the pigeons. The Engineer seals his zip-lock full of egg salad and stuffs it in his coat pocket.

I say, "I don't know the name of the film." I look at my wrist, at a watch I'm not wearing. "I have to get going," I say.

The Engineer takes a swig from the Styrofoam cup. Yankl lights up a cigarette, eyes me suspiciously. I leave the men on the steps of the shul.

CUMBERLAND CINEMA, Yorkville: snazzy bars with fifteen-dollar martinis, sushi chic restaurants up the yin-yang. Thirty years ago this was hippie central. Now it's crowded with stretch SUVs, the air thick with the perfume of the rich. And galleries sell authentic Native Canadian Art at twenty grand a hit.

I make my way through the sea of festivalgoers and head to the rush ticket line. On the sidewalk by the idling limos, a young woman with a black headscarf smokes a cigarette. Her face is striking. She has high cheekbones, a diamond stud in the left nostril, and eyes ... well, they're the sort of black that draws you in, dangerous, the way fire is dangerous and you can't help but stare at it. She speaks Arabic to another woman. What are they talking about?

They're not the only ones wearing headscarves. There are dozens, it seems, and men, too, wearing their Muslim-yarmulke things. I realize I've never been around so many Arabs in my life. I stare at the woman's black boots. They have a thin white stripe running down the side. I wonder what her feet look like underneath. She takes a drag of her cigarette, and our eyes meet for a moment.

In the rush ticket line a couple of old men stand directly behind me. For a second I think it's the Engineer and Yankl. It's not. But I imagine them leaning over and whispering.

"Another *Shoah*," the Engineer says.

"Hitler's heirs," Yankl pipes in.

I look back toward the sidewalk. The Arab woman stares at me. I feel incredibly uncomfortable. It's like she can see right through my skin. Like she's strip-searching me.

JEWS WARN EACH OTHER about the scary goyim. Arab murderers. Neo-Nazi skinheads. Moonie abductions. Asian gangs with knives and guns. But as a kid I was afraid of the Israelis. Rumour had it former military generals from the IDF ran Bialik Hebrew Day School. It's no wonder I was scared shitless as a kid.

Do up your shoes! Close your mouth! Open your book! What did I say on January 15? So what if that was four months ago? In 1948 we had no pens, no paper. We memorized every scrap of military intelligence. Entire codes! Maps! Hideouts! And you, Shalom Garfinkel, can't remember the strategy Joshua used to invade Jericho? The one I drew on the blackboard in such detail? It was a work of art! Practically Picasso! Remember this! Inscribe it in your mind! Your blood! The only reason I don't snap off your right arm right now is because it's illegal. Not that it's unethical, but i-lle-gal. When I break this ruler in half, I am breaking your arm.

I'm next up in line. The woman behind the ticket window speaks into her microphone. "How many?"

I imagine Yankl leaning toward me, urging: "Don't go inside. Please?"

He'd ask this with such desperation it'd be hard to say no.

If only I'd stayed at the synagogue and endured the rabbi's talk, the "So when are you and Judith getting married?" questions, the "one luxury a Jew cannot afford is time" preachings. What the hell am I doing here, spending twenty bucks on a film? I turn back to look outside, catch the woman in black putting out her cigarette. She walks coolly past the line and heads into the theatre. This is pathetic. It's a friggin' movie, not a Nazi rally. You're thirty years old. They're not going to brainwash you in ninety-two minutes.

A knock against the glass. "Hello?" the ticket seller says.

"One, please."

I push my money under the window. Follow the Arab woman into the theatre. I can smell her, I'm sure: sugar and cardamom. Were she to unravel her headscarf, I'd be drowning my nose in her rivers of hair.

THERE'S NO QUESTION Bialik was different from the world I saw around me as a kid. In Grade Three I was convinced my teachers were from another planet, their otherwise normal bodies taken over by strange, Hebrew-speaking beings. I mean, why else were they in Toronto, teaching me about a country godknowswhere?

That year I wrote a telegram to the powers that be and slipped it beneath the door of the principal's office:

Dear Dr Bialik [STOP] When the aliens recruited you from the outer orbits of Vulcanis why did they send you here to torment me [STOP] Sincerely Laika [STOP]

I didn't know any better. Didn't know Bialik was a Labour Zionist school with roots in the Jewish National Workers Alliance, its birthplace somewhere between Czarist Russia and working class immigrant New York. At the age of eight, I couldn't comprehend the significance of these factions; the difference between secular and Orthodox lay in the road that separated Bialik from Etz Chayim, the all-girls *frum* school across the street. (Their otherness, their hidden playground. And they wore plaid skirts that made them oddly resemble the Catholic girls I fell in love with daily on the bus.)

What does it mean for a child to be sent to a Labour Zionist school? We were thrown into the waters of secular Jewish culture— Ben-Gurion and Singer, Shemer and Herzl, Amichai and Ahad Ha'am. We lived and breathed modern Hebrew, the almighty love of Israel. I became adept at the world of mixed messages. By night I lived in Forest Hill: Village of Jaguars, Ralph Lauren, the smooth skin of the pampered. In the days I went to a school that preached universal values of social justice and a commitment to class struggle in the name of the Jewish state. Is it any wonder I was confused?

BEHIND ME the black and blue hijabs frame women's faces. To my left three men, their heads covered with white knitted skullcaps. They speak Arabic, musical chatter punctuated by hushes and accented

English. To my right and directly behind I can hear smatterings of uptown Toronto-Yiddishkeit, the restrained Anglo intonations, slight Jewish accent, sound of my lousy and insignificant youth. "Did you see Mabel?" "I got it at Holt's," "You should've seen the lineup at Daiter's, it was *reee-dic-u-lous.*" The music of these voices, Arab and Jewish: the twang similar, the kvetch familiar.

I look down at the program. *Divine Intervention* is directed by Elia Suleiman, a Palestinian who lives in Paris. Apparently the more incendiary scenes were filmed in France; it's hard to get a movie permit in the West Bank to blow up an Israeli tank. This film could be a useful education. Sort of the same way I feel about certain books I ought to read but never do. *War and Peace. Beowulf. The Rise and Fall of the Third Reich.* This film ought to be *good* for me, I think.

My cellphone beeps. I've missed a call. Judith. She's probably wondering if I'm done with the rabbi yet. She's the one who pushed for me to meet with him in the first place. It started the other night after the Shabbos at shul. The Minsk hadn't made me feel right; in fact, it made me angry. I showed her the Aleinu prayer and sulked in the corner of the kitchen with Max the cat.

I wasn't going to talk, so Judith did. "You're confused. Maybe the rabbi can help put you back on track."

I told her that the rabbi isn't going to help, I question things, there's nothing wrong with that.

She said, "The rabbi asks questions too."

"About his chosenness?"

"It's Shabbos," she said.

"So what?"

"So why can't you just enjoy yourself?"

"Because," I said, "going to shul once every four months makes me feel like an intruder."

"Do you want to become more religious?"

"God no."

"So what exactly is the problem then?"

I said nothing. Stroked the cat instead.

"Jesus Christ you're a bore," she said.

And what do you say to that? I felt the bony ridges of Max's spine and let him rub his cheek against my hand.

She said: "Questioning is healthy, but once in a while an answer is in order."

"All right, what's the question?" I said.

And she said it: "I need to know. Do we have a future together?"

My hand stopped on Max's thin neck. I wanted to say, "How did we get from talking about the rabbi, Israel and my problems with Judaism onto us?" But I didn't say that because she's right. The questions—Judith, Israel, my faith—have become stupidly inseparable. "Okay," I said. "I'll go see the rabbi."

Judith would be interested in this film. I think to call her back and invite her, but the film looks like it's sold out. And besides, having to talk to her will only complicate things. I prefer to watch my films alone. Now I can sit back and let someone else's drama take over.

Perhaps this will inspire something. Maybe when I talk to Barak next time he won't say, "You North American ignoramus, you have no idea what's going on here." *Teach me something Palestinian* I think, and the thought is ridiculous, as naive as a tourist walking into my city, Toronto, saying *Teach me what it means to be Canadian.*

I close my eyes and let the pre-show buzz of the audience wash over me. "Have you seen the new Sukorov?" "Juliette Binoche was an angel." "Won-Kar-Wei *speaks* Hong Kong." I look at my watch. Five minutes. A surge of heat and electricity jumps near my crotch. I pull the phone out of my pocket. Judith again. This time I decide I'd better answer it. I let it vibrate in my hand, one, two, three times, and feel a tap from behind.

"Do you mind taking your hat off?"

Without turning around I know who it is. I've never talked to her, and yet I know it's the woman in black. I don't need to turn around. But I do.

"I don't mind at all."

I try to say it cool, catch her in the eyes. She nods curtly, without a smile. "Thank you," she says. Her diamond nose ring gleams. I remove my brown sailor's cap and try to flip it playfully onto my lap. It falls on the floor.

Moron, I say to myself.

The phone has stopped ringing.

ELIA SULEIMAN STANDS next to the festival director anxiously rocking back and forth on his feet. The forty-something director scratches his right temple, looks down at a fly that's landed on his black leather shoe. Is he listening to the festival director gloat over him, or is he focused on the insect climbing the tear in his left sock? He's accomplished, arrogant-humble, a man who has simultaneously helped his people's struggle while becoming the toast of Paris's smarty-pants culture (I mean just look at his swank and cool black Armani suit, tieless of course).

Suddenly he hacks into a blue handkerchief. I can see the blood flying, the phlegm going forth into cotton. I wonder if he's going to make it through his own screening. He stands in front of the microphone, stroking his throat beneath a silk scarf. Suleiman manages to eke out in a whisper, "While the film is critical of the Israeli occupation, I have employed a Jewish sense of humour in creating it." After a fit of coughing he pauses dramatically and says, "The irony in the film is a symptom of a people living in ghettos." He returns to his seat in the front row. The film hasn't even started, and already I'm squirming in my seat.

I'M TEN YEARS OLD. Three days ago our Hebrew teacher Mrs. Orlovsky mysteriously disappeared. Rumour has it she's contracted a rare flesh-eating disease. Either that or she's fled from fear. I can't blame her. The twenty-four kids in Class 5b are rambunctious, full of simmering adrenalin. But is it really our fault? The teachers of Bialik command us to sit still for eight hours a day to study Hebrew, Yiddish, French and English. At lunchtime we're given forty minutes to run, scream and hit each other like maniacs in a small concrete parking lot surrounded by tall fences. This fun and barbaric event, otherwise known as recess, is our only release.

We're children, wild in body and thought, locked into learning.

(Four years ago on my first day of school, I was seated in a small plastic chair welded onto a desk. I expected Mrs. So-and-So to come around with a key at the end of the day and unlock us from our studies.)

Jacob sits next to me. He's the baddest of the bad boys. He karooms spitballs off Rachel Haber's face, plants thumbtacks on Danny Finkleman's seat, smears wet gum in the hair of Becca Greenbaum, girl of my dreams. The rest of us are full of blah-blah and I-Scream. The lack of teacher means a few minutes of chaos, an eternity of freedom.

Mrs. Blintzkrieg enters the room but we do not shut up. She stands at the front of the class, her arms folded against her chest. Calmly, she presents a challenge: She'd like us to be so quiet she can "hear a pin drop." The howling continues.

Mrs. Blintzkrieg is high up in the rankings of Bialik. She teaches classes in every grade because her love for Israel is unquenchable. I've never had her before. The tales about Blintzkrieg are tall, even though she's shorter than Napoleon. Everyone knows who she is: the awe of her myth, the terror of her reign. Some say she was a secret commando-paratrooper (that's where the stocky legs come in handy—sturdy landings). Some say she single-handedly conquered a hill in Jordan during the '67 War. I think she's the long-lost grand-daughter of Theodore Herzl. You can see him in her thick, bushy eyebrows. In her coal-black eyes that burn when she's singing the praises of Zion.

Blintzkrieg: "Sit down! I'm going to call your mother! Do you want to go to the principal's office? You wild African monkey, Jacob! You have a heart of darkness!"

She can yell at the top of her lungs without shaking. That is, she makes the entire room shake but is herself immovable.

Blintzkrieg flicks off the lights and turns on the film projector. The effect is magic—we're immediately silent and calm. Who doesn't like a good movie? From the rusty whirrs and clicks of a sixteen-millimetre projector radiates a cone of light.

10-9-8-7-6 ...

The film is grainy black and white. Most of the others let out a groan—BORRRING!—but I really like black and white.

5-4-3-2-1 ...

In the first scene some freakishly thin man with a single tooth smiles at the camera. A few of us break out into laughter—"What a weirdo!" "Loser!" "Who's his dentist?"

"Shut up!" snaps Blintzkrieg.

I figure this film must be a precursor to the Marx Brothers and Three Stooges, a "How the golden funnies came about." But if this is comedy—and that's what black and white is for, comedy—this is the strangest act I've ever seen. People are so skinny their bones push through skin like sharp knives. It *must* be a joke—no one's supposed to look like this. When the uniformed soldiers laugh their asses off, the thought is confirmed: *I should be laughing!* I force a giggle when the soldiers pull out their guns and press them against the heads of the skinny clown-men. The roll over and play dead routine. Dead! Dead! Dead! Now that's comedy.

The tall grey factories are endless, vast cities of industry, but what on earth are they making in there? Imagine the contents of trains: entire city blocks of chocolate, swimming pools of maple syrup. I fiddle around in my chair, reach into my brown corduroys for that piece of milk chocolate I snuck out of the house this morning. It's warm and melted. In the darkness I lick the tinfoil.

One of the soldiers opens a metal door and a pile of bodies falls out. The soldiers slap-knees-guffaw, but this seems not so funny. Especially when a little girl climbs out from under the pile and asks for her mother. Well, I don't know for sure if she asks that. There's no sound, right? But she's doing that thing I do when I'm so tired it feels I have something stuck in my eye and the world might close unless I rub myself open. One of the soldiers laughs and another bends down to offer her something. She looks at the soldier mistrustfully, but takes it anyway. I mean, I would too—looks like it's a piece of chocolate or nougat. She eats it and the tears in her eyes turn into a hint of a smile. The laughing soldier pulls out a gun and shoots her in the brains.

Now Mrs. Blintzkrieg can hear a pin drop. She can also hear thirty-two heartbeats, the rapid breath of children, light sobbing.

"This could've been you," says Blintzkrieg, pointing with her ruler to the girl lying next to the heap of corpses. A shadow turns the ruler into a machete, a sabre, the arm of a monster.

Becca cling-clangs out from her desk. She's likely running to the bathroom to puke. Jacob puts his head down and closes his eyes. I feel this yanking in my stomach, like a hand's reached inside me to pull my insides out. The images continue on the screen. A doctor with Siamese twins. The shine of a soldier's boots, the sheen of his black suit. Rabbis with gold stars, humiliated, pummelled. I cannot take my eyes off what I'm seeing. Don't want to. As though by watching I could come up with an answer.

God, I think. And then: *Is this God?*

IN A FIELD in Nazareth, Santa Claus chugs through an obstacle course of tall grass and large, sharp stones, chased by four Palestinian teenagers wielding rocks, bats and insults. Santa's breath shakes in stops and starts; he's out of shape and far too hot in his thick red and white Claus-skin. He carries a broken wicker basket on his back. It's full of stolen presents, and he occasionally throws one back at the children to delay them. They don't flinch when the wrapped gifts sputter down the hillside all shiny and glossy. Don't snap up the bait of gift-wrap, promises of the new, the good. They only want Santa Claus's red ass.

The chase takes Santa and his young pursuants farther afield and up a hill. He trips into a hole, pulls himself up, scoots, fat and slobbery, toward the grounds of a monastery. Here we see what is really getting at Santa of Nazareth: a meat cleaver, stuck in his chest. He finally crumples at the base of the monastery; the afternoon sun slithers down his head. The caption below the scene tells us where we are: the Holy Land.

I find these opening images strangely disturbing. There's something creepy about this Santa with a kitchen knife in his breast. He gets under my skin, crawls inside my head and whispers, *You wanted an education? I'll give you one.* I reach into the pocket of my jeans hoping to find some chocolate or candy. Nothing. Shit. I'm diabetic and I'm wondering if the discomfort I'm feeling is simply the beginnings of a low blood sugar.

Some of the audience is laughing. Now the main character, what's his name, throws an apricot pit out the window of his car. The pit blows up an Israeli tank. *May this seed grow into the orchard of our homeland!* In another scene, the same guy inflates a balloon with Yasser Arafat's face caricatured onto the surface. The balloon rises magically above a West Bank checkpoint. The balloon defies gravity, rises above the gun-in-the-face, shit-in-the-pants questions of soldiers. It travels to Jerusalem, ascends the Dome of the Rock and smiles like an idiot. The man beside me in the black knitted cap lets out a giant, "Hooray!"

Hooray?

A French tourist asks an Israeli police officer for directions to the Holy Sepulchre. The officer doesn't know the way, so he yanks out a bound and gagged Palestinian prisoner from the back of the paddy wagon. Blindfolded and handcuffed, the prisoner points left, then right, then right again.

The Arab next to me is howling. "Real Mel Brooks!" I think he yells. The Jews in the audience must be less impressed. I think I see some get up to leave—are they wearing yarmulkes? Part of me wants to join them. This movie is bullshit, I'm thinking. Yankl and the Engineer were right. This is manipulative, not artistic at all. It's not even funny. But I'm staying. And I don't know why.

"It's not like this," I want to say to the Arab man.

"Of course it's not," I imagine him saying. "Nowhere in Palestine can an apricot explode with such force!" He laughs hideously, I'm sure of it, revealing three gold teeth.

"It's easy to make Jews out to be the bad guys," I would reply.

"You're the *gonifs*. You took our land."

Mel Brooks was one thing. But to speak to me in Yiddish? And to say *that*?

"I didn't take your land," I'd say in response, doing my best to keep a level head.

"Your forefathers did."

"My forefathers were in Canada. And besides. This is a movie. Things are not that bad there."

"And when were you there to know?"

BLINTZKRIEG KEEPS US on a steady diet of Holocaust films for what seems like a week. I don't sleep for two. I can't see the point in it. Every time I hear a car drive by it's the Gestapo. I'm guilty. They'll know me by my prick.

"Shalom, open up in there." It's my mother.

"What do you want?"

"It's time for you to go to bed."

"I'm still doing my homework."

That's what Mrs. Goldberger would call a euphemism.

On the floor by my bed there's a brown plastic bowl with warm water and flour. Four thin strands of newsprint lie on the floor next to the bowl. I dip one in, just like Mrs. Goldberger taught us in art class. I want to be an *artiste*, I've decided. Carefully I stick the pasty newspaper around the tip of my penis. Perfect.

"You're my little Einstein," my mother says proudly from the other side of the door. "But can't I see you for a minute?"

"Come back in five." The strip is soft and warm, a bit uncomfortable and slightly stingy. This is a worthwhile sort of pain. It's going to solve all my problems, and really, it's not so bad. I mean how big can a foreskin be? I fan the strip with my hand, hoping it'll cool quickly.

"It's ten after eleven. Please open the door."

"Almost done," I say.

I stand up to look for my Superman Underoos in the mess of my room. Suddenly the shelves on my wall start to shake. My Rawlings centrefield special tumbles from above. Three glasses break—root-beer mugs I've stolen from the local Burger Shack. The floor starts to tremble and I'm waiting to be swallowed whole like Korach was in the desert. I'm convinced: God is punishing me for breaking His covenant. The ritual of hot-newspaper-on-prick has doomed me. That's when I notice my mother in the room, holding the bowl of water and flour. Her look is one of shock.

That night phone calls are made.

The next morning Mrs. Blintzkrieg is very, very nice. She asks me how I am, tells me to take a seat. "Please," she says. Then she shows us a new film.

This one is not like the others. For starters, there's a pretty song. A youth choir sings from the lousy projector speaker, *eretz zavat chalav ud-vash: the land is flowing with milk and honey.* "This is life on a kibbutz, a Zionist collective farm," a voice like Alistair Cooke on *Masterpiece Theatre* announces. Men and women dance gently in the wheat fields; a butterfly flutters lazily in the valley; sun sweetens the olive and orange groves. In the field the workers are busy working, the bees busy bee-ing. Everyone wears silly white hats to keep out the sun, the same goofy ones Gilligan wears on *Gilligan's Island.*

In the next clip there's a one-eyed general. He marches into Jerusalem with a group of other soldiers. I'm searching for Blintzkrieg among the fighters, but I can't see her anywhere. She announces to the class: "From the ashes of Europe we rose to build a nation in the desert and swamps. We arrived, cultivated and liberated the Middle East. Israel was not a land of milk and honey—*we* were the milk and honey. The land was fallow and empty. Our labour, our love: That's what made the soil bloom."

I adjust myself in my seat. Blintzkrieg's words are strong, and there's relief in that strength. For a moment, the sting is gone. And the film cools the burning between my legs.

A MAN MY AGE places his right ear to the chest of his father in a Ramallah hospital. He listens for the life-drum that says, *Everything will be all right, child.* It's a strange thought, but it occurs to me I've never thought of a Palestinian in these terms. Never imagined a man my age, eyes dark like mine, hoping his father will continue to live.

I think of my father's cancer, post-surgery. How I went to visit him, watched him sleep with respirator and IV. In that moment it all seemed ridiculous, the questions of faith, history and culture. What mattered was him: morphine in the veins, and the question of whether or not the doctors had removed enough of the tumour.

I feel a kick at the back of my seat. It's the Arab girl. Is she adjusting herself, or trying to get my attention?

I don't turn around.

MEGAPHONE IN HAND, an Israeli soldier dances drunk toward the West Bank checkpoint. He barks out orders while obnoxiously blaring a siren among the rows of parked cars. "Get out of your vehicle!" A driver emerges from a small black compact. The soldier demands the man take his leather coat off.

"Good quality leather," the soldier says, evaluating the coat, its supple skin smooth in his hands. He puts the jacket on. A perfect fit.

The soldier shoves the Palestinian into another car and makes the driver from that car sit in the first. This game of musical cars goes on for some time until the soldier pulls out a young Palestinian boy whom the soldier commands to sing, "Am Yisrael Chai" while dancing a traditional Israeli number. *The Nation of Israel lives, the Nation of Israel lives,* sings the soldier off-key, helter-skelter, his right arm dangling on the shoulder of the Palestinian boy, who's doing his best to keep up. The boy struggles to get the words out. They're a fist in his throat, they trip up his feet. And the soldier keeps him dancing, criss-crossing, Israeli style. A hora.

"Five, six, seven, eight!" Mrs. Blintzkrieg exclaims. Dance, dance, dance! The words demand to be screamed, they're pushed out of my lungs by the song itself. There's Motti Engelblott, Grade Four physics genius from Haifa in his tight blue Adidas short-shorts, chopped-egg breath and voice like a crow. Here's Yuval Nirifar, King of the Klutzes, thin as a rail, kicking up a storm. He can barely keep up. They sing it their way, Jacob and I sing it ours, on the auditorium floor, our hands locked into each other, chanting while we stomp, "Am Yisrael Chai! Am Yisrael Chai!" *It fires you up, a shot of Hebraic adrenalin mainlined to the body's furnace. When we exclaim the nation of Israel lives, we're announcing, "We live. We're alive."*

The soldier repeats the chant with the boy, dances him to the front car, pushes him in with a bunch of strangers.

What the hell is going on?

Out of a sandstorm emerges a woman dressed in a black ninja suit. Her head is enshrouded in a black and white checkered burqa. Five Israeli soldiers stand at attention and aim their automatic pistols. Target practice in the Judean desert. She fearlessly faces the men.

They fire and she spins into the air. The bullets slow down and surround her head, freezing in mid-air while she pulls out two poisoned darts from her ninja outfit. The darts, emblazoned with the emblem of a crescent moon encircling a star, are flung at two soldiers, stinging them dead on the spot. With her badass sling shot she stones a soldier to death. Ninja-woman juggles three grenades as bad flashy dance music pulsates. She tosses the grenades in the air, throwing one onto the ground to destroy herself while two land on a couple of soldiers. A flag of Palestine appears on the ground and Ninja-woman reappears.

Most of her face is covered. And yet I'm sure I've seen Ninja-woman before. I think: I know those eyes. I whirl around for confirmation, but the Arab girl isn't there. What the hell? I look at the screen. The captain, the last remaining soldier, fires an M-16, desperate to bust some Arab ass. Ninja-woman pulls out a metallic shield—a map with borders identical to the ones I drew as a kid. She uses the shield to defend herself from the bullets. Her sleek legs wrapped in tight black leggings. Her large black boots with a thin white stripe.

The girl. Ascended from seat to screen.

Ninja-woman floats in the air. She coils her burqa around the captain's gun, strangles it out of his arms. When an Israeli Apache rises from the valley behind her, she throws the map like a boomerang, blowing the chopper to smithereens. The captain stands amidst the circle of dead soldiers, incredulous. Ninja-woman disappears into the stone landscape. Boy, did she do good. Boy, can she throw a supernatural kick in your face punch or two. And eat those bullets like sandwich, like supper.

I'M STUPID AND HUNGRY. When I get hungry I space out, blood sugar plummeting. I ask stupid questions. I approach the director and tug at his sleeve. Elia Suleiman turns from a small crowd of admirers. His brown eyes pierce me. *What do you want?* they ask.

"Are things really that bad?"

I don't know why I'm asking this question. Why I can't just go home, turn on the internet and fill my head with facts so I don't sound like an idiot. But I have an urge to talk to the man who made this film. The director ignores my question, returns to his admirers and continues with his conversation.

"Mr. Suleiman, are things really that bad over there?"

He scans me from head to toe to make sure I'm real.

"They're worse," Suleiman replies, coughing into his handkerchief. While his eyes are terrifying, his voice is delicate, a soft hand on the neck.

"How so?"

We stand in the theatre staring at each other for a few seconds. My question stupefies him. This is not the sort of thing Elia Suleiman encounters in Cannes or Ramallah. "To find out more you can read. Or better yet, go see for yourself what it's like."

Two women escort the director away from me. I'm scratching my head, thinking, what the hell do I do now? Looking around at the people spilling out of the cinema, I have that sense of being affected while knowing that another reality exists: Yankl and the Engineer, the rabbi and the synagogue, around the corner from my house. I feel a tap on the shoulder.

"What would you like to know?" a voice asks.

It's Ninja-woman, only now she's back to how she looked before the film. She's my age, I decide. I consider asking for her autograph. Or the usual banal questions: How long was the shoot? Where'd you go to acting school? Instead I say: "I'd like to know how bad things are over there." I know the statement is ridiculous. Maybe I hope to prove the film is wrong, a lie. I search my pockets for LifeSavers, a candy bar, something. I must've taken too much insulin this morning.

She touches my shoulder. "We should get together," she says, sliding her right hand toward my left elbow. She pulls lightly, as though she were offering to guide me through a crowded market in a foreign country. "We should have coffee," she says, lightly tugging my skin.

I know she does not mean this the way most people in Toronto do: One day, in the next few months, perhaps we can accommodate a rushed and caffeinated forty-five. She writes her telephone number on the back of my ticket stub. Her handwriting is slanted and she crosses her sevens. I put her number in my shirt pocket and excuse myself. I head toward the rear exit that will take me to an alley, short-cut to Bloor Street. I feel warm and faint. When I remember I haven't asked her name, I turn around but she is lost in a sea of people. I pull out the ticket stub and read beneath the row of numbers.

"Rana."

CHAPTER 4

Self-portrait. Age ten.

I love Jesus. I love him so much I've dressed up like him for Purim. I wear a long white bathrobe with a tiny white towel for a loincloth. I've constructed a crown of thorns from broken pencils stuck with duct tape to a headband.

Mrs. Goldberger stops me in the hall, asks me what in G–d's name I think I'm doing.

I bring my finger to my mouth and shush her. Cross myself solemnly (like the two Catholic girls I see on the bus). Keep walking the halls of Bialik. Listen to the complaints of teachers, the uninspired sounds of children, empty, without direction.

Bialik: eight hundred children crammed into thirty classrooms on three narrow floors. I pass the halls of grey lockers. Seek the graffiti of washroom stalls, the secret messages. An occasional shriek—a screaming teacher, chalk whipped point-blank at a rebellious kid. On the top floor: fluorescent-lit classrooms. The staff room, where the teachers drink coffee and speak to each other, civilized. Downstairs to the first floor where the Grade Ones and Twos obediently study and sing. *Blessed are their ignorant brains, for they know not what they are learning.*

Why am I dressed like Jesus? He was an unusual Jew. He not only loved his neighbour but he even loved a prostitute. This fact I learned from *Jesus Christ Superstar.* He so intrigues me that once I asked Mrs. Blintzkrieg the question, "Why doesn't Israel try to love its neighbours?" She said, "Yeshu died on the cross. That's the fate of those who turn the other cheek." End of discussion.

When I get to the basement I knock on the door of Tommy Salami's janitorial chamber. I'm this week's juice monitor and I'm here to pick up twenty-four grape juices for my class. Tommy is Italian-Catholic and doesn't speak English. He's fifty-two years old and has hair growing out of his nostrils. I wonder what he thinks about working in a school full of crazy Zionist kids. When he gets home at night, what does he tell his wife? "Every morning they scream 'Hatikva' at the top of their lungs." Or: "They dance like they're being chased by murderers." Or: "It's illegal for them to eat pepperoni on their pizza. Do you hear me, Rosa? Ill-e-gal!"

Nobody answers the door so I knock again. I'll admit it: In spite of Blintzkrieg's logic, I can't help but think there is something cool about Jesus. To Love Thy Neighbour: Isn't that just another way of saying, hey, you're different, I'm curious, can I get to know you better?

Nobody answers. The door's unlocked so I venture inside. It's crazy but I've never talked to Tommy before. In fact, I've never talked to a non-Jew other than Deolinda, the Portuguese woman who comes to clean our house every Wednesday morning. There's a whole world of non-Jews out there. That's what Mrs. Blintzkrieg says. She also says that just about all of them hate me. History proves it up the yin-yang.

Still, I want to talk to Tommy. I'd like to convince him I'm not so different. I'd like to convince myself of that too.

Tommy Salami's room is windowless with a single dim light bulb screwed into the ceiling. This is where the lunch juice for the children of Bialik is stored. This is also where Tommy spends his off-hours smoking and playing solitaire.

Git yer grape juice! Sweet-tooth apple! Sourpuss lemon! Orangutan orange!

I sit on a crate. Pull back the metal foil of a juice, and drain it in three giant sips.

Deeeliccccciousss. Highly illegal, of course.

"What are you dressed as?" a voice asks.

"I'm putting the Jew back in Jesus," I say, wiping my mouth.

"That's funny," says the voice. "I thought you were dressed as an old geezer from the JCC."

"Who are you?" I ask.

"Seek, and you shall not find," says the voice.

"I want to perform miracles," I say.

"What kind?"

"The kind that make people like each other."

"That's retarded," says the voice. "If I were going to perform a miracle, I'd turn concrete into grass."

Pushed against the corner of the room is a table covered in puke-green paint. Tommy's desk. From beneath it emerges a thing. Jacob. His face is scraped and scabbed.

"Grass," he says, wiping snot and blood from his nose. "We could use some." I try to make a kind Jesus face like the glowing ones I've seen on Sunday-morning TV. "Grass is necessary for so many things."

"It doesn't hurt the knees," I say.

"It helps things grow," he adds.

"It would help me improve my moonwalk."

"Coo-day-tit."

"What?"

"A coo-day-tit. What the Maccabees did to the Syrian Greeks."

"You mean an armed rebellion against the powers that be."

Jacob says, "I mean what I mean, the way grass is green. So you in or not?"

He picks up a metal trash can and holds it between us like an offering. I can make out a pair of torn grey wool socks lying in the bottom. They're Tommy's, I figure, because they're smelly and big. There's something incredibly sad about those socks.

I decide there must be two kinds of Jews: the ones who fight those who hate them, and the ones who love and forgive. A Jacob or a Jesus. There are times for each. But which one? And when?

"So what do you say?" he asks.

I place my hands on the trash can along the edges closest to him. Our arms crossed, we stare each other in the eyes. Clutching bent tin in stale darkness. A pact.

"Will you call me Jesus?" I ask.

CHAPTER 5

On the outside, the café is small and unassuming. When I open the door, I enter another world: Arabic music and walls of baklava, bowls full of Turkish delight. People drink dark coffee out of small cups poured from blue metal pots. I sit down at a table in the corner. On the other side of the restaurant sits a man with dreadlocks, a black and white *kaffiyeh* tied around his neck (recently purchased at an Urban Outfitters clearance sale, I suspect). He talks to a table of six.

"At 4 A.M. there were bullets everywhere. I was standing there, stupid, not knowing what to do with myself. I felt this hand pull me down to the earth. It was Yala. She yelled, 'Idiot! Do you want to get shot?' and I said, 'Yes, Yala, that's why I'm here!'"

The men and women at the table laugh. They are hippie-anarchist types. They drink coffee, eat falafel and talk to each other in a familiar manner. A surrogate family, bound by the causes of the oppressed.

"Where was this?" demands a man at the end of the table. His hands shake when he speaks. He has blue eyes and is clean-shaven. There is a gash across his chin. He seems to be the only one not laughing. He is also the only one not wearing a kaffiyeh.

"Nablus," says the dreadlocked man.

I flip through the maps from Bialik in my mind. Nablus= Shechem. Ancient city, where God made His promise to Abraham.

And I will assign this land to your offspring.

I'M A BIT UNCERTAIN about this meeting. When I dialed her number, I felt I was committing a crime. Coffee would be more than coffee, a conversation more than get-to-know-her-chatter. "I want to know what's going on over there," I'd said to Rana at the cinema. But why did I need to talk to *her*? What did she know that I couldn't read in a book or the newspaper?

"We met," I said on the phone.

Before I finished my sentence Rana replied, "Have you ever tried Arabic coffee?"

I could hear two male voices fighting in the background.

"No," I said.

"Thursday." And she gave me an address for a place I'd never heard of.

When I hung up the phone I was like a kid waiting for his birthday. I counted the days until our meeting—three. On the wall by my desk, the stern face of my grandmother, black and white, Korets, Poland, 1926, stared back at me, unimpressed.

I WALK UP to the cash and order a "Blood of the Pigeon," Bedouin tea. As a kid I was enamoured of the Bedouin. A roof of stars, a floor of sand and stone. This seemed more Hebraic than Jews in their Forest Hill mansions, heated swimming pools and leather car interiors.

"Aren't you going to have a dessert?" asks the man behind the counter. He squints at me, cleans his teeth with a toothpick.

"The tea is just fine."

"You *must* have a sweet," he says.

"I'm okay, really."

"Here," he says, looking both ways to make sure no one is looking. He hands me something wrapped in wax paper. He whispers, "You're not allergic to nuts, are you?"

"No." I accept his gift. I don't want to offend him, so I don't tell him I'm diabetic.

"Pistachio and honey," he whispers.

"Thank you," I say.

"Basir," he says.

"What does that mean?"

"It's my name."

He pours himself a cup of coffee, winks at me when his wife comes into the store and counts the pastries.

"Fat as a rat," she snarls at him.

Basir says nothing, picks his teeth.

JACOB AND I would go to the Jerusalem at Bathurst and Eglinton after school, a quick detour on the way home. The Jerusalem was run by Lebanese, not Israelis, but Jews were quick to point out this was some of the best falafel in the city. "The Jerusalem makes really good falafel," say the Jews of Forest Hill, but I always thought there was a hint of discomfort in that statement. Why would a Lebanese family name their restaurant "Jerusalem"? Why not "Beirut Palace" or "Hezbollah Snacks"?

Basir prepares falafel behind the counter. When he looks at me I pretend to take a small nibble of the sweet. It'll send my blood sugar skyrocketing if I eat the whole thing.

Basir asks, "How is everything?"

"Fantastic," I say.

A chair falls at the table next to me. The man with shaky hands and the dreadlocked activist are at each other's throats. Friends try to pry them apart; the shaky man tries to land a jab, swipes only air. "Fraud," "Fuck your mother" and a list of Arabic curses (I can only imagine) fly out of his mouth. Without a word Basir's wife grabs both men by the arms and escorts them outside. Slams the door behind them.

Basir announces, "Everything is okay."

I take a bite of the baklava. This time I swallow.

RANA SITS ACROSS from me, eyes closed, sipping coffee. Oddly enough, she isn't wearing a headscarf today. I wonder if you can just do that, wear one whenever the impulse grabs you. She has not woken up yet, she says. I'm still anxious about the two goons kicked out of the café. The rest of the people at their table appear rather funereal.

I decide that any questions related to suicide bombing, such as "Have you ever loved a bomber?" "Have any of your relatives ever blown themselves up?" or "Do you have suicide bombing fantasies?" might be best left by the wayside.

"How's the coffee?" I ask by way of breaking the silence.

"It's okay." Rana speaks in a thick accent. She leans over and whispers, "My mother just mailed me a package of the real stuff from Jerusalem."

The way she says this—secretive, confidential—reminds me of an article I recently read saying that coffee can hide just about anything from bomb- and drug-inspecting dogs. I try to get this thought out of my head.

"So why do you want to know about Palestine?" she asks.

"I'm looking for something to write about."

"When were you last there?"

"Where?"

"Palestine."

"I've never been."

She looks at me like I'm from Mars.

"I'm Jewish," I blurt out.

I look around the room. Nobody's stopped their conversations; the anarchists are quietly discussing Venezuela, Darfur and Afghanistan. Basir's wife dusts old boxes of dried tahini and falafel on the shelves. She barks orders at the young Asian girl washing dishes at the back.

Only Basir watches Rana and me. He strokes his clean-shaven face as though it were fully bearded. Can he hear me?

"Jewish," she says, stirring her coffee, which does not need to be stirred. Her stirring is an attempt to decipher meaning from vague statements. She laughs. "I thought you were Mohawk. You have slits for eyes." She licks her spoon and shakes her head.

"Disappointed?"

"Sure," she says. "I've been in Canada one year, and I never met an Indian." She takes back the rest of her coffee. "I know a few Jews."

"From where?" I ask.

"Israel. I was born there."

"Right."

"So you're Jewish and you haven't been," she says.

"No."

"Not for that birthright thing they send you on for free?"

"Nope."

"Never worked on a kibbutz, studied in a yeshiva?"

"Never."

"Interesting."

"I suppose."

"And why haven't you?"

"Never wanted to."

"And now?"

"I just wanted to talk to someone about what it's like over there."

"Talk? Like this is what you call 'therapy'?"

"I don't see it that way."

"You wanted to talk to a Palestinian."

"I wanted to hear a perspective I'm not familiar with."

While we enter uncomfortable pause land, I decide to say what I should have said ages ago: "Hey, I've been meaning to say, you were a dynamite Ninja-woman."

"Excuse me?"

"*Divine Intervention.* You were amazing, whirling around in the sky like that."

Rana laughs, shakes her head. "You're funny, you know." She takes me by the hands. Holding them together she blows inside them as though they were cold.

"I'm not cold," I say.

She unfolds my hands, opens them to the light. Says, "I'm not an actress."

"But the film."

She removes a pouch of Dutch tobacco from her jean-jacket pocket and starts to roll up a cigarette. "I'll tell you a few things about my country. But, if you are, as you say, a writer, I can't say I have a story you're going to want to write. My life," she says, twisting paper stuffed with tobacco, "is no different from anyone else's." She licks the cigarette closed.

RANA WAS BORN in the north of Israel in an Arab town named Tamra. She was raised Muslim and has five siblings. I ask her what it's like growing up as an Arab in Israel.

She says, "That's the problem right there."

"Right where?"

"What you just called me. Arab-Israeli."

"Oh. Sorry." What the hell is she talking about?

"We have Israeli passports, unlike the Palestinians in the West Bank or Gaza, and we can work in Jerusalem or Tel Aviv. But we are still second class." She explains that her ID card is different from a Jew's. It's marked "Arab" as opposed to those whose nationality is marked "Jewish."* "It is a deliberate act by the Israeli government to

---

* Since the time of our meeting, the Israeli government has changed the ID cards and replaced the nationality with a number. It is thought that this code contains the ethnic background of the card carrier. Source: Susan Nathan, *The Other Side of Israel*, p. 35.

segregate. And why do they call us Arabs? I am neither Arab nor Israeli. I'm Palestinian." Rana's voice is angry, irritable. She is quickly waking up.

I've never heard of such a thing. Ethnic identity cards—in Israel? Surely there has to be a sensible reason for this. After all, Israel is a democracy, the only one in the Middle East. It's not like Arabs—I mean Palestinians—within Israel don't vote or don't have government representatives in the Knesset. Okay, it might not be a completely equal society, but which country is? I feel like I need to know more to respond to this. I nod to Basir and tell him I'd like one of those coffees Rana is drinking.

She goes on to explain there's no constitution in Israel. There was supposed to be one created in 1948 (as guaranteed by the Israeli declaration of independence), but the first prime minister, Ben-Gurion, kept putting it off—it's an issue still unresolved until this day. Instead there are eleven "Basic Laws" the judiciary follows. "It would be very inconvenient for Israel if there was a constitution. It would mean Palestinians would have legal rights." Rights such as freedom of expression, equality, health care, education and welfare are not ensured in law. "Legally protected or not, I'm treated like a security threat wherever I go. If I'm at the Tel Aviv airport, I'm guaranteed a three-hour search. Minimum."

I think about what she says regarding the lack of constitution in Israel. Maybe it's not only a Palestinian issue. It likely has to do with the fact the religious right would never stand for a secular constitution. The laws of Halakah cannot be secondary to the laws of the state, the Orthodox would say. A real problem, admittedly. But intentionally racist? I have trouble believing that. As for the airport thing, what can I say? Post-9/11, it sucks to be Muslim.

Rana says, "Have you heard of the Jewish National Fund?"

"Of course. They plant trees in Israel."

"Trees?" She shakes her head.

"Yeah."

Every Friday at Bialik I was told to plonk whatever change I had into a little blue and white box called *Keren Kayemet*. The donations helped to plant trees in arid areas such as the Negev desert. We were required to give money, but it was something I always looked forward to doing. What a thought it was: the desert, that dead furnace of a place, miraculously transformed to provide oxygen, life to the Jewish people. I felt fortunate to contribute. God, Mrs. Blintzkrieg, the entire history of the Jewish people nodded their heads in approval when I put my quarter into the Keren Kayemet box. The miracle of Israel born because of my grandparents' donations; Israel sustained, still growing, because of mine.

Rana tells me a story I know: In 1901 the JNF was set up to buy land in Palestine with the idea that Jews should buy as much of the land as possible. She asks, "Do you know how much land was actually purchased by Jews by the time the State of Israel was formed in 1948?"

"I have no idea."

She rolls the unlit cigarette between her fingers as though it were a pencil.

"Less than seven percent," she says.

"So the JNF wasn't all that effective," I reply.

"No. So in 1948, one would expect the JNF to turn the land over to the state. After all, their mission was complete, right? There was a Jewish homeland."

She explains that during the '48 War the Israeli army destroyed over four hundred Palestinian villages. Over seven hundred thousand Palestinian refugees were created in the process. Today they and their descendants number over four million. "They fled," Mrs. Blintzkrieg taught us, who always made sure to add, "And they ran away so they could join the other Arab nations. So they could throw us into the sea." It was a miracle—and thanks to the supreme organizational power of the Jewish Yishuv—that Israel emerged victorious.

Rana tells me a slightly different version: "Some of us fled because we were afraid. Many of us were driven out by the Israeli army. There were massacres, rapes. Entire villages were razed to the ground. It was the Nakba. The catastrophe."

Rana studied land assessment at the Hebrew University in Jerusalem in the late 1990s, so she knows a thing or two about this. She explains that Israeli law called the people who left their villages during the war "absentees."* Anyone considered an absentee lost the rights to his or her home. The assets, bank accounts and land of absentees were transferred to an official body known as the Custodian of Absentee Property. Thus, with a stroke of a pen and the help of some bulldozers, the Zionist dream had come true: Palestine was an empty land for the people without a land.

The Jewish National Fund played an important role in making sure the newly formed state of Israel remained Jewish. Following the '48 War some 160,000 Palestinians continued to live in Israel (among these included Rana's parents and grandparents). Israel had a challenge: It was a democratic country, but it wanted to ensure that the land would remain in Jewish hands. Millions of dunams' worth of absentee property was handed over to the JNF by the state. Rana explains, "The JNF is not a government organization. They can legally pay heed to their mandate—to lease land to Jews, and only Jews. I, as an Arab-Israeli citizen, cannot acquire land the JNF owns." Today the JNF owns approximately thirteen percent of the country.

---

* According to Absentee Property Law 5710-1950 (1), an absentee is a person who legally owned or held property in the area of Israel, who following the United Nations partition plan in November 1947, became a citizen of an enemy country (i.e., Lebanon, Egypt, Syria, Jordan, etc.), or who migrated to enemy territory, or who was a citizen of British Mandate Palestine and left his or her ordinary place of residence for an area outside the country prior to September 1, 1948, or who left for a place in Israel that was controlled at that time "by forces which sought to prevent the establishment of the State of Israel or which fought against it after its establishment."

Rana explains that another eighty percent of Israel is in the hands of the state. These state lands, combined with the JNF, are managed by the Israel Land Administration—a state body that controls and leases property to its citizens.* While the ILA in theory, leases land to all Israelis regardless of ethnic background, the reality is much different. "Go to the ILA website. You'll see that almost half their representatives are from the JNF. You can bet they make sure their policy to 'redeem the land' for the Jewish people is met." Rana says the ILA makes it virtually impossible for Palestinians in Israel to lease property—most available land goes to neighbouring settlements, moshavim or kibbutzim where only Jews live.† "While we—in Tamra—are forced to build on top of each other. We become a ghetto," Rana says.

Basir brings coffee in a large blue porcelain ewer on a silver platter. He pours me a small cup and waits me for me to try it, as though it were wine. I take a sip and nod my head. It's fine, but I don't really care. I want to know where this is going.

Rana asks, "What would you say if a Canadian institution controlled ninety-three percent of the land in this country and said it would only sell it to Protestants?"

I don't know what to think.

"But they plant trees," I say, nearly choking on the words.

"Yes," Rana says. "They plant your fucking trees."

She pauses, puts the cigarette in her mouth.

---

* Land in Israel is leased for forty-nine-year periods. The number *forty-nine* comes from the Torah, where it says every fifty years the land must be redeemed or returned to its original owner because, "The land must not be sold in perpetuity, for the land is Mine" (Leviticus 25:23). Source: Hussein Abu Hussein and Fiona McKay, *Access Denied*, p. 145.

† The same argument is advanced in greater detail in Susan Nathan, *The Other Side of Israel*, pp.155–56, and Hussein Abu Hussein and Fiona McKay, *Access Denied*, p. 153.

"Canada Park," she says. "Do you know this?"

"Of course. It was the pride of our school. Canadian Jews raised something like fifteen million dollars for that forest in the 1970s."

"The JNF planted those trees on top of three Palestinian villages that had been destroyed in 1967. That's what your Canada Park was for."

RANA CONTINUES TO TALK, but I don't know how much more of this I can listen to. The question, "How much of this is true?" keeps flashing in my head. I reassure myself by saying, "What is the other side of the story?" There has to be an explanation for what she's telling me. I decide I'll look into this later.

She asks, "Do you go to synagogue?"

"Sometimes."

"So you're a believer."

"I like the songs. The idea of a sacred space." I hate explaining what I think about this religious crap. I can't decide if Rana is judging me for caring about it or not. "And you're Muslim?"

"Yes."

"Do you pray?"

"I don't practise."

I think to ask her about the headscarf but my mind is fixed on something else. I take another sip of coffee. It's sweet, spicy and unfiltered. The caffeine goes straight to the head. Emboldens me.

I say, "Let's go back to the War of Independence. The Nakba, as you call it." The Bialik education comes back full force. I remind her of the 1939 White Paper: The British offered Palestinians an independent state to be jointly ruled by Palestinians and Jews. It also put a strict limit on Jewish immigration and land purchase. The offer was incredible for Palestinians (and a huge defeat for Zionists), and still the Palestinian leadership refused it. Then in 1947, the UN passed a resolution proposing forty-five percent of British Mandate Palestine go to the Palestinians, and fifty-five percent to the Jews. Jerusalem and Bethlehem were to be made international cities. The Jews went for it, and the Palestinians didn't. "They never missed an opportunity to miss an opportunity," Abba Eban once said about the Palestinians. In 1948, when Israel declared independence, seven Arab nations launched a war against the Jews, Palestinians leading the way. Israel won the war. "How is that land expropriation?" I ask. "Isn't the Nakba that Palestinians didn't take what was offered them? Jews needed a country. And they were willing to share it."

Rana says, "I can sympathize with the Jews' need for a home. But how would you feel if someone came to your house and said, 'Would you mind leaving so we can live here? Don't worry, there's a house for you on the next street over.'" I say nothing. She continues. "And of course the requests weren't quite so polite. In Deir Yassin, over one hundred women, children and men were rounded up by the Jewish Irgun and shot dead. The rest were paraded through the streets of Jerusalem, then forced to cross over to the Arab part of the city. The Jews wanted to scare the shit out of us so we'd leave. And that wasn't the only place that happened. Even if the UN resolution had been accepted, it would never have been enough for the Zionists. Ben-Gurion wanted the West Bank from the start, and after '48, he wanted Sinai, Beirut, even Damascus. The Zionists were colonialist aggressors. Bottom line."

I feel as though I'm being personally attacked. To call Zionists colonialists is flat-out wrong. Zionism, as I'd been taught, is the belief in a country with a Jewish majority that lets Jews live without the anxiety of pogroms, discrimination and hatred. The creation of Israel was essential for the survival of the Jewish people. Even though I'd had no desire to go to Israel as a kid, I considered myself a Zionist for this very reason. Wasn't the tragedy of the Holocaust that Jews had had nowhere to go? Europe had just tried to annihilate us and we simply wanted to live in peace. And the Arab nations weren't all innocent and friendly, either. While the Jews (according to Rana) were driving out Palestinians, almost a million Jews were kicked out of Arab nations like Iraq, Syria and Egypt. If it hadn't been for Israel, where would those Jews have gone? Rana mentioned the massacre at Deir Yassin—which admittedly I hadn't heard about—but what about the '48 massacre at Kfar Etzion, where over a hundred Jews were murdered?

Still, I don't say anything in response. It's not that I think Rana's right. But I'm listening to her, and I understand something I've managed to overlook: People lived in that country. They are not statistics, abstract numbers in the pages of a history book. At Bialik we weren't even taught about them. From what I can remember in my early years, the land was empty before the Jews came. When I was slightly older, Arabs were mentioned (they were never called "Palestinian"), but only as nomadic tribespeople who might have wandered through Palestine from Syria on their way to Egypt. The word *refugee*—let alone *Deir Yassin*—was never mentioned. The words *PLO, Yasser Arafat* and *terrorist attack* were. While the Palestinians were mourning the Nakba, we were singing "Hativka" and wearing blue and white scarves to celebrate Independence Day. "There were some Arabs who lived there before we came," Mrs. Blintzkrieg said in Grade Seven. The way she said "some" I imagined (in my twelve-year-old mind) twenty, thirty people. Not a million people with cultural traditions, tribal ties, an ancient connection to the land.

I'm down to the end of my coffee. Basir looks at me and raises his right eyebrow. Rana excuses herself so she can smoke her cigarette. I watch her gently open the door, then slam it behind. Her point of view rattles me. Bialik has hidden certain truths from me. But I've been avoiding things too. The questions, the difficult ones. Have not wanted to read them in black and white newsprint, the daily articles and pictures, kaffiyehs wrapped around the necks of men, a stone thrown at the glass walls of my faith.

WHEN SHE RETURNS, I change the subject to something more personal. I ask her about her university days, and about Jerusalem. Where'd you live in that city?

She tells me she lived in a Jewish neighbourhood on a street called Mekor Chayim. "It was one of the best places I've ever lived," she says.

"Did you live alone?" I ask.

"No. I rented half a house. Shared it with a crazy Jew named Shimon." She laughs at the thought of him.

"You rented from a Jew?"

"No. I rented from Abu Dalo, a Palestinian."

"Really? So a Palestinian and an Israeli shared the same house?"

Rana pauses. Says, "It is a bit of an unusual story, I suppose." Abu Dalo owned the house. It had been in his family for ten generations. In 1967 during the Six Day War, the Israeli army was approaching Jerusalem. Abu Dalo and his family fled to Beit Safafa, a Palestinian village. They stayed there for a week until things were calm again. When they came back to the house, Shimon and his wife, Dina, were living in Abu Dalo's living room. The belongings of the Abu Dalo family were scattered outside on the front lawn.

"What did Abu Dalo do?"

"For two weeks he slept outside the house with his family in a makeshift hut. By the second week, he executed a plan: In the middle of the night he would sneak into the house through the root cellar. He would re-occupy."

"Did he have a gun?" I ask.

"Abu Dalo barely had enough clothes to wear. But he snuck in anyway. Made it all the way into his old bedroom."

"And?"

"He locked himself in there for a week. He told Shimon he wanted his house back."

I have too many questions. What did he eat? How did he relieve himself? Why didn't Shimon come in with a shotgun and blow Abu Dalo's head away?

"So what happened?"

"Abu Dalo started to built an extension to the house for the family to live in. Eventually, they worked it out. They decided they'd share the house."

"Were there courts involved?"

Rana hesitates. "I don't know. Maybe."

She says it was hard to get a straight story from either of them. Abu Dalo was engaged in one shady business deal or another and Shimon never talked to her unless he was drunk. Otherwise he'd refer to her as "The Arab," *ha-aravi*. Dina was worse: She never said a word to Rana. Still, they shared a semi-detached house, with separate entrances. Relations between them were tolerable, until the second intifada. Rana had met and married a Canadian Muslim by this time. As tensions got worse (in Jerusalem, and between her and Shimon), she found it easier to leave. In fact, she felt compelled to do so.

"I become too angry in Israel," she says. "It's impossible to remain calm about anything there."

I'm stuck on this house. In my mind, it's a dilapidated building with apartments crammed on top of each other. How many doors? How many rooms? How did Abu Dalo build an extension, illegally, without Shimon's consent?

"Is this unusual? An Israeli and a Palestinian—sharing the same house?"

"I guess so. Though it seemed kind of normal at the time. I mean, I was just living there and going to school. But it is pretty interesting. You should go see it."

Rana seems older than I am right now. The setting sun emphasizes the lines on her face. I wonder what she's doing in Canada, how she feels about being away from her home, if indeed she still considers it that. We sit in silence, but this time I'm less uncomfortable. Something is becoming clearer in my head. A need, a question, a place. A plan is forming.

She says, "Before you go to Jerusalem, will you do me one favour?"

"What?"

"Would you take me to your synagogue?"

CHAPTER 6

It's Friday afternoon, and the Keren Kayemet box is passed around the windowless classroom. We sing, the Hebrew consonants sticking in the back of our throats:

I shall tell you girl
and you too, boy
how in the land of Israel
the land is redeemed:
A dunam here, a dunam there,
clod after clod
the land of the people is bought
from the North to the Negev.
On the wall there hangs a box,
a blue box,
Every penny in the box
redeems land ...

Twenty-four children scream in Hebrew, trumpet a song whose meaning eludes us. We sing out of key, out of memory. And while the harmonics suck, the soul is loud. Our ten-year-old voices attack the words, our bodies rock back and forth at our desks, pounding tables, drumming thighs, repeating the plea:

On the wall there hangs a box,
a blue box,
Every penny in the box
redeems land ...

Mrs. Blintzkrieg stands in front of me as I fake-drop a quarter into the box. I have major doubts about this—a voice tells me we should wait until next week—but Jacob demands full speed ahead.

We've practised it time and again. You simply press your index finger against your thumb, thereby creating the illusion of a quarter. Then you make a slight rattle of the box, simulating deposit. I'm doing okay here, I think—Blintzkrieg coolly walks past, keeping an eye on the rest of the class—but I don't want to let my guard down. I lower my hand toward the slot and rattle.

A dunam here, a dunam there ...

Blintzkrieg pulls a move so quick I nearly have a heart attack. She takes a quick step toward me and slams her metal ruler against my desk.

"Shalom Garfinkel, do not cheat the land of Israel! Where is your donation?"

I suck the yelp back into my throat and nearly piss myself.

"I have no money this week."

"The nation of Israel would not survive without this blue and white box," Blintzkrieg declares, grinding her ruler into my desk. A sharp pain shoots up the length of my right arm. She calls upon Tiferet Grabinsky to recite the historical importance of the Keren Kayemet box.

Tiferet Grabinsky is all smiles and privilege. She's the cat's fucking meow. The Mercedes among the Chevys. She has shiny red pointed shoes that give new meaning to the term "goody two-shoes"; a "Strawberry Shortcake" lunch pail; and her smarter-than-thou glasses, pointed up at the sides, making her eyes look like they're constantly smiling.

Tiferet stands up and proudly begins, "In 1901, following the first Zionist Convention in Basel, Switzerland, the Jewish National Fund was created in order to buy land for the Jewish people in Palestine." Tiferet's glasses sparkle red when she speaks. "For over forty years Jews from around the world donated money to Keren Kayemet. The goal was to buy as much land as possible for the Jewish people in Palestine. This was enormously difficult, as many rich Arabs preferred not to sell land to Jews, for whom this land is holy and ever promised."

"Very good, Tiferet," says Blintzkrieg. She eases her grip on the ruler. The pain in my arm slowly disappears.

"I'm not finished yet, *gveret* Blintzkrieg." Tiferet clicks the heels of her red shoes and starts to rise, hovering a few inches above the floor. "The symbol of the Keren Kayemet box is of utmost importance. The JNF represents the hope of Jews all over the world, from India to Indiana, from Orange County to Odessa. This small box contains the entire spirit of the Jewish people."

"Good answer." Mrs. Blintzkrieg grimaces. Tiferet bats her eyelashes and lands back on the floor. "But if this box was only a symbol, we could do as Shalom did and only pretend to donate." She turns and looks at me. "Right?"

Jacob makes eyes at me. It's now or never.

"I'm sorry Mrs. Blintzkrieg. It will never happen again," I say. Jacob slumps down into his chair. As he has suspected, his best friend is a complete chickenshit.

Our strategy, in Jacob's words: "The opportunity presented itself when caught by higher authorities (i.e., the teachers of Bialik, *putuh*, may they rot in hell) will be to declare our position, that we are discontented Jews unhappy with the prop-u-ganda forced upon us. We salute Hank Greenberg and Sandy Koufax, who prove that people of the Hebraic faith are more than great hairsplitters of Talmud and warriors of the land. We first and foremost demand a return of all wanton tennis balls stolen from our possession with the lame excuse they promote eye injuries. And furthermore, and finally, we demand a baseball diamond, a soccer field, a swing set, a slide, and some friggin' grass."

I have failed our cause. But instead of doing nothing, Jacob leaps up from his seat and announces: "*Gveret* Blintzkrieg, I need to confess. I stole Shalom's money."

A gasp arises from the class.

"Shalom had two dollars he was going to give to Keren Kayemet this week. I stole it from his jacket, unbeknownst to him."

"Is this true Shalom? Did you have two dollars in your coat?"

I'm flabbergasted by Jacob's false confession.

"Shalom, you dim-witted moron, answer me!"

*Every penny in the box
redeems land ...*

I say nothing. Mrs. Blintzkrieg walks over to Jacob.

"Well?" she asks. "Where's the money?"

Jacob stands up theatrically, nodding to both sides of the class as though he were about to perform a magic trick. He pulls a perfectly crisp two-dollar bill from his Bible. He declares, "This is ransom money."

"What are you talking about?"

"Until tennis balls are returned to their proper owners. Until we can play football and baseball without scraping our skin on concrete—I am withholding this donation from the Jewish National Fund."

"Jacob, don't be an idiot."

"In the name of Hank Greenberg and Sandy Koufax, I hereby declare the beginning of the Recess Revolution!"

We all nod in agreement with the Prophet Jacob.

Mrs. Blintzkrieg lunges for the money. Jacob, who has excellent reflexes, hops away from her hand and steps onto his desk. "And now, the disappearing act." He tears up the red two-dollar bill and chomps on it. Jacob declares, "When I shit this money out, I will save it in a container in the science lab. Only when you put green grass and a couple of trees in this parking lot will I donate this shit-ass money to the people of Israel!"

Blintzkrieg points her finger at Jacob. The class holds its breath. For what seems like forty days and forty nights, Jacob stares at her stubby digit. We all stare. That finger is everything: What we do, think, say. Jacob smirks, shrugs his shoulders and jumps down from the chair. He calmly lets himself be led out of the room.

Now a deeper silence invades the class. We fear the worst.

Rumour Numero Uno: One month ago, Danny Fingerbaum, in an act of impressive rebelliousness, wrote a note on a small piece of paper and put it inside the Keren Kayemet box instead of the requisite change. The note read: **THIS IS BULLSHIT. YOU TEACHERS KEEP THIS MONEY FOR YERSELVES.** They say Blintzkrieg took Fingerbaum into an empty classroom. For forty-five minutes she interrogated the poor kid until he broke down weeping. But Blintzkrieg didn't just want his confession. She demanded a five-page treatise on the importance of Keren Kayemet L'Yisrael. She didn't want us to admit our guilt; we had to change our minds.

Rumour Numero Deux: In the storeroom next to our class there's a large grey metal closet. None of us have ever seen it, but we know it's there. They say Blintzkrieg put so-and-so in there for an entire hour for having cheated on a test. We know what Jacob has done is a thousand times more serious. There's no doubt in our minds: Blintzkrieg must, at all costs, crush the rebellion.

I can't help but imagine the scene.

The closet is five feet in height and three feet wide. There are six shelves full of course books, mostly the primer Tiferet recited from. Beneath the bottom shelf there is maybe two feet of space. I wonder how Jacob would fit in there. He'd probably go limp, play dead on the floor. Blintzkrieg would have to pick him up from underneath his arms, push him forward one scrawny leg at a time. Realizing it's game over, Jacob would pull his legs into the darkness. Blintzkrieg would slam the door and say, "This is what we do to thieves."

In my mind Jacob turns to me, flashes his little devil's smile and says, "Don't worry buddy, I can take this." Blintzkrieg turns the key in the door handle.

After a few minutes she returns without Jacob, and we continue with the afternoon pre-Shabbat proceedings. I can hear him breathe even though he's in the room next door. What does Jacob see in that closet? When we make the blessing over the wine, I hear the sound of a black Sharpie marker. The Sharpie is something Jacob carries with him to be used for impromptu graffiti. Only I can recognize the sound of marker against metal.

I am here. He-neni.

Jacob writes these words in English and Hebrew. He wants, more than anything, to be heard.

CHAPTER 7

I decide it's best to take Rana to the Minsk when no one is praying. She's cool with that—she only wants to see inside. All her life she's lived among Jews, but she's never set foot into a shul. This is a pilgrimage. To witness what's behind closed doors.

I'm nervous walking through Kensington Market with her. What if we run into Judith? Yankl? What will I say?

There's nothing wrong with what I'm doing, I tell myself. A friend is simply interested in seeing the synagogue.

We stroll past the punks drunk on beer, the teenagers stoned on pot, the fishmongers, the bread-makers and nut-sellers. Rana has never been to Kensington and she's enamoured of its lack of apology.

"Really!" she exclaims. "Finally, somewhere with life."

We walk through the mess of shopkeepers and shoppers, the vintage Day-Glo clothes, coffee culture, tea culture, Chinese-Portuguese-Vietnamese-French-English spittle-prattle. We pass my apartment on Baldwin.

"I live here," I say, pointing to the beige, beaten door. I look at the upstairs window. The apartment lights are out.

IN THE MEN'S SECTION of the synagogue, she is full of questions.

"What are the silver crowns for? How many Torahs are in the ark? Why do women sit upstairs?"

She flips through the *Five Books of Moses*, opens it randomly to a page, scans it, then puts it down on a bench face up. I hand her a prayer book from which she reads the title aloud in Hebrew: *Siddur l'tfeelot*. Her accent is thick, her pronunciation precise, the way my teachers might have read the passage. She returns the book and asks me to sing a prayer.

"Here?"

"Why not?" she says.

I open the book and recognize the song right away. Sing in a low, hushed tone. As though prayer itself were illegal.

Sim, sim, sim shalom
Sim shalom tova u-bracha

Rana sits in the front pew, resting her head in her arms. I'm standing at the foot of the bimah. We're both facing east toward Jerusalem. It occurs to me I've never seen a woman in the downstairs section before. It's allowed when there's no group prayer, but it still feels weird. A Muslim-Palestinian woman—in the men's section of an Orthodox shul?

Once, on Purim, I came to synagogue wearing Judith's black lace dress, eyeliner, and hair done up pretty. When I entered the men's section I was terrified. I had entered forbidden territory. Purim celebrates Queen Esther's saving of the Jewish people and encourages one to dress up as a character in the story. It even allows for cross-dressing—the one day of the Jewish calendar that does so. I felt exposed dressed as Queen Esther. Until the whisky. Yankl poured the shots, and we got so drunk we couldn't remember what was right and what was left anymore, just as the great sages command us to do on this holiday. Judith and I danced (stumbled, twisted) downstairs to Ronnie Wiseman's Hasidic reggae band, Kedushah, a white handkerchief joining our hands, the skin that cannot touch.

Rana closes her eyes to listen.

The prayer is beautiful, typically melodic. It's in a minor key, as many of the prayers are.

(At my youngest brother, Joseph's, bar mitzvah, I was the *chazzan* for one day only, leading the congregation in song, in chant.)

Establish peace, goodness, blessing and life ...

I look up. The rabbi leans against the doorframe, folding his arms under his chest. How long has he been watching?

"I see you've brought a guest," says the rabbi, fingering the *tsitses* that hang at the bottom of his white shirt. He gathers a bunch and presses them nervously in his hand.

"A friend," I say. "She's from out of town."

"Where are you from?" he asks, looking at Rana.

She says, "Jerusalem."

The rabbi's eyes immediately light up. He walks toward us. "Jerusalem," he says. "What street?"

"Mekor Chayim."

"Ah, fantastic. Do you know the Shapiros?"

"No."

"What's your name?"

"Rana."

I always imagined the rabbi was born ebullient, kind and generous. As though he popped out of his mother's womb with a smile on his face, singing, "Praised be Hashem!" But it is with great difficulty he says, "*Welcome.*" He says it in a way I've never heard him say it before; a hushed tone, an accident. The rabbi looks at me, then at her. He wonders what the hell I'm doing.

"Jonathan," he says, "you were going to come by the other day to talk."

"I'm sorry, Rabbi. Something came up."

"Life is short," says the rabbi grimly, looking straight at me. "Time is the one luxury a Jew cannot afford."

"I'm thinking of going to Israel," I say.

This takes me by surprise. I hadn't meant to say this. That is, the plan to go wasn't really a plan yet. Of course the rabbi's pleased, though slightly guarded in his tone.

"*Mazel tov*. Is Judith coming with?"

"I don't know if she can come. I'm thinking of going for some time."

"Well," the rabbi pauses, twisting a lone *tsitse* around his index finger until it turns red from the pressure. He does not look at Rana. "I have work to do in the basement, a mail-out of letters. Come and help if you like."

When the rabbi leaves the sanctuary and heads downstairs, Rana turns to me. "Thank you," she says.

"For what?" I ask.

"For not being afraid," she says.

She kisses me on the cheek, lets her lips stay a quarter second longer than a casual kiss among acquaintances. It feels like an ember has been deposited on my skin.

"I'll call you," I say. The words stumble from my mouth.

Rana pushes open the sixteen-foot-high doors in the main hallway. The light blinds me. I think she turns back to look but I can't be sure. The door clanks shut and I see the *chumash* open on the wooden bench. I pick it up and read the passage. It's from the Book of Joshua.

And they exterminated everything in the city with the sword:
man and woman,
young and old,
and ox and sheep and ass.

CHAPTER 8

In the basement of the Minsk are rows of plastic brown tables. On one sit four piles of letters numbering in the several thousands. Sarah sits between the rabbi and me at a round table stuffing envelopes. The rabbi and I fold the letters into three.

"What are you doing?" the rabbi asks me.

"Reading," I say.

"We need folders, not readers." The rabbi continues to fold his letter; he does it quickly and accurately. At the line containing the word *Gaza* he makes the first fold, and at the line containing the words "two thousand years" he makes the second. When I fold the letter it never comes out quite evenly. Sarah glares at me when I make her envelope stuffing more difficult than need be.

"Shouldn't I know what I'm folding?" I ask.

"Sometimes it's easier to criticize and harder just to do," says the rabbi.

True, I think. As usual there is more than a grain of truth to what the rabbi says.

"He's lucky he can read," says Sarah. "If I could I'd be reading too. I never got an education. That's why I cook and sew, I'll have you know." Sarah continues to stuff and lick the envelopes. She's been doing it since nine this morning. It's a wonder she hasn't dropped dead from glue poisoning. "Nineteen forty-five, Montreal. It was a different world then. Albert would come by and take me to the dance, and later for ice cream. Rocky road. With real marshmallows."

"What's a real marshmallow?" I ask.

Sarah ignores me. "Even in winter we ate ice cream." While her words wax nostalgic, her tone and eyes don't miss a beat: They follow the rhythm of her tongue that licks the envelope. Her face has a look of complaining even when she isn't complaining. "Boy I wish I'd been lucky like you, getting an education."

"Indeed," says the rabbi, folding with incredible precision, "Jonathan, you are a lucky, lucky man."

"Thank you, Rabbi and Sarah," I say, doing my best to follow the rabbi's lead.

"Sarah, did you know Jonathan is going to the Holy Land?"

"So what, everyone goes."

"It would be my first time," I pipe up.

"I was fifty-six when I went," says Sarah. "I hated the place. It's too hot and everyone's crabby. It's the land of the kvetch. Imagine. An entire country of crazy Jews."

"The first time," says the rabbi, doing one of the things he is best at: ignoring naysayers. "That indeed is something." The rabbi pauses and looks at the stack of letters. "Well, we've done a third. Three thousand more to go."

"I'll be licking until my tongue falls off," says Sarah. She pauses and looks at me. "Say, you're not hungry, are you *bubele*?"

"Why, you have something to eat?"

"I have chicken soup. Noodles. I could put something not so bad together for you."

"I'm okay, Sarah." Really I'm starving, but I feel I should be going soon. The last thing I want is the rabbi to ask me why I brought a Palestinian into his shul.

"Come on. Let me feed you. You're like the son I never had."

"I thought you had a son."

"Three of them," she says. Sarah gets up and waddles across the synagogue floor to the kitchen.

"Israel, Israel, Israel. This is big news, Jonathan. What will you be doing there?"

"There's a house I want to write about."

"Speaking of houses, if you need anyone to stay with, or have a killer Shabbos, let me know."

"I will."

"A yeshiva, too, if you want to study. You know there's nothing like it, studying Torah in the Holy Land."

The idea sounds appealing. I imagine the joy the mystic Shlomo Halevi must have experienced, reading from the Tanakh in the early morning Galilee light. Then I think about Halevi's Lecha Dodi, and the Book of Joshua lying open upstairs. I don't remember the Bible being so bloody and ruthless when I read it at Bialik. Granted, the last time I read it, I was thirteen years old. I used to fall asleep whenever the Tanakh teacher Alon Eloni spoke. While he read about flaming chariots, wrathful punishment, divine death, his voice was calm. His words were like hands, gentle on the shoulders, soft on the soul.

"So tell me. Why didn't you come and talk to me the other day?" the rabbi asks.

"I was busy with some research," I say.

"What kind?"

I ignore his question and respond with another. "Can we talk Torah?"

"Of course. Nothing would please me more."

"The Book of Joshua."

"A good book," says the rabbi.

"I was wondering, why did God command Joshua to brutalize the Canaanites?"

The rabbi pauses with the next letter in mid-fold. He rocks back and forth on his chair. He closes his eyes and speaks to me this way.

"Nowhere in the Bible does God enjoy seeing any of His creatures killed. Even when the Egyptians drowned in the Red Sea, they who terrorized us for four hundred years, God scorned the Children of Israel for celebrating. He shouted, 'Why are you rejoicing? These are my creatures!'"

"So why do the Jews slaughter the people of Jericho?"

"The Canaanites were idol worshippers."

"Do idol worshippers deserve to be killed?"

"They also conducted the sacrifice of children. They were evil people, Jonathan, not followers of the Law."

"Isn't our job as Jews to witness?"

"That's right. It's God who judges. We listen to what He says."

"Amalek, I can appreciate that. They were trying to annihilate us. The story of Esther, okay. David and Goliath? No problem. But an innocent people—the entire citizens of a city? Why would God command Joshua to do that?"

Sarah re-enters the room carrying two steaming Styrofoam bowls of chicken soup, one for the rabbi and one for me.

She commands, "Don't put any salt in."

"All right," I say.

"It'll ruin it."

"That's fine, Sarah."

"Always, you put salt on everything. Taste it first."

I do. I burn my tongue.

"Blow on it! *Shmendrik.*"

I blow on a spoonful of soup. Taste it. It needs salt. Terribly.

"It's wonderful," I say.

A stack of letters falls over. Sarah starts to gather them in smaller piles.

"For the love of Joseph," she says. "I go away for three minutes and all chaos breaks loose. What happened here?"

"Jonathan and I are engaged in Talmud."

"Talmud schmalmud. What can I know? I never learned how to read," she says, taking a small pile of letters for herself. "My tongue is sticking to the roof of my mouth. Garfinkel, your turn to lick."

The rabbi turns to me. "Judith is concerned."

"What's Judith worried about?"

"She thinks you're depressed."

"I'm just uncertain about things."

"Like what?"

"Like why Joshua had to kill all those people."

"Why do you have to focus on this one story?"

"One story? Doesn't this *story* sound familiar?"

"What are you talking about?" asks the rabbi.

"The Promised Land, from the beginning, has been about occupation."

"Let's talk about your trip to Israel. What's this house all about?"

"I want to understand something about that country."

"Understanding is good. It can bring peace."

"That's right. The house is peace."

"It's good to want peace," says the rabbi. "Baruch Hashem, first we need to find peace in ourselves."

"And how do we do that? Please don't say through reading Torah."

"Reading Torah helps."

"How?"

"Right mindfulness, Jonathan. You study, put your mind into it, you make an effort to be good."

"The Book of Joshua teaches me nothing about how to be good."

"Torah keeps you focused on being a better person."

"Don't you understand what I'm trying to say?"

"I hear you. You're concerned about occupation. Everyone talks about occupation, like it directly affects *them*. Because we Jews have done something terrible to this planet. Polluted it with our *horrendous* occupation. Because no one else ever does anything wrong ... except for the Jews. Why on earth are you, Jonathan Garfinkel, who lives in Toronto, Canada, so worked up about this? You haven't even been to the country you criticize."

Sarah has stopped folding letters. I stare at my feet.

There was a rule my Baba had in her house: No one was allowed to mention the words *Arab* or *Israel* at the dinner table. Were that line to be crossed, she would turn to my grandfather and simply say, *"Genug."* Enough. And he would know to shut up. Maybe the rabbi is right. Why do I care about the occupation? What does this house mean to me? Why, in the fourth year of the second intifada, do I want to go to Israel?

Sarah, illiterate, voice of reason: "Shut up you two, and eat your chicken soup."

CHAPTER 9

In our flat on Baldwin Street I sit in my small, dingy office. The radiators gently hiss. People buy bread in the bakery below—poppyseed inquiries, change exchanged, banter between customer and baker. Their voices are so close it sounds as though they're stuck in this tiny room with me. Cramped with dusty books, old photographs, stories from my life. But their voices are not crying, "Help, it's small in here!" They are not saying, "Why is it so difficult to think in this apartment?" Their choices—sesame or rye, brown or white—are clear and well-defined.

I have not told Judith that yesterday I spoke to Barak about Rana and the story of the house. He was intrigued, and agreed the house might be a strong metaphor for the situation in his country. Still, he was skeptical. "What are you going to fill the house with?" he wanted to know. "What is the *story*?" He wanted to see some scenes before he made any kind of proposal to a theatre for the residency. I told him I'd email him when I had something and we left it at that. I hung up the phone, stared at my computer screen and started to type.

What. The. Hell.

Yesterday and today and still nothing written. In truth, I'm relieved. Part of me is hoping to fail, to not be able to write anything of interest so I can say there is no story here. There is no need to tell Judith. No need for me to go there without her and pursue a story that is beyond the logos of our covenant. I look at the photo of my grandmother keeping guard of my desk. What would she think? "Go or not go," she'd probably say. "Just write something that bursts with life. It's time for you to grow up, shmendrik. To write something real, *mit chayim.* The Yiddish word for 'life' is plural for a reason: It's complicated. It isn't just one note."

To go to Israel and look for the house of Shimon and Abu Dalo is to leave this apartment. If I leave, will I come back? The one window in my office looks out onto a red brick wall. Judith's painted yellow and green stars on it to give me more light. This apartment is one of the only places I've ever considered home. In part it's the shared history, the story of two lovers absorbed by the walls. What Judith and I have created together, what we fight over, what we forget. But it's more than the sum of two people's lives. Home is also in the architecture, the street, the neighbourhood history. The morning after our first night together, we drank dark Cuban coffee on the roof and watched old Toronto below us. The Saturday afternoon Marxists shouted through their red and white megaphones. The punks wandered hungover toward Planet Kensington. The hipsters shopped for vintage clothing. I remembered coming to the Market as a kid with my Zaida Ben. The Jewish butchers used to slaughter chickens and geese, a buck a head. That morning on the roof, it was February cold.

Within four months of our meeting I moved in. It didn't matter that she'd lived there for ten years; I felt I'd come home. In my study, books and papers sit quietly on their shelves. In the corner rests the desk I used as a kid. When I want to write I close the door. I can hear Judith quietly tip-toeing past. Sometimes I hear her stop. I imagine her pressing her ear against the door, listening. What does she hear?

INSTEAD OF DRAFTS for a play my desk is littered with possibilities for a trip.

1. Phone number for El Al airlines, Toronto.
2. Phone number for Samer Shalabi, a Palestinian cameraman in Ramallah.
3 Books Rana has recommended: Amira Hass's *Reporting from Ramallah: An Israeli Journalist in an Occupied Land.* Norman Finkelstein's *Palestine and Israel: The Myths and Realities.*
4. A map of the country (I stare at the names of cities—*Bethlehem, Haifa, Safad*—speak them in my mind. Something is etched, somewhere in the hippocampus, so they say. It's memory, my brain that's affected, which is me I suppose).
5. A photograph of my grandfather stirring a bowl of his homemade mustard. Behind him hangs the poster, "Visit Palestine."

The photograph makes me think of the last time I visited him. He's been dead four years now. We listened to the radio in his kitchen, eating thick pumpernickel bread with fresh butter. Zaida Ben wrote letters to dignitaries the world over informing them of his plans to save humanity from complete and utter destruction. I have a letter I carry with me, folded three times in my wallet. It's the one he wrote to Boris Yeltsin shortly before his fall from grace in Russia. Please ignore the folds in the paper and the yellowing lines.

February 15, 1998

Dear Mr. Yeltsin,

In 1993 I wrote you a letter congratulating you on your victory in the newly formed Federation of Russia. I understand you are a busy man, and that is why only your secretary was able to get back to me, but I am nonetheless grateful for her response.

Now that you are losing popularity in the second largest country (in area) in the world, I wanted to bring to your attention an idea that might help your position in the polls. But before the proposal, the facts:

1. *We live in a world that is not sustainable. This is in part due to the burning of fossil fuels, which is creating this dire situation known as Global Warming (now to be referred to in this letter as "GW").*
2. *It is ESSENTIAL we start looking to the future. In fifty years from now, the streets of Winnipeg, Canada, will be flooded due to GW. What remains of this great prairie city will be nothing more than small islands of people living in tribal situations.*
3. *Flooding will also mean famine and poor health due to malnutrition and excessive water (cholera, malaria, etc.).*
4. *I do not hesitate to predict similar conditions for your country.*

PROPOSAL: to turn our northern cities into natural grain storage facilities. As average winter temperatures in Churchill and Irkutsk are minus fifty degrees centigrade, grain can be stored without any electricity or concern of it rotting. In the event of thermonuclear or environmental disaster, we would be prepared if we each had several thousand kilotonnes of wheat, rye and millet at our disposal (I understand you might grimace at the sound of millet, but it is a nutritious and fair-tasting grain made even better with my homemade mustard—see enclosed sample packet). Regardless of what grains we choose to store (you may prefer barley or flax seed, for example), I do believe this mission ESSENTIAL for our survival as a human species. I have included various diagrams and maps of

Churchill's port and grain storage facilities (see figures 1a through 3c) for your reference.

I am an environmental chemist, son of Romanian immigrants, though my father spent most of his years in Odessa, a city you are likely familiar with. He told me the Black Sea rolls in "beautifully" toward the port that is Odessa. As a scientist I am no authority on beauty, but I can assure you that in fifty years there will be no food left to feed the inhabitants of Odessa if we do not start acting NOW.

Your comrade,
Benjamin Berck, environmental chemist

It was a bitter cold February. I arrived in Winnipeg to visit Zaida Ben and found him surprisingly weak. At the age of eighty-four he was clearing forty inches of prairie snow in minus-thirty-five-degree weather and felt unusually tired. I convinced him to go to the doctor, who said Zaida's shortness of breath was the result of a heart attack. The fact of his failing body enraged Zaida Ben. He was convinced he had successfully reversed the aging process by eating a daily diet of Red River cereal, organic apples and borscht. He slept in regimented segments of no more than two hours at a time, drank green tea and could often be found in the headstand position at all hours in strange places.

"The necessary transfer of blood," he claimed once when I found him precariously balanced on the *Yellow Pages* in the kitchen.

It was a bad winter for Zaida. Three weeks before my arrival, the Manitoba government revoked his driver's licence. A police officer found him driving the wrong way on a one-way street in River Heights. Fortunately he was only driving twenty-five kilometres an hour. Zaida Ben said he was gathering samples for an experiment, a particular shrub had caught his eye. Now the car lay dormant, dead in the garage. After the heart attack the doctor wanted him to stay in hospital. Zaida demanded to be sent home. The doctor said, Ben, you're going to die. For the first time in his life, my Zaida listened.

He was confined to a bed with an oxygen mask, IV tubes and a morphine pump plunged into his veins. His eyes: bloodshot. He didn't respond to my questions. I leaned over the hospital bed and bent at the waist, the way one bends for Aleinu in the synagogue, pressing my ear to his chest. I listened for his heart. It was still there, faint, the echo of a life. Suddenly Zaida Ben grabbed my hand, yanked off the oxygen mask and whispered into my ear, "This is going against all my theories."

He knew he had only a short time left. He dictated his mustard recipe to me. His mustard is famous in our family and among any friends who have tried it. It has an unusual mix of spices, a peppery horseradish smell that brings tears to the eyes and warmth to the chest. It is good on just about anything—meat, cheese, eggs, blintzes. Even kasha, boiled buckwheat, absorbs its piquant taste. The catch is that Zaida Ben has never told anyone the ingredients, until now. He whispered beneath the sound of the machine that monitored his heart.

Boil the demerara sugar for one minute on low, no more.
Stir gently, never be cruel to the flour or the wine.
Use forty-eight percent oriental mustard seed.
And so on.

He survived the hospital episode, but it still shocked him to realize he was going to die. When we returned to his house on Queenston Bay, he invited me in to the kitchen for the first time while he made the mustard. He led me through the finer points of the process. I snapped a picture of him, black and white in 1/60 speed, standing over the smooth metal bowl, stirring whole-wheat flour with a metal whisk.

The man moved one frame at a time. The epic expedition to the
sink to haul water (four cups) made him pause halfway, consider the
piece of lint on the floor and the label on the stove in his tiny red
"microscript" that read: "Warning: Extra *extra* hot!" He continued on
to the sink and wiped the sweat from his brow. He paused, contemplating an *Ideas* special on CBC radio.

The CBC announcer commented on the recent effects of global
warming, and a physicist interviewed discussed the perils of winning
the Nobel Prize. Zaida Ben muttered, "Grain silos, they're already abandoned, why don't they just use them, for Chrissakes, they're just sitting
there, fill them up with GRAIN!" He was enraged his ideas weren't
taken more seriously. His huge belly drooped over his cracked leather
belt. It lent weight to what he was talking about, but it also seemed to
mock him. His head (hairless) was crammed with ideas no one would
ever hear but his family, who had long grown tired of his rants.

In those final days, Zaida Ben often spoke about the Arab-Israeli
crisis. He had always been a passionate supporter of Israel. One of the

treasures in his museum-like basement (pack rats make wonderful archivists) was a black, orange and gold poster that said, "VISIT PALESTINE." It was printed in 1935 in Jerusalem. I imagined the head of tourism in Palestine bellowing this as a Biblical-like commandment: *You better come or else,* was the message in that poster. I brought it up to show Zaida. He told me it was originally designed by a Zionist development agency. The artwork debunked the myths I had been taught as a child. The crowded houses inside the walled city of Jerusalem showed concrete evidence of a populated land— hardly a land without a people as my teachers at Bialik Hebrew Day School had intoned.

Zaida: "My mother wanted to move to the Holy Land in the 1920s. The aliyah idea was debated in my family, and many fights arose as to whether we should leave or stay."

In the end, Ben's father won the argument and they stayed in Kildonan, Manitoba, where they continued to farm barley and wheat. His mother worked as a mid-wife, delivering the children of Ukrainian and Scandinavian immigrants. The Berckoviches endured the Great Depression; Ben skinned muskrats and groundhogs to earn a living, a buck a skin. And you could cook the varmints over fire for a meal.

My grandfather expressed enormous regret about never making the move to Palestine. He, like his wife, was an ardent socialist, and believed he belonged on the kibbutzim of the Promised Land, tilling collective farms, working the soil.

ZAIDA BEN'S EYES WERE RED from medication and lack of sleep. In the foreground, a clothesline held a thin line of snow.

He picked up the phone and dialed an endless array of numbers.

"I'd like to purchase a one-way ticket to Jerusalem," he said into the mouthpiece.

I could hear the woman on the other side of the phone saying there are no tickets to Jerusalem, only Tel Aviv.

"One ticket to Jerusalem," my grandfather demanded. His voice sounded stronger, more determined than it had since his heart attack five days before.

She explained to him that El Al has no international flights to Jerusalem. My grandfather said she was lying.

"Why the hell would I lie to you?" she yelled.

"Because you're an anti-Semite," he screamed.

I grabbed the telephone receiver. Started to talk in Hebrew, which I knew my grandfather wouldn't understand. Hebrew in his day was the language of prayer.

"My grandfather is dying," I explained.

"Your grandfather is a pain in the ass," she said.

"He wants to make it to the Holy Land before he passes on."

I could hear the ticket agent on the other side of the phone light up a cigarette. Her voice had a twang of annoyance that grew as she spoke. "Look, there's a thousand and one *meshuggeners* who want to come to the Promised Land before they die. Tell the guy to buy a ticket to Tel Aviv. Otherwise he can wait in his grave until the Messiah comes to take everyone on his big Moshiach plane and drop them off at the Wailing fucking Wall."

I covered the mouthpiece and asked, "How about a ticket to Tel Aviv?"

"I want to go to Jerusalem," he said.

"You can take a bus to Jerusalem. It's only forty-five minutes away."

When I said this to him, I realized that, like me, he knew Israel only in the imagination: in posters, maps and newspaper articles. The distance from Tel Aviv to Jerusalem might be only eighty kilometres, but in our minds they were worlds apart.

"I want to go to Jerusalem," he repeated, his voice quivering.

The late-afternoon winter sun turned into shadow; darkness passed over my grandfather's face. He took the phone from my hand and slammed it on its cradle.

I was required to ensure my grandfather remained calm—doctor's orders.

"Is the mustard okay to sit like this?" I asked.

"The problem," he said suddenly, pounding the table, "is Arafat. He's a terrorist and he deserves to die."

"When do you think the mustard will be done?" I put my hands on his bony shoulders and massaged him.

"We need to slaughter every last Arab!"

"I'm covering it with wax paper."

"They cannot be trusted." He picked up the phone and held the receiver against his heart and said, "They always carry daggers. And they smile when they kill you."

He hung up the phone for the last time. I covered the mustard with wax paper and left the bowl to settle in the fridge.

The next morning we sat on the old green couch. Baba hadn't sat there for two years and still it smelled like her. I'd found an eight-by-ten colour photo of an astronaut in the basement. He wore an orange space suit and carried a helmet in his hand.

"Ilan Ramon," Zaida said when I showed him the picture.

"Who?"

"Mark my words: He'll be the first Israeli in outer space. The man is a real hero. Unlike you," he said irritably.

I held my grandfather's head in my lap, studied the lines in his skin: the past, faint, pockmarked. He drifted in and out of consciousness. He had been on a two-day diatribe about a country neither of us had been to. "Only an Israeli could be so brave and smart," he said about Ilan in one breath. In the next: "Arabs are too stupid to fly into outer space." Zaida Ben was right. I was cowardly. I did not utter what I was thinking: How could a diehard socialist, desperate to save humanity, want to wipe out all of Arabia? I did not say anything because I didn't want to upset him. I sat in silence trying to ignore my anger.

"They are beasts," he explained to me, which is when the conversation finally ended. Holding Zaida's head in my lap, I read the newspaper and fell asleep with him, my head resting against the back of the sofa. When he awoke he was confused and wanted to know what time it was.

"It's afternoon," I said.

"Have we missed breakfast?" he asked.

"Yes."

"I've never missed breakfast in my entire life."

I flipped on the TV. There happened to be a special on Yitzhak Rabin, his life and times flashing before us. The images of his assassination lulled Zaida back to sleep. Dreaming of Red River cereal. The wings of an airplane ascending toward heaven. Sky service. Room service. Help. Help. Help.

On the floor the Palestine poster lay in its black frame. The Dome of the Rock, half emblazoned in sun, half in shadow. Beyond it were the houses and hills of Jerusalem, and outside the walls of the old city, sand and rock painted orange. Beside the poster lay the photograph of Ilan Ramon. He stared at me, his black eyes intent on space. He held his NASA helmet proudly. And the orange of his uniform looked like the sand that surrounded Jerusalem. Zaida slept in my lap. I imagined the heat against my face, my hands touching hot stone.

VISIT PALESTINE. VISIT PALESTINE.

CHAPTER 10

I'm leaving, I say to Max the cat, who rubs his right cheek against my left shin.

Max, blind and seventeen, doesn't really give a shit about this drama. He swipes his claw at me, knocking the passport out of my shirt pocket. Judith sits up in bed, startled.

"Oh. It's you." She says this as though disappointed.

"Who else?" I ask.

"I was having a dream. I'm so tired. Up all night on a shoot." She falls back on the bed.

When I returned from the travel agent today, I thought of the first time Judith invited me inside her apartment. The smell reminded me of the dry sauna at the Bloor JCC when I was a young boy, sitting with my grandfather on hot cedar planks. The heat made the insides of my nostrils burn. It was a feeling both comforting and alarming—as though I were being baked, my limbs slowly turning into bread.

I pick up the passport from the floor and sit in the doorframe. The hard wood pushes into my back. I look at Judith and think about Rana: how she looks when she sleeps. Does she curl her hands toward her mouth? Does she stretch her arms wide across the bed? Max sticks his tail in my face, brings me back to the moment. His soft fur, his gentle purr. I stroke him, listen to the record of Judith's sleep.

WE'RE IN THE BATHROOM. I don't know how to say this. So I talk about something else.

"I was speaking with the rabbi. He wants us to help with the phone-a-thon. After the fire last year, the shul really needs help." Last year a bunch of arsonists piled religious books up in the women's section and lit them on fire. Fortunately a Chinese restaurant owner called the police before the whole synagogue burned down.

She pauses in mid-scrub and looks at me. "It's terrible what happened. Like Nazi Germany, right here in North America."

I haven't told Judith about Rana. I have not told her anything. Judith plucks her eyebrows.

"You'll have to tell me more later. I have to get to set."

When she's not a theatre director Judith works in film as a script girl. The money's good but the hours are a grind. It's 8 P.M. now and she'll likely be there all night. Judith applies foundation to her face.

"Will you do the dishes?" she asks.

"Sure."

"But when you do them, will you actually do them?" She applies the foundation in rapid, jagged motions, not gentle at all.

"Of course."

"This afternoon I had to wash them all over again. I can't stand it, being your mother."

"My mother never washed my dishes. We had a dishwasher."

"Whatever."

I walk to the kitchen table and pick up one of the sample phone-a-thon letters. Sitting at the table, I start to read.

"What's it say?" asks Judith. She enters the kitchen and starts putting away clean dishes.

"Some sort of bullshit about the problems of Israel are the problems of all Jewish people. You know, the Minsk didn't used to be so political when I started going there five years ago."

She turns on the hot water and washes a dish.

"I said I'd do them."

"I used this one," she says. "I just want to make sure you do your own."

Her hand circles a clay brown plate, more gently than when she'd washed her own face moments ago. The plate is part of a set my mother gave us when I first moved in with Judith. I remember the plates from childhood—they were the meat dishes in our kosher kitchen. Now they're used for anything—cheese, Portuguese sausage, prosciutto. I put down the piece of paper and say, "Sometimes the rabbi can be such a moron." Judith drops the plate and it shatters on the floor. The pieces scatter across the black and white tiles of the kitchen. For some reason this makes me laugh.

"Shit," she says.

"Don't worry about it." I immediately regret my cackle.

"It's broken."

"There's another five of them."

"Four."

I get up. "It's okay, Judith."

The smell of smoke suddenly invades the room. The bakers must have burned their last batch of bread before closing. This is a smell I hate; charred crust, burnt dough. It makes the room stuffy, the air acrid. I join her down on the floor and pick up the larger pieces with my hands, trying to avoid her glance.

I ought to say, "Judith, I bought a single plane ticket to Tel Aviv today."

Instead: "The rabbi thinks they'll get over five hundred people out to the fundraiser if we help with the phone calls." I stand now, sweeping, my focus completely on the blue broom and Judith's pale, long fingers that cradle the yellow dustpan she holds as she crouches to the floor.

"Sounds romantic," she says. "A helluva date." The tip of my broom meets her dustpan. She tilts it forward then back to let the broken pieces fall toward her. With a careless *ka-junk* she dumps the remains of the plate into the garbage, banging the rim of the metal can. We're still crouched on the floor when she asks, "Who's Rana?"

I feel like she's just ka-junked the shattered plate into my mouth. "I met her. At a movie. She's a friend."

She doesn't look at me. "You should bring her by. I'd like to meet her."

Judith gets up and starts to pace the kitchen, gathering the things she'll need for set: clipboard, suitcase on rollers, stopwatch. She's moving quickly. It makes me nervous.

"I found a book of yours," she says. "Norman Finkelstein."

"I haven't read it."

"There were notes scrawled in the margins in your handwriting."

"Okay, I've read some of it."

I don't know why I feel defensive. I've read a few chapters, but it's not like I agree with the guy. His sweeping condemnation of Israel puts me off. Why can't I just tell her that? Instead I find myself defending him, adopting his point of view.

"Jonathan, he's a self-hating Jew."

"His parents were survivors."

"I don't care if his parents were survivors." She points her finger accusingly. "It says Jews massacred Palestinians."

"Some did."

"He accuses Israel of having an *apartheid* system."

"He's allowed to have an opinion. And besides, it's strong scholarly work."

"Israel is not South Africa. You of all people should know that. Don't tell me you're becoming ... a ... a ... a whatever." Exasperated, Judith starts stuffing the necessities into her suitcase: running shoes, paper, calculator.

I say, "I'm just trying to understand some other perspectives."

"Don't you know what's in the Hamas constitution? They want to drive Israel into the sea."

"Not all Palestinians are Hamas."

"What do you do with her?"

"Who?"

"Your friend. Rana."

"We meet for coffee from time to time."

"She calls here."

This is news to me. "She does?"

"She hangs up when I pick up the phone. Today I called the number that came up." Fucking call display. Judith is holding the yellow stopwatch in her hand as though she were timing this conversation. "You're not having an affair, are you?"

"She's married, for Chrissakes. To an orthodox Muslim."

"So she is Palestinian?"

"Yes."

Judith zips up her suitcase. "I don't have time for this right now. I have to get to work."

The thing about decisions is you can't think too much about them. Otherwise they don't make any sense. Jacob and I talked about this the other day when we were playing basketball at the Bloor JCC. We were doing our one-on-one thing, what we've been playing since we were kids. Last week he finally said it straight: "You're turning into a fucker. There comes a time when you grow up and become a man or remain a boy. But you can't be both. Make a choice for God's sake. Marry her or don't."

I grab Judith by her left arm. She's trying to get her jacket on.

"What do you want?" she asks.

In all fairness, my decision hasn't been too sudden. In fact, this one feels long overdue.

"I bought a ticket."

Judith won't look at me. She struggles to get her arm away, pushes me, then shoves her right arm into her jacket. She rifles through her suitcase and realizes something's missing. Judith hurries to the back of the apartment to find whatever it is she's looking for, leaving me with the dishes. I turn on the hot water, close the drain and throw ample soap into the sink. I look at myself in the small mirror above the tap. Are Rana and I having an affair? Sure, our encounters have become more frequent in the year since I've met her. We rarely meet in the same place. Our conversations are filled with awkward pauses. Sometimes we'll be talking and her hand will brush up against my wrist for a moment. Intention and accident: blurred boundaries, confused moments. No, Rana and I are not having an affair. Though perhaps our attraction is the kind Judith, or any lover, fears.

As I wash yesterday's soup pot, the burning smell from below becomes stronger. They must've forgotten this batch. I consider calling the bakery to tell them, but I can hear Igor and Stepovya fighting over whose fault it was. No matter. By midnight they'll be into the vodka, and by three they'll be tearing into each other against vats of rising dough.

I told her about the ticket at least. But I haven't told Judith about the house. For months I've been wanting to tell her, not knowing how. My lack of courage is pitiful. But I know it's because she wouldn't want to hear it. The house is not her version of Israel—it's the Jerusalem I'm interested in. I finish washing the pot and leave it on the rack to dry. The phone rings and Judith picks it up. I can hear her frantic voice. "I have to get to work," she says to whoever's on the other end. Why did she bother answering, only to say that? She puts down the phone and returns to the kitchen.

"There's something I never told you," Judith says. "Last year, when there was that fire at the Minsk, I went by the next day to help gather the burnt books with the rabbi. They were still warm from the fire. Why would anyone do such a thing here in Canada? There were so many people helping out—punks, Marxists, old people—everyone in the Market was there for the cleanup. We were on the steps of the synagogue when a young woman shouted from across the street, 'This is the fault of Zionism!'"

"That's terrible."

"That woman was young. She had black hair and wore a black headscarf. About your age, I would say. She was Palestinian."

Judith rezips her briefcase. She leaves the apartment, slamming the door behind her. I can hear her feet on the iron steps pounding their way to the street.

The phone rings. I don't answer it.

ARRIVAL

The Jewish mystical tradition claims that the very air of Israel makes one wiser. The land will, it is said, stubbornly "refuse" to bear fruit unless the Jews, its natural caretakers and the inhabitants for whom it was created, dwell on and cultivate it. History bears out this notion. Modern Israel was a land of desert and swamp for centuries until waves of emigrating Jewish Zionists in the mid-nineteenth century began tilling its soil. Only then did the land blossom and give forth its produce: "For the Lord will comfort Zion; He will comfort her waste places, and will make her wilderness like Eden ..." (Isaiah 51:3)

—RABBI YECHIEL ECKSTEIN, *JEWISH VIRTUAL LIBRARY*

CHAPTER 11

I'm waiting in the brightly lit terminal of Ben-Gurion airport beneath the trembling fluorescent lights. I don't feel the earth alive beneath my feet. I've been pulled to the side to be questioned by a young female Israeli security agent. Her partner, a short, buzz-cut weasel of a boy straight out of the army, conducts the luggage search.

"So this is your first time in Israel?" she asks in English.

"That's right." I decide to speak in English and see what happens.

The weasel rifles through my books. Fortunately I left Finkelstein at home. The other officer hounds me with questions: What's my father's name, where's my mother from, do I know any Palestinians, am I a member of the International Solidarity Movement? She looks me in the eye. I don't tell her about Barak or the proposed play. Barak is not expecting me for another two weeks; I've come early to do some research, to familiarize myself with the country. I certainly don't tell the customs official about the house. Don't tell her because I don't know the story yet.

It bothered Judith that I was going to Israel to look for the house.

"I don't understand why you need to to do this," she said the night before I left. She avoided looking at me by filing her nails.

"It's an interesting story, don't you think?"

"Don't you think," she said, vigorously filing, "that you should stay here so we can work on things with us?"

"This is really important to me."

105

"And our relationship isn't?"

"Look," I said, taking her left hand. It was like ice. Usually her hands are much warmer than mine. "We'll work on things when I get back."

"And when will that be?"

"A couple of months. We'll have to see how this residency goes."

"But you do want a future with me?"

I paused, fiddled with my diabetes necklace. The clasp had come undone. I could feel it against the back of my neck. "Yes."

She put the nail file down on the table and looked at me. "That's good." She wasn't convinced. "We'll see," her voice said, and she tried to catch me in the eye, the same way the security agent is right now.

I remain tight-lipped with the officers, play up the stupid, ignorant tourist. My short answers bother them. They dump out the entire contents of my waist pouch. There are two phone numbers in my money belt written on a small piece of paper and the weasel's studying them. One number belongs to Ruthie, Jacob's ex, a recent convert to Orthodoxy and Zionism. She's offered to help me find a place to stay in Jerusalem and I'm meant to call her once I've arrived. The second number belongs to Samer Shalabi, a Palestinian living in Ramallah. Does the weasel recognize the area code as one outside of Jerusalem? Maybe Samer's on some kind of wanted list. I don't know the guy, never talked to him, but a friend of a friend worked with him on a documentary about suicide bombers. Samer is a respected cameraman, and my hope is he'll take me on a tour of the West Bank. To see the other side, get a sense of the Palestinian daily life before I begin my search for the house. I've been advised by Rana not to tell the authorities I'm planning to travel to the West Bank. Truth be told, the idea of entering Palestine terrifies me. Fortunately the weasel puts down the phone number and moves on to more pressing matters like my notebooks.

The female security agent rifles through my passport. Stamps, visas of the world illuminate the pages: Georgia, Turkey, Ukraine, Mexico. *Is he suspicious?* ask her black opal eyes.

She says, "Is everything okay?" Again she stares at me. It feels like she's undressing me with a cold metal fork.

"I'm fine."

"You seem nervous."

"I don't like customs inspections."

"If you've got nothing to hide, there's no reason to be afraid," she says. She flips back to the Georgia visa. "You look like you've passed through a few borders in your time."

"I like the world."

The security agent speaks into her radio in rapid-fire Hebrew. I don't understand.

"Is something the matter?" I ask.

The weasel empties the contents of my rucksack.

—3 empty notebooks, two graph paper, one blank

—2 toothbrushes, one red, one blue

—1 digital camera

—1 pair shorts

—1 pair sandals

—3 pairs underwear, 2 T-shirts

—1 container, Zaida's mustard

—insulin, 2 zip-locks full

—180 needles, 5 mm, extra-sharp

—1 yellow Duo-Tang from Bialik

On the cover of the Duo-Tang is a cut-out picture of the old city of Jerusalem pasted on with glue. In orange, blue and green marker the word *Yerushalayim* has been written in Hebrew block letters. He opens the book. It's a Grade Four Hebrew assignment about the history of Jerusalem. I brought it with me instead of a guidebook. It sounds funny, but I wanted to compare what I had written in Grade Four with what I see now (there's also a handy tourist map pasted into the back of the Duo-Tang). The officer smiles as he flips through the pages. He shows it to the other officer.

"*Atah medaber ivrit?*" she asks.

I reply, *"Nachon."*

"Why didn't you just say so?"

"My Hebrew's a bit rusty," I say.

"Where did you study?"

I tell her.

"And you've never been to this country?"

"I keep putting it off for one reason or another."

"Now's not the best time to be visiting, you know."

"Isn't it always a good time to visit the Holy Land?" I've been here five minutes and already I've adopted the rhetoric of Yosef.

The sternness of the security officer becomes a restrained smile.

She says, "What's the purpose of your visit?"

"I'm a tourist."

"For how long will you stay?"

"I have an open ticket."

"Do you have an address?"

"I thought I'd start off at a hotel."

"No reservation?"

"No. Is there something wrong with that?"

"No." She pauses. "Next time just say so."

"Say what?"

"Enjoy your trip." She hands me back my passport, leaves me and the other agent to finish repacking.

When I'm outside the airport I decide I will call neither Ruthie nor Samer. A hotel sounds like a perfect way to unwind and prepare myself for whatever lies ahead. I head out to the collective taxis marked "Jerusalem."

CHAPTER 12

A young, shirtless man takes my backpack and flings it into the back of the van. His blond-streaked ponytail bounces against his tanned back as he heaves one suitcase after another through the open door. He shouts, *heeyah! heeyee!* and pauses to laugh when the driver makes fun of his pants, which droop below the waist. An old Texan couple on a pilgrimage to Bethlehem watch their four pieces of leather luggage recklessly tossed into a haphazard pile. They're appalled by the young man's look, the revelation of a navy blue thong when he bends over. *Britney Spears is one thing,* the elderly Texan likely thinks, *but a man with hip-huggers and that thing-thong?* The pony-tailed dude makes fun of the driver wearing tough-guy black aviator sunglasses, *You're a fat-ass, a shit-prick, I fucked your whore of a mother,* and other terms of endearment in Hebrew, holy language of my ancestors.

When I board the van the long hair sits next to me, a towering bottle of Johnny Walker Black between his legs. Turns out he's neither working for the van company nor headed in any particular direction himself. His name's Yonni and he's been touring the world for two years now. This is his grand return to the Holy Land.

Yonni celebrates his homecoming by doling out shots of Scotch in the bottle cap to passengers on the bus. The puritan Bible-thumpers ignore his pleas to join us for a drink, pretend he isn't there. No one's sure what to make of this young meshuggeneh's arc or action.

The German businessman cordially takes back one drink, no more, and Fat-Ass, driving the van, downs two before we leave the airport parking lot. Bad-ass Hebrew trance invades us from four speakers, plus a sub-woofer at the back, which is helping to demolish whatever hearing I still have. Yonni opens a second bottle, Chivas Regal, so that he and I can go *tête à tête*, and really get down to matters.

Yonni pours Scotch the way he talks: jitterbug, shake-street, so concerned with the ecstatic he forgets where he is. I'm the one responsible for keeping the cap still, but already the driver's made me spaz a few times. Yonni has no notion of limits, keeps pouring over the edges of the cap so my hand is doused in whisky. No matter. If I don't lick it he will, which he's doing right now, strange dog-man that he is. This hand-licking gesture is uncomfortable and disgusting. But I try to be okay with it. See, I need something from Yonni. I want real things to happen. Stuff not found in guidebooks, tour groups or media images. I want an authentic Israel, not the one from the maps of my childhood.

He also might make a good character in a play.

"In Goa I rode the back of the dragon," Yonni confesses.

"That's nice."

"And in Colombia, I saw the electric dynamo assault the centre of the universe."

I try to look out at the countryside; exits to such and such settlement, which and whatever town. I admit it: I'm nervous. I look around at the other passengers in the mini-bus. No one's body seems unnaturally large beneath their clothes, although the Texans are pretty damn fat. Everyone is a potential terrorist, Ruthie explained in a recent conversation. Nowhere is safe. Bombers can attack moving vehicles by simply racing up alongside the car you're in. It happened to a friend of a friend. She wanted to go for a swim in the Mediterranean. Ended up scattered along the highway, barely enough of her left to bury.

I'm looking forward to a hotel. I want to decompress before setting off to look for the house. Tomorrow I can take in some ancient sites, walk through the markets, kill the jet lag. Then I'll call Ruthie. Honestly, I don't know about Samer. The thought of visiting him scares the shit out of me. Yonni puts a Lucky Strike in my mouth and holds a butane lighter to my face.

"I don't smoke," I explain.

"Today you start," he says.

"But I don't want to."

"You are too nervous, too uptight American."

I don't argue with him and I suppose it's true what my mother always said: I am a terrible victim of peer pressure. The cigarette tastes awful. But I will say it calms me, keeps me focused. Perhaps beneath this veil of hedonism Yonni has a trace of goodness, of angel, and he's really looking out for me.

"Mission control said it was okay to come back," Yonni says.

"Good for mission control."

"Jerusalem, Land of the Great Pussy." He pats my knee. "You will come with me," he says, smirking, smoking, eyes sprinting the length of the highway, *forward, forward, forward,* like a kid kicked out of a carnival and left to his own parking lot devices. Smash-up derby thoughts, Ferris wheel head.

AT THE WELCOME TO JERUSALEM sign the driver yells, "Get out." He's had enough of Yonni. The door is opened, and Yonni grabs his two duty-free bags of booze—the entirety of his luggage—and jumps out. I'm left to pay for both our journeys.

I'm jet-lagged, disoriented. Yonni is shirtless and crazy.

We walk into the cool March day.

IT'S A GOOD HOUR'S or so blister-walk to downtown Jerusalem. Aided by a half-bottle of Chivas Regal, we make it to the pedestrian walkway of Ben-Yehuda. Yonni leaps onto a box of oranges. This is a rough translation of what he says:

Pussies of Jerusalem, I missed you!
Your holy, holy smell!
Your sweet, sunny taste!
O, pussies of Jerusalem!
Etc, etc.

Rather than attracting a wild throng of Jerusalemite women, the only excited reaction comes from a teenaged boy in ripped jeans, bleached blond hair and Coke-bottle glasses. He comes running out of a store screaming, jumping onto the box of oranges and embracing Yonni madly. Brothers, I presume. His name is Alon.

The three of us head to Alon's electronics store to begin the Holy Land festivities. Yonni removes his left shoe and pulls out a piece of hash the size of a hockey puck, then removes his right shoe and pulls out a rather large bag of cocaine.

I slump into my chair—I'm drunk, I think. I don't react well to drugs or alcohol, though I seem to have found myself okay with cigarettes. I wonder where I'm going to sleep tonight, if these two will let me. They catch up on the past two years.

"Aloni," Yonni says, pinching his brother's cheeks. "I was fucked up."

"Two years, we thought you were dead," Alon says, weeping into a hash joint.

"The truth is, I was." Yonni snorts cocaine off the glass counter.

"Why do you always talk like such a moron?"

Yonni stands up straight and looks his brother in the eye. He slaps him and laughs. "You are a man now." Then Yonni, inexplicably, starts to cry. "Damn you, for turning into a man."

The door opens and in walks a woman wearing tight cream linen pants, giving strong emphasis to the contours of her panty line.

She wears a near-translucent white shirt, pink-sunset lipstick. Her eyes are green (possibly fake) and her hair is a thick mess of curly red (likely not). She walks straight up to Yonni and does not say a word. When she's three centimetres away from him, she spits in his face. Yonni laughs.

"Still an animal," she says.

"Still a whore," he says.

"How were the twelve-year-old blonde girls in Thailand?"

"Delicious."

"Caught some diseases, I hope?"

"Nothing you haven't given me already."

She says, "You're a pig."

He says, "You should go home."

"I am." She grabs his crotch, full-fisted. "I just wanted to see if you were still here."

It is the exit to end all exits. She spins around on her heels and plants a stiletto right into Yonni's bare foot, inducing much screaming and embarrassment in the boy. Grinding it in for effect, she takes a few steps forward, fixes a look at me, and without saying a word, asks, *Who the fuck are you?* The door slams behind her. Boxes of software catapult to the floor.

"Bitch," says Alon.

"I can't believe it," says Yonni. He sits down, massages his bloody foot.

I ask, "Who was that?"

Yonni says, "I'm still in love with her." He wipes blood with the white shirt that was stuffed in the back of his pants. "Galia, I'm still in fucking love."

CHAPTER 13

Yonni and I leave the store high as Qassam missiles—wavering, uncertain where we're going to land. I'd indulged in some hash in the end, unable to resist the drug's sweet smell and the annoying laughter of the brothers. There's no doubt about it, it sucks to be sober among morons. The hash seems to have loosened my tongue a bit and made my Hebrew comprehension better. Conversation has now shifted mostly from English to Hebrew, with me shuffling along, almost keeping up.

We head right, left, then left again down some narrow alley. I have no clue where I am. A fat Russian man plays "Oczy Czerny" on the accordion beneath a storefront canopy. His grandchild fusses with the old man's laces. The rains of Jerusalem have started, and the Russian song feels out of time, out of place. When I imagined Jerusalem as a child it was always sunny and hot, the way it is in *Ben-Hur*. The Russian man horks phlegm like it's one of the notes in the song. The grandchild ducks for cover. This is not Biblical. The streets are empty, cold and damp. It's raining like hell.

After snagging a few Becks at the corner store, a couple packs of Lucky Strikes, Yonni takes me into his apartment building— ramshackle concrete, unlit and damp. We climb six flights of stairs, two by two by two. The stairs are uneven; concrete cracked at the edges. The smell of piss lingers in the air. A woman sobs, glass shatters against the wall. A baby wails, a man shouts, *Listen to me.*

When we enter the apartment we find three ruffians in their early twenties sitting around doing fuck all. A few needles scattered on the glass table. Empties, tinfoil, an ashtray piled high like an ashen tomb. John Cale's *Vintage Violence* blares from punched in speakers.

"Kikes," a guy called "Goofball" declares when we enter the room. "Who the fuck are these kikes?" Goofball has a pink and yellow mohawk with a Magen David shaved into the right side of his head. There are Auschwitz-like numbers tattooed into his left arm.

"I live here," Yonni declares.

"Shit, he lives here," says Rat-face. Rat-face looks like a rat. I'm not sure if it's male or female.

Skyward says, "Tis is te funniest ting I've seen in years." Skyward's got two wandering eyes, both gazing up; even when he looks at you he's not really looking at you.

"Yes, this is very fucking funny." Yonni turns off the stereo.

"Like I said, te funniest ting I've seen in years," Skyward says, motioning with his hands to Rat-face for a smoke.

Yonni says, "Don't smoke in my apartment." Yonni's finished one smoke and is on to another. He walks over to the corner dresser and pulls out a nine-millimetre pistol from the top drawer. He points the gun at Skyward.

"Who's tis loser?" Skyward points at me, waving off the gun like it was nothing more than a fly.

"He's a Canadian," says Yonni.

"What's he wanting?"

"He's sleeping on the couch."

For one moment—and only a moment—I let myself take my eye off the gun. I had decided not to do the hotel thing in the end, thanks to the white leather couch that Yonni had advertised as the best place to sleep in the world—except for perhaps a hammock in Mexico on a Grade-A *sensimillia*, which he likened to the experience of flying.

My abode for the night is covered in ash, tinfoil and a brown, smeared substance that is either heroin or shit.

"What's he want?" asks Goofball.

"Why don't you ask him?"

"Hey Canuckian," Goofball says in broken English. "I know all about you."

"That's nice," I say. Nobody but me seems to be nervous about the coked-out maniac waving a gun around.

"You're Anne of Green Gables," Goofball says. Rat-face, who is missing his left hand, is rolling a joint with his right.

I thank him, adding that I've never read the book before.

"You've never read *Anne of Green Gables*?" Skyward asks, cooking up something special on a tarnished silver spoon.

"I saw the TV series. Or the movie of the week. But only part of it," I confess, not sure if I should be ashamed or not for missing out on this vital Canadian cultural export.

"*Anne of Green Gables* changed my life," confesses Goofball. "She, like, has the truth."

"The truth?" I ask.

"She's got innocence," offers Rat-face.

"And faitt," says Skyward, eyes blinking. As he cannot pronounce "th" properly, he makes Anne's faith somehow more earnest.

"Faith in what?" I ask.

"Humankind," says Goofball.

Yonni cocks the gun and points it at Goofball. He speaks in Hebrew: "Look, I'm sorry to interrupt our Hour of Eternal Canadian Hope, but you're in my apartment cooking with one of my grandmother's silver spoons she brought all the way over from fucking Odessa. So get the hell out of here before things get really messed up."

Fortunately Galia walks in. She's dressed in the same impractical outfit as before (just imagine six flights of stairs in those heels), only now she's carrying a small cardboard jeweller's box tied neatly with a red bow. It fits into the palm of her hand.

"What do you want?" asks Yonni.

"This is for you," she says.

"What is it?"

"It's a 'fuck you' present."

"Huh?"

"A you-were-gone-so-go-to-hell gift."

"Enough of this. Can't you see I'm busy?" Yonni waggles the gun, aiming it at nothing, gesticulating questions with lead. Does he even know what he's holding?

Galia puts down the box and slowly unties it. I hold my breath as though my life depends on whatever is in that box. Inside is a black and white picture of an old woman, yellowed along the edges. Standing next to an elm and a maple, she's holding three white lilies.

"Baba Chasia," says Yonni, shoving the gun into the back of his jeans.

Galia says, "You remember the picture."

"Of course. I saw it every day we lived together. For two years."

"She's dead."

"What?"

"When you were off in Thailand screwing twelve-year-old girls, Chasia died."

"Galia. Why didn't you tell me?"

"How was I supposed to? You didn't leave a number, email, nothing. You just disappeared."

The four of us are watching this tender moment. Yonni, smoking in his non-smoking apartment, steps toward Galia and holds her against his shoulder. They start to cry.

"Boo!" shouts Goofball. I think I'm the only one who jumps. "This is absolutely disgusting."

"Gross," announces Rat-face.

"I think it's kind of sweet," says Skyward. His eyes are in a permanent state of Groucho Marxism.

"Anne of Green Gables would know how to handle this situation. This is not what I would call a very Canuckian moment," Goofball says, turning to me. "What do you make of this shit?"

Galia and Yonni start to kiss. The sound of face sucking face echoes through the apartment. The gun drops to the floor with a loud *thwock*. None of the punks go for it. Rat-face turns on the stereo, and Goofball turns to me, waiting for an answer to his question. When I say nothing (the booze, hash and jet lag, my head an overscrewed screw-top), Goofball puts forth his hypothesis.

"Anne has a special thing all of you Canuckians have, a tenderness, a way of being-in-the-world that is just, well, nice. Galia and Yonni? This is made up. Desperate. Bullshit."

"I see."

"We lack your nicety here in Israel."

"Hmm."

"You Canuckians are very, very nice."

"Not all of us," I say.

"See, even your denials are friendly." Goofball smiles. Skyward laughs. He and Rat-face are engaged in a wicked game of thumb war. "If you want to be Israeli, you should say like we do here: 'Go fuck yourself.'"

"Go fuck yourself," I say.

Goofball rolls his eyes and blows smoke at the shattered balcony window. "Pathetic."

He whacks me in the nose with his hand.

"Ow."

"Does that hurt?"

"Yes."

"Good." Goofball flicks my right ear.

"Fuck off!" This guy is getting on my nerves.

"No. That just won't do."

Now Galia and Yonni have retreated to the bedroom. Dishes tumble, cupboards crash, books slam against the floor. He screams, "I love you," she says, "I hate you," she sings, "you bastard," he trills, "you delicious eggplant," and so on. Skyward gives Rat-face a massage. In spite of my lame Canadianness, Goofball offers me a cigarette and invites me onto the balcony for a smoke. He picks the gun up off the floor and shoves it in the back of his pants. I feel almost relieved.

"So. You came to Israel to learn how to be tough," he says, lighting my cigarette.

"Not exactly." The cigarettes are tasting better and better all the time.

"Sometimes Jews come from abroad to fight in the army."

"I don't want to join the army."

"That's cool. I hate war."

Goofball must be twenty-five, twenty-six. Like all Israeli men, he served from aged eighteen to twenty-one.

"What did you do when you served?"

"Allow me to demonstrate," Goofball says. He pulls the gun out from his pants and points it at his head. He smiles. "Delete," he says, and pulls the trigger. Click.

"What the hell are you doing?"

He pushes it forcefully against his head, barrel against rough-shaven skin.

"Delete." Click.

"Hey. You're going to kill yourself."

He cocks his head, stares at me. It's only now I realize his pupils are gone.

"Delete." Click.

"Put the fucking gun down, you crazy FUCK!"

Goofball eases the pistol away from his head. "That was rather well said. My perception of you Canuckians is changing already."

My hands are shaking. "That was a very elegant use of the word 'fuck.' Forceful, strong. Almost Israeli." He twirls the gun around his finger. "You really shouldn't worry, though. I unloaded this months ago. I'm a pacifist." He aims the gun against his right temple, then points it at me. "Delete," he says, clicking the empty pistol. Thunder erupts from the dark skies.

WHEN I EXPLAIN to Goofball why I'm in Israel, about the house ostensibly shared between the Israeli and the Palestinian, the story seems ridiculous, impossible.

"Are you a reporter?" he asks suspiciously.

"Nobody's paying me to be here, if that's what you mean."

"So why are you looking for this house?"

"A good story," I say.

"Whatever," Goofball says, unimpressed. "People come here from all over. We're the hot story, a number-one music video. They don't know a fucking thing. They only see what they already know."

Velvet Underground's *Loaded* blares feedback from inside. Rat-face and Skyward dance, hold each other nice and slow.

"I don't know what I know," I say, and this is the closest to anything truthful I've said in a long time. "I guess I'm trying to figure that out."

"It's all rather simple," he says. His left eyebrow bulges slightly red with pus from two silver hoops. "Everybody thinks we're interesting because we've had war here for sixty years. And we'll have it for sixty more. But all we want is to be normal like you in Canada. An end to heat. To be *cool.*"

As if on cue, the skies of Jerusalem open up and sheets of rain descend upon us. We stay outside and smoke another cigarette. Our shirts are soaked and our skin is cold. Water slopes to the sides of the street; small streams dart alongside the curb seeking drainage. He asks where I learned Hebrew, and why.

"My parents wanted me to have a Jewish education," I say.

"You were forced to."

"Yes. But it's strange. I don't mind that. I mean. I'm glad I speak Hebrew."

Goofball spits from the balcony and we watch his phlegm travel six storeys below. He lowers his voice. "I used to be a commando."

"What did you do?"

"That's not important," he says. "But when I was done, I did what many young Israelis do: I went to India, took a boatload of acid and pressed *delete, delete, delete.*"

"Did it work?"

"What do you think?"

I look at the numbers on his arm, the Star of David etched into his head. Of course memory cannot be wilfully erased. And yet I also can't help but think of my grandfather. In the months leading up to his death his mind unravelled, eroded, full of holes. He couldn't remember the name of the town his father was from, the names of his daughters, his own birthday. It's infuriating, really. Memory abandons us when we need it, assaults us when we avoid the past.

"Have you been to the West Bank?" I ask.

"Yes," he says.

"Could someone like me go?"

"You mean to a settlement?"

"No, I mean a Palestinian town. A city. Anything."

"Why would you want to do that?"

"I'd like to see what it's like. For real."

"It's not some sort of summer camp."

"I figured that."

"Look," he says, clicking open and shut his lighter, "you can support or not support the occupation. But for a Jew to go there, it's crazy. They don't give a shit what you think."

He tells me the story of two army reservists travelling from their outpost to Jerusalem a few years back. They got lost driving through Ramallah when a mob swarmed them, beat them, bludgeoned them. Their bodies dragged through the city streets.

"In this country, we cannot afford to be Anne of Green Gables."

Goofball and I smoke in silence. Jerusalem is getting colder by the drop.

CHAPTER 14

"Everyone uppp!"

The voice comes hollering from above, cracked and tinny.

"This is the supreme commander of the Israeli Defence Forces. We are announcing with great alarm that there is movement on the Egyptian, Jordanian and Syrian borders. All men and women to their stations. Calling all to the defence of this country!"

It can't be later than four in the morning. It's still dark out and I've been handed a set of army fatigues I dutifully put on. In spite of the fact I'm still half asleep this registers as fairly exciting. I've always wanted army clothes but my mother likes camouflaged outfits almost as much as she likes toy guns. "War," she likes to say, "is a waste of time for smart boys like you."

After ten months locked away in Bialik, I, at the age of eleven, have begged and pleaded with my parents to send me to a Zionist sleep-away camp. Camp Shalom.

On the downside: We have to go to synagogue once a week (though sometimes we do services on the muddy, mosquito-infested beach). Hebrew singing class is mandatory. We have to learn dopey Israeli folk dances and perform them for our parents on Visitors' Day. Every morning we stand at attention at *mifkad*, flagpole, to sing "O Canada" and "Hatikva." On the upside, there's an endless amount of grass to play on so I can practise shagging flies and do my Laika moonwalk. There's Arnon, too. He's a pretty good counsellor. He taught me the meaning of blue balls.

"If you spend too long with a girl and there's only some *action*, it's not necessarily better than *no action* at all. Because if she starts to get the *fire* going, and doesn't let the steam whistle *blow*, then you get what is commonly known as *blue balls*."

I can't say I really understand what blue balls are, but at least I'm learning things they don't teach at Bialik. Like what I'm doing right now. Lying belly-first in the mud, anticipating gunfire from the enemy. This has to be the best thing I've done all summer.

I CRAWL WITH the other boys of my cabin: Neil Silverblott, Danny Fingerbaum, Brian "the Fridge" Mandelstam and Johnny Kugel. Led by Arnon (with an official black Maglite flashlight), we inch our way through the rain-soaked camp.

Arnon: "Over there, do you see them?"

I can make out a few figures darting through the forest wearing white towels on their heads. Arabs. I can't see their faces, but I assume they're counsellors. Gunfire rings out from the loud speakers above. I'm lying next to the Fridge. He farts. We laugh.

"A fart could kill us all," Arnon scream-whispers. The rest of us shut up.

Arnon has actually fought in the Israeli army, so we take his insights seriously. He wears a real army shirt with the name *Tzahal* inscribed in yellow Hebrew letters over the heart. While we wait at the base of a hill for our first attack, he speaks to us in whispers. He teaches us that pride, camaraderie and humanity are intrinsic to the Israeli army.

"It's the best time of your life," he says, as he hands out water-gun Uzis from a black canvas bag. "You'll never do anything like it again. And the friends you meet, you make for life."

I look at the boys in our mock unit. I feel something lying here in the mud with them. It's certainly a thousand times better than synagogue prayers and singing lessons. Sure, it isn't baseball, but in some ways this beats the hell out of waiting around in left field for a fly ball to come your way. My heart thumps against the earth. I feel myself, alive, not so different from the living, breathing muck I lie on top of. Although the gun is only plastic, it feels solid in the hands. I like this. Purpose. The Fridge turns to me and smiles. It's the first time any of the guys seem to have noticed me.

"To the forest, men," Arnon says. "And take no prisoners."

AT DAWN the different battalions meet up in the main area of the camp by the flagpole. According to the rules as laid out by the camp director, the day will be a glorified version of Capture the Flag, which happens to be my favourite game. Our battalion is called the Dayan division, named after Moshe himself. Each battalion must look for clues scattered throughout the camp; little scrolls of paper with codes and maps that point to the next clue. The map we receive at the start of the day renames the camp. Over the hill is the Golan. The Ping-Pong table is Jericho. The muddy beach is Haifa, and the mess hall Tel Aviv. The synagogue is Jerusalem, and the flat open field the Negev, which flows into Sinai, the place where grass lies parched and dead. The head counsellor, who wears a black patch over his eye à la General Dayan, announces through a megaphone the various missions we must carry out. Looking at the camp director's eye patch, I admire this fact: The most famous general in Israeli history could only see through one eye. This is the heroism that is Israel. The hero I want to be.

Each team gets rewarded for successful missions. Points for finding a clue, discovering the final flag, the amount of "spirit" a team demonstrates. We gather in a huddle and start to chant. Our heads pressed together, we scream:

Ruach, ruach, we've got ruach!
Spirit, spirit, we have spirit!

I look at their faces. The Fridge lets out a howl. Fingerbaum spits words. *Kleine* Kugel stomps his tiny feet on the earth. Arnon, with his huge Goliath hands, claps our backs, urging us louder.

Now the wind sweeps across the Negev, and the sight of Arabs fleeing through the early morning forest raises my adrenalin. My excitement an inward scream, loss of breath, swallowed laughter. Through the forest we chase the enemy toward the Jordan River. My Uzi, Arnon's cone of light, the imagined spray of bullets. I follow the path, deer tracks, toward Jerusalem.

CHAPTER 15

We came here to this country, which was settled by Arabs, and we are building a Jewish State ... Jewish villages arose in the place of Arab villages. You do not even know the names (of these villages) and I do not blame you, because those geography books no longer exist. Nahlal arose in the place of Mahlul, Gvat in place of Jibta, Sarid in the place of Haneifis, and Kfar-Yehoshu'a in the place of Tal Shaman. There is not one single place built in this country that did not have a former Arab population.

—MOSHE DAYAN IN A SPEECH TO HAIFA STUDENTS AT THE TECHNION (TECHNICAL UNIVERSITY) MARCH 19, 1969[*]

The McDonald's in Central Jerusalem might not be the best place to meet a Palestinian in a gold Mercedes. After all, the Golden Arches are a prime terrorist target. As I wait, Israeli security forces are standing in front of the restaurant, frisking, and unzipping the bags and clothes of breakfast customers. Surely the Mysterious Mustafa will be eyed suspiciously.

I do my best Goofball. It's a survival technique I've picked up in my three days in Jerusalem. Leaning cool against a bus post, smoking nonchalantly, following the curve of lips with thumb, I try not to let my terror get the best of me. The driver I'm waiting for will take me to Qalandia checkpoint to meet Samer, the Palestinian cameraman. The Israelis won't let him leave the West Bank for

---

[*] Quoted in Nur Masalha, *The Politics of Denial,* p. 210.

"reasons of security." I talked to Samer on his mobile yesterday morning, hungover on the floor of Yonni's apartment. Yonni and Galia shopped for breakfast, and the punks scattered to the streets. I explained to Samer that I wanted a "tour of Palestinian life," to get a sense of the day to day in the West Bank. "A crash course," I explained, "on the realities of the occupation."

Go to the McDonald's near Ben-Yehuda. Wait outside discreetly. At 10 A.M. a gold Mercedes will arrive to take you to the checkpoint. The driver's name is Mustafa. He is a trustworthy man.

At 9:59 A.M. a black Mercedes grinds to a stop in front of my black sandals. Now the black window rolls down with elegance and grace—beautiful, tinted and electric.

"Mustafa?" I ask.

"No," says the driver, "I am Mohammad." He wears black-tinted sunglasses. I think my mind is becoming tinted. "Please, get in the car."

"But what about—"

"Get in."

I comply, Mohammad puts his foot to the floor, and we careen down the street, screeching around tight street corners. I want to know what happened to Mustafa, but Mohammad is too busy talking in rapid-fire Arabic on his cellphone.

We speed out of the city. I had forgotten that the maps we used to draw in Bialik neglected an important detail: Israel is really damn small. Within five minutes we're on a highway. Mohammad takes time away from his cell to point to Beit Hanina to the left, the such and such settlement to the right. Within fifteen minutes we're stuck in a mess of traffic going nowhere.

"Where are we?" I ask.

"Checkpoint," he says, pushing numbers into his cellphone. Mohammad lets it ring but nobody answers.

"Are we really going to drive through this?" I ask.

A gold Mercedes pulls up next to us. Mohammad rolls down his window and proceeds to swear at the driver in Arabic. I know he's swearing because the only Arabic I know is curses. The two immediately become engaged in a wicked screaming match. Mohammad closes his window.

"What are you fighting about?" I ask.

"We do not fight," he says. "We scream only because we love each other very much. We are brothers."

I have grown comfortable in the plush leather seats. I have even begun to like Mohammad. I have a good feeling about this bearded man. There's a photograph on the dashboard of his two children wearing Adidas and Nike outfits and one of his wife in a traditional Palestinian wedding dress, framed in a band of red and yellow elastics in the shape of a heart.

"Get out," Mohammad commands.

"Where am I going?"

"Do you have a passport?"

"Yes." I'm holding on to it for dear life.

"There." He points to a group of four soldiers, eighteen, nineteen years old with M-16s, eyes scanning bags and ID badges. "You walk through. There you will find Samer."

"How the hell am I going to find Samer?" I ask. I don't even know what he looks like. And while there is an hour of traffic trying to get through the checkpoint to the West Bank, there are at least three hours on the other side trying to return to Israel. "You'll know Samer when you see him."

Perhaps my desire to take a tour was not well thought out. I don't make sound decisions when I'm hungover, and I'm wondering what I actually hope to achieve by crossing over to the other side. I want to say to Mohammad: I've never been to the West Bank. I don't want to end up like one of those mutilated Israeli soldiers lost in Ramallah. I'd rather not become a decapitated moron, a limbless news item. And besides, I promised my mother I wouldn't do anything dangerous on this trip. "You had to wait until the fourth year of the intifada to make your first journey to the Holy Land? You have to go *now* of all times?" Mohammad looks at me, tilting his sunglasses down toward the end of his nose. "Well? What are you waiting for?" he asks. I open the door and leave the car. Before I can even say *shukran*, he has reversed the Mercedes onto the highway and sped off south toward Jerusalem.

I WALK THROUGH the maze of cars and people toward the checkpoint. Someone sells chai from a silver pot. At the checkpoint an Israeli flag proudly flaps above a mess of concrete, camouflage and barbed wire. Soldiers check cars and their occupants, slowly, slowly. There hasn't been a suicide bombing in two months, and tensions are supposedly low, making this one of the "better" days at Qalandia. I pass tables with fake Levi's, Kelvin Klein T-shirts, homemade orange pop. A tin roof–covered walkway marks the pedestrian passageway between the Occupied Territories and Israel, and I walk through with Palestinians. The Israeli soldiers don't ask for anyone's passport— who's going to bomb Ramallah? On the opposite side of the checkpoint people have stopped bothering to honk. *What's the point?* their eyes say. *Life is this waiting.* Behind the cars lies an open field of broken glass, blown-out tires and rusted metal. This junkyard home: the West Bank, prologue to a nation.

Amidst this rubble and chaos stands a man well over six feet in height with a completely shaved head, wearing a blue-and-white Reebok track suit with red vertical stripes. He spots me immediately and approaches to shake my hand. He smiles goofily.

"Fucking shit," he says. "Let's get the hell out of this mess."

I do not argue with the man they call "Samer."

THE WEST BANK. Say its name and it conjures images of boys throwing stones at slightly older boys with guns that shoot rubber bullets, tear gas or grenades. American and Israeli flags doused in gasoline, an effigy of the West. Men wearing kaffiyehs spraying bullets straight into the air, mothers weeping for their martyred sons, coffins carried through the howling crowds.

Samer's Land Rover is equipped with white armour and bullet-proof glass windows. In blue, he has pasted the word *TV* half a dozen times around the vehicle. I feel at once reassured and nervous.

"Are we expecting snipers?" I half-joke as he opens the door for me. He doesn't smile.

"This place is hell, my friend. Welcome. Can I smoke?"

I pull out a fresh pack of Lucky Strikes and offer him one.

"Finally. A fucking Canadian who smokes. Today is already full of miracles."

I don't tell him I am new to the habit, that I only started smoking two days ago. Cigarettes keep you sane, keep you breathing in the here and now.

Samer pulls the Land Rover out of the mess that is Qalandia check-point. Soon enough the tour begins. "This is the refugee camp," he says, pointing to the ramshackle concrete disasters on our immediate right, "and this is the settlement." He points farther up the road toward a hill. The buildings are monotonously replicated row upon row; white stucco facade, cookie-cutter windows, red-shingled roofing. There is an eeriness to their architecture. The suburbs of North America have been transplanted into an occupied war zone.

"This road is the one the army uses to go from the settlement to start their shooting in the camp," Samer says, pointing at a road that leads up a hillside.

"When does this happen?"

"Whenever they feel like it."

We turn up the road and Samer parks the TV tank in front of the Muqata, Arafat's compound. Arafat's compound! We hang out with a couple of Palestinian soldiers who guard the inner gate to where Yasser and Company are holed up. Samer's the life of the party, cracking jokes, smoking cigarettes and high-fiving the guys. They know

Samer because he's a cameraman who has been hired out by many North American TV networks, including CTV, CBC and NBC. If there's anything going on in the West Bank, he's there—Jenin, Hebron, Nablus—all the hot spots.

The compound is a ghastly collection of ruined buildings. Dangling rebar creates a surreal image: a frozen waterfall that might start to flow at any moment. Behind us, Palestinian Authority soldiers conduct feeble military exercises in the courtyard. They remind me of the Woody Allen film *Bananas*; the clothes don't quite fit, and I'm suspicious as to whether their guns actually function. Not that it matters. There is so little left to guard here.

I have no idea what we're talking about, but I'm one of the guys. "The Canadian Writer" is how Samer introduces me. I excuse myself and head off in search of a bathroom but discover the building that might have once housed a toilet has been blown to smithereens. I sidle up beside a broken wall and proceed to piss discreetly. Gazing up at Arafat's bunker, I spot a haggard face framed by a small window. The face wears—am I imagining this?—a black and white kaffiyeh. He looks down at me and sees my golden stream of urine. This makes him laugh. I quickly zip up my pants. Did I just see *the man* himself? That is, did Yasser Arafat just watch a Jewish tourist piss on his compound?

"RAMALLAH," Samer explains as we get back into the Land Rover, "is the paradise of the West Bank. It is quiet. Here there are no problems. Except at the compound."

I can't tell if he's serious or not. He lights up our cigarettes with a gold Zippo lighter. I ask him where he got it.

"At the store," he says, annoyed by my question. As if they don't have stores in the West Bank or Zippo lighters.

We drive the main avenue of Ramallah, past a giant Coca-Cola sign and a Lipton Tea billboard. Adolescent boys wear Eminem shirts, sell blackmarket DVDs and Tweety Bird balloons. In the middle of the road there's a roundabout. Four white lions lie about in different poses. I figure they're some ancient symbol for the city. According to Samer, the Chinese government mysteriously delivered them as a gift during the days of Oslo in the mid-1990s. Nobody knows what they mean.

When we stop at a café for lunch, I am embarrassed about the Zippo question. Sitting down on a plastic chair at a wooden table, ordering a Thai chicken sandwich with french fries, I realize I hadn't expected to encounter the normal in the West Bank. A sign for the Palestinian beer, Tabyeh, advertises "on tap by the pint." People sit, talk, read the newspaper, drink coffee. Scenes of ordinary life that aren't portrayed in the media, yet this is the banality that everyone dreams of—and fights for.

Samer and I discuss politics, sneaking in bites of food between arguments. He launches into his analysis: "Freedom is a very complicated situation. You have to understand that's all we're asking for here."

When Samer talks, he looks you in the eye. His words sound weary from overuse—the same arguments for too many years. "Before this intifada you could be sitting in your house drinking coffee and say, 'Let's go to Bethlehem,' and you could. Now you need special permission to cross with your own car. I have a friend who went from Bethlehem to Ramallah to cover a story. On the way in, the soldiers said it's okay, you go in, no problem. On the way back, he wasn't allowed to return to Bethlehem, where he lives, because he had a criminal record. It took him ten days just to get home. The bottom line is the power is out of our hands. Some soldiers are easy, some are strict. You don't know who you're going to encounter."

I ask, "What about the need for security, for Israel to defend itself against terrorist attacks? Doesn't Israel have a right to do this?"

"The justification is bullshit. It's about controlling a people and keeping them in one spot, isolated, helpless and dependent. Some days the Qalandia checkpoint is only open until seven at night. Other days it's until midnight. Or it's twenty-four hours. It's whatever they want. They make life impossibly unpredictable. We live with complete uncertainty." Samer talks about the seven-hundred-plus-kilometre "security fence" that Israel is erecting around and through the West Bank. Israel justifies it as a means to discourage would-be suicide bombers from entering the country. Samer comments, "If this wall was about security, they'd build it at the pre-'67 borders. Instead, Israel puts it in strategic places to get good farmland and more water. It's a land grab."

I ask him if the average Palestinian supports suicide bombers. I mention the television images of families being honoured when their children choose to be martyrs.

"Listen, when you see a mother on TV saying I am so happy my son blew himself up, this is bullshit. She is saying this is something she supports in order to feel okay about the tragedy she has to live with."

I don't buy it.

"We made a film and interviewed the family of a bomber. The kid was brilliant. He was going to the university in Nablus and was thirteen days from graduation. The kid was top in his class, and the first in his family to be in the university. You think his parents were happy when he blew himself up? It took us two hours just to calm them down so we could ask any questions. They live with an emptiness inside them. You can feel it when you walk into their house. Nobody wants this situation."

We're headed into murky territory here. "Why aren't more Palestinian intellectuals speaking out against the violence?" I ask. "Where are the peaceful demonstrations?"

"The first intifada was something like this. It was rooted in the universities, and many students and intellectuals spoke up. Since then most of the intellectuals were either arrested or deported by Israel." He dips a french fry into some ketchup and holds it in front of me like a teacher holds a ruler. "You have to understand this intifada is different. Most Palestinians, myself included, don't support the suicide attacks. The bombings advance the political agendas of groups like Hamas. Some believe there is no other choice. The circumstances are terrible. We aren't allowed to leave the West Bank or Gaza and soon we won't be allowed to leave our own cities or villages. They are building a cage around us, this 'separation fence.' Think about it: People are blowing themselves up to get a country. It's the last act of a Shakespearean tragedy. It's shit man, total shit." Samer pauses, puts down the uneaten french fry, and opts for a Marlboro instead. He offers me one too.

"Look, I know you're a Jew. When you called me from that apartment in Jerusalem, I could tell from the numbers." Samer lights up. Nobody is paying attention to us in the busy café. I shift in my seat. "Am I going to kill you because of this?" He takes a long drag of his cigarette and stares me in the eyes. He exhales and starts to laugh. "Fucking shit man, of course not. What matters is whether or not you're a good person. Which I think you might be." He throws me his lighter and laughs some more.

I feel like I've just passed through another checkpoint. The difference here is that once I have crossed this border with Samer there is hope for trust, the possibility of friendship. After paying for my lunch Samer takes me to his apartment, which overlooks a valley where more construction is underway. In spite of the hopelessness of the situation, people are still building their futures. I try to imagine the house in West Jerusalem, and wonder if the Palestinian or the Jew takes care of it. What kind of shape are the walls in? Do Abu Dalo and Shimon fight over the small things, like where a plant should go, whether or not the music's too loud, if a room should have carpeting or hardwood floors?

At home, Samer speaks in a different tone, quieter, as he looks out into the valley. "If I didn't believe in peace, I wouldn't be here with my family. It won't happen tomorrow. But when it does, it will be because Israelis and Palestinians have learned to see each other as human beings. As equals."

Sitting with his wife and two daughters, we drink one pot after another of Arabic coffee. I think of Rana, her long fingers cradling a cracked cup at the Arabic café in Toronto. While Samer and I sit contemplating the beautiful view and the apartments being built in the valley, we do our best to steer clear of the issue of our religions, beliefs and backgrounds. Life feels utterly fragile at this moment, too precious to pollute with ideology, politics and history. Samer takes his youngest girl, Sama, onto his lap. She laughs with her entire body, trembling with joy.

CHAPTER 16

I have plans. Samer says he knows a driver who can take me deeper into the West Bank. I want to see Hebron. I want to see over 100,000 Palestinians living next to a few hundred Israeli settlers, protected by the army. I want to visit the refugee camp in Jenin, sight of an alleged massacre by the IDF in 2002 during Operation Defensive Shield. I want to witness, to listen, to take it in. Coming to Ramallah has opened something inside me. If Ramallah is so different from the media images, what are the Jenins and Hebrons like? I want to find out.

Samer drives me to a hotel for journalists and says he'll come back for me later; he has a story he needs to cover. In spite of my protests he insists on paying for the hotel room. "You're my guest," he says. I go up to the room and lie down. At eight o'clock that night I get a phone call. It's Samer and he's in a panic. A double suicide bomb has just gone off in Ashdod, killing ten. I'm to meet him at a local bar.

I'm in a panic myself. I have no idea where Ashdod is, but if my Palestinian guide-friend is in a state, then I assume I should be worried too. Leaving the safe confines of the hotel, I wonder what the bombing mean for us in the West Bank. Will the army be coming in soon? I follow a side street to the local bar. Look for some sort of indication of what's to come but I can't even read the street signs: They're in Arabic. I feel vulnerable. Life changes on a dime here. You can be caught in the wrong place at the wrong time. Jenin, Hebron? I'm terrified walking three blocks to a bar. I pass a group of six men. They wear black leather jackets and smoke strong cigarettes. Their conversation stops. They're watching me. Are they wondering where I'm from? Are they out celebrating the news that ten Israelis have died?

Over pints of Tabyeh beer, Samer explains it's going to be difficult to travel in the West Bank now. His tone is stern and matter of fact. "Better go back to Jerusalem for a few days. Then call me and we can try to arrange something else." I don't object. It's very crowded in the bar and the other patrons are drinking and chatting away as though nothing has happened. The news comes on—Al Jazeera—and the bar shuts up. Dozens of us sit in silence. A ceiling of smoke rises and settles in the air above our heads. Our eyes are glued to the large-screen TV. We're waiting for the results of the bombing as though anticipating the outcome of a shoot-out at a World Cup final.

As soon as the town Ashdod is mentioned (I can see it on the television map, red arrow pointing near Tel Aviv), the bar-talk resumes, and so does the drinking. "People can relax now," Samer explains. "The bombing is far enough away. There'll be no curfew. Not tonight, at least."

I wonder what Rana would think about the bombing. "People are desperate for a country," she once explained in Toronto, echoing Samer's earlier comments. But I never pressed the issue.

I'VE BEEN STAYING at Max's the past few days. He's a friend of Ruthie's and he lives in Nachlaot, Central Jerusalem. Max is very generous. He's put me up for as long as I want. I have a small, windowless room, and a desk with a lamp.

Max is a kind and open-minded frum originally from Minnesota. I'm happy to learn that not all religious Zionists believe in transferring every Palestinian to their brethren Arab states. While Max practises Judaism and its rituals to the tee, his bookshelf has a wealth of literature on Palestinian and Muslim culture. His interest is genuine.

"We're living in the Middle East, not North America or Europe. One should get to know the neighbours. In thought at least." When I tell him about my excursion to Ramallah, he listens with interest and responds wistfully, "In the nineties, we used to go." He leans over and whispers, "They make the best falafel."

He tells me Judith called earlier in the morning. I was out at Mahane Yehuda, the Jewish market, buying gargantuan oranges for breakfast. It's been a week, and Judith and I made a deal to talk at least that often. Max says I should call her back as soon as possible; she was concerned because of the bombing. I look at the clock: 11 A.M. She knows via Max I'm okay, so I can call her later. I need to get the day going. I want to find the house.

It's a sunny spring Jerusalem day as I set off. The almond trees are in flower, and the smell of apricots and oranges fills the air. Hyacinths and irises bloom in the parks while security guards holding bomb-checking devices smile in front of the cafés. I walk to the neighbour-hood of Katamon. In my sweaty palm is the address of the divided house: 83 Mekor Chayim.

When I reach Emek Refaim I take the Bialik Jerusalem Project out of my shoulder bag. I flip through the pages while waiting at a traffic light. In perfect Hebrew handwriting I describe the old city, its four quarters in meticulous detail. The diagram is exactly how we were taught in class:

Jews   Moslems

Christians   Armenians

It's peculiar, the ten-year-old mind. It didn't envision a city beyond the old gates. I had not pictured traffic whizzing by, trucks wheezing diesel, traffic lights for the blind. I also had not imagined people leaving their respective quarters—the Jews stuck in theirs, the "Moslems" (how we wrote it) theirs. My imagined Jerusalem was a neat and orderly affair. The good guys were in the upper left quarter, the bad guys in the upper right. And in the lower hemisphere were the neutral ones, the unknowables, the ones who posed no threat. So the diagram could just as well have looked like this:

Jews (good guys)   Moslems (bad guys)

Christians (neutral)   Armenians (Who the hell?)

When I was making this project I remember writing in pencil (very lightly) the word *Shalom* in large block letters behind the four quarters, so the name touched each of the four groups. Was I simply writing my name behind the project? Or was I trying to insert peace into this city—the word linking the disparate nations? What was I thinking when I realized what I had done and fearfully erased the four Hebrew letters? So afraid I tore the paper, then taped it back together. Evident when held up against the blazing spring Jerusalem sun, as seen today.

WHEN I REACH Mekor Chayim Street, I feel like I'm on the outskirts of town, even though it was only a twenty-minute walk from Max's. The section of the street I'm on is quiet and poorly paved. I walk to the end of the street but the numbers only go up to sixty-six. I ask a young woman if she knows where I might find eighty-three, and she looks at me like I've asked whether two and two add up to five. I stop a young man to ask if any Arabs live in the area—he shakes his head and continues walking. I come to a house at the end of the road. An elderly couple sits outside in the garden drinking lemonade. These people, if any, will know.

"I'm looking for Abu Dalo," I say. "Do you know him?"

"Abu Dalo?" asks the woman, stirring sugar into her lemonade. "It's an Arab name?"

"Yes."

"Arabs haven't lived here since the 1950s."

"Most of them left in '48 or '49," adds the man. He rubs his fingers on the lining of his yellowed gums, picking food from his teeth.

"Where did they go?" I ask.

"Beit Safafa," the woman answers. Her hands are tough and fleshy. "It's an Arab village. Just follow the railway tracks south a few hundred metres and you're there."

I'm perplexed. Rana never mentioned this. "I have a friend who lived in an Arab house owned by a man named Abu Dalo. She said it was on Mekor Chayim."

"That's this street. And we're telling you no Arabs have lived here for fifty years."

I'm getting a little frustrated when the man says to his wife, "Why doesn't he go to Ketter?"

"Who's Ketter?"

"Ketter's lived on this street forever," she answers, stirring more and more sugar into her lemonade. "Ketter knows everything."

DAVID KETTER'S HOUSE is hidden behind a wall of ivy and wrought iron. He greets me suspiciously, standing on the other side of a two-metre fence, trying to decide if my mission is trustworthy. *Who sent you? What do you want?* he asks with his eyes.

Ketter is a soft-spoken man. When I say I'm looking for a house shared between an Arab and a Jew, Ketter raises his right eyebrow. When I mention that the neighbours claim no Arabs have lived in the area since the early 1950s, Ketter simply nods his head and strokes his grey moustache, thin above the lip. He wears prescription sunglasses and runs his long fingers through some eucalyptus leaves.

"I don't know what you are talking about, but perhaps you could come inside and we could look at some maps and figure this out," he says, more to the flowers than to me.

Ketter's garden is a meticulous work of symmetry, with cacti growing beside the artfully placed stone footsteps. I sit in the back-yard, and he brings out maps and tea. We speak Hebrew, and he encourages me by correcting my grammar, teaching me the words I've forgotten since I was a child. Ketter was born in this house in 1931 and fought in every war from 1948 to 1986. He is now retired and spends his days drawing the various weapons he's fought with over the years—detailed pencil sketches of grenades and Mausers, secret arms caches to hide weapons from the British. Ketter's also writing a book about the history of his street—a book no one will ever read.

Ketter is a Zionist from the old school. He is secular, detests the religious extremists who are coming from America, and has a fascina-tion with maps, weapons and gardening. After various maps from the past five decades reveal no clues, he takes me to his collection of arti-facts in the tool shed.

When he was fourteen Ketter became a member of the Haganah. He was responsible for burying weapons beneath the earth in this backyard to fool British arms inspectors. Gardening and sharpshoot-ing were taught to him at an early age, he says matter-of-factly. In his tool shed, empty shells are used to hold pens, pliers and screws. He shows me a model grenade he's building, a replica from the 1950s. He recounts the bombing of the King David Hotel with pride. "The world called us terrorists, but we were fighting for our survival. It was the birth of a nation."

Ketter's worst memory of the early days is the executions the Haganah carried out on Jewish informers to the British. "We were Jews butchering Jews," he says, placing a dab of white glue to a piece of metal falling off the model grenade. He adds, "We knew what had to be done. The same way Ben-Gurion knew he had to blow up Begin's arms cache in the Mediterranean, we had to kill the traitors. That's how it is when a country is born."

Behind an old radio from the 1930s that Ketter is trying to refurbish, I notice the same coloured photograph from my Zaida's basement.

"Ilan Ramon," I say, pointing. I feel a rush of pride that I can identify him.

Ketter nods his head slowly. Mournfully he says, "Yes, a great, great man."

"Did you know him?"

"My son, all of Israel knew him." Ketter places his hand gingerly onto the edge of the worktable. "He was our light at a time of despair. When the Palestinians rejected Barak's peace and started the second intifada, there were bombs going off every week. We lived in complete fear. That we could put a man into outer space was a kind of solace. It reminded us we are still capable of greatness. Miracles, even."

Ketter fiddles absently with a clamp. Though a secular Jew, Ramon had chosen to observe the laws of Kashruth in space. He kept Shabbos, Ketter tells me. Child of Holocaust survivors, he took a small, digitized Torah with him. Even in outer space, the Jewish faith can live.

I remember the news clips from a year ago. The horror people felt when the shuttle burned up as it re-entered the Earth's atmosphere. None of those astronauts stood a chance. And the most surreal detail of the day: The space shuttle *Columbia* exploded over Palestine, Texas. Body parts, metal, engine detritus, scattered on the streets of that town.

WE RETURN TO THE TABLE in the garden. Ketter's wife comes outside with a plate of sesame seed cookies and we pore over the landplot maps. He looks at me, flustered. As far as he's concerned I must have misunderstood Rana. "This house you are searching for does not exist." Ketter dips a sesame cookie into hot, sugary coffee. "We don't live together, do you understand?"

"But perhaps there's an exception?"

"Maybe in certain neighbourhoods, in Akko, or Yaffo. But not in the same house. And not on my street!" What baffles Ketter most of all is the idea that there is an Arab landowner on Mekor Chayim. He goes over the maps again and again.

"I don't understand how you can be so adamant there will never be peace," I say, licking the sesame seeds stuck in between my teeth.

"That's because you are an idiot," says Ketter, eyes still fixed on the maps.

"Thank you," I say graciously.

"No offence." Ketter looks straight at me. "You are Canadian. You have no idea what life is like here. There can never be peace. We must live here, and they want our land."

It is difficult, perhaps impossible—this argument between generations and geography. Ketter has known bloodshed and anti-Semitism. He's defended his country and nearly died for it. I know nothing of war or discrimination. Know only what I have read in newspapers, books, what I've gleaned from Bialik. Know maps I have drawn over and over again, abstractions on the page that I am trying to understand in the flesh. I can't truly understand the situation because I have never lived it.

"Look, we offered them land, but they want all of it."

"And negotiation?"

"There is none. It is ours historically, and we have won every single war there is to be won. They terrorize us, and now Europe wags its finger and calls us the terrorists. Europe—where all these problems began." Ketter pauses and looks at the map. "Hold on a second." I can see the wheels in his head turning. "This Arab you speak of must live in the neighbourhood Mekor Chayim, not the street." Ketter juggles the model grenade in one hand, reaches for a cookie with his other. "But to find this, I will need another map."

CHAPTER 17

Ketter phoned me this morning. After several unsuccessful forays into the Jerusalem city archives, and a stab-in-the-dark walk south and west of Mekor Chayim Street, questioning anyone I saw about Abu Dalo, I was beginning to lose hope. Then Ketter found a map in his basement.

"There," says Ketter, pointing at a street way off to the side of a 1951 housing plot map. It's an unmarked dead end and he thinks there are houses of Arabic origin there. I hike through a field of yellowed grass, hop over the old railway tracks. A dirt trail cuts through grass fields that grow stones, stones and more stones. Silence—a commodity rarely found in this country. Barbed wire, broken fences, abandoned concrete structures punctuate the open space. Even the distant shopping mall and billboards seem restrained in their shouting.

I follow the dirt path to a narrow unpaved road, turn right and ask the first man I see, a shock of white hair, stooped over and digging earth, if he knows where a man named Abu Dalo lives. He does not stand up, barks in Hebrew, "The asshole is over there."

He's pointed to the other side of the street to a small stone bungalow. Its front lawn is littered with broken bricks and burnt rubber tires. There's a door to either side of the house—I assume separate entrances for each apartment. I choose the one on my right and knock. A woman opens the door slowly, peering out from behind the chain.

She is in her mid-thirties and covers her long black hair with a blue headscarf.

"What do you want?" she asks me suspiciously in Hebrew.

"I've come to see the house," I say.

"What house?" she asks.

"This one."

"There's no room to rent, if that's what you want."

"I don't want to rent a room. I want to see the house that Rana lived in."

"Rana?" she asks. "Who's she?"

"She lived here five years ago." Thinking up something quick I add, "She asked me to take a picture of where she lived."

"I don't know Rana."

"You don't?"

"What did she do wrong?"

"She did nothing. She moved to Canada. We're friends."

"You speak English?"

"Yes, of course."

It's as though the neutrality of my native tongue has relieved her—she's calmer now, and she unchains the door. "Do you want to come inside?" asks the woman.

Her name is Mary, a Christian Palestinian. She has no idea who Rana is, but is willing to let me take pictures. I take shots of the uneven, sloped floors, of the crooked brick walls. I try to imagine this place with an entire family, but it's too small to imagine more than one or two people living in it.

"Where's Abu Dalo?" I ask, assuming Mary is his daughter.

"Abu Dalo lives in the house behind this," she says. "He owns this house, and the house across the street."

"You mean—there's more than one house?"

"Yes. Abu Dalo owns three houses."

So Abu Dalo is some kind of business tycoon?

There's a knock on the front door. A man with spiked white hair wearing a navy-blue track suit speaks Arabic to Mary. She translates.

"This is Abu Dalo," she says. I'm so excited I jump over to him and shake his hand. He's taken aback by my enthusiasm. "He wants to know what you want."

I give him the Rana story again, this time with a bit more detail. I mention she was studying at a college in Jerusalem. It doesn't register.

"Rana?" he says, shrugging his shoulders. Turning to Mary he asks, "Who is Rana?"

"She lived here for a few years," I say.

Abu Dalo shrugs his shoulders again. His expression says, *I don't know what this crazy foreigner is talking about.*

I say she shared a house with some other Palestinians and a Jew named Shimon.

"Shimon?" says Mary. "He doesn't live here."

"Where does he live?"

"Across the street."

She points at the white-haired man who directed me to this place. House #3. Things are not making sense.

The "interview" with Abu Dalo goes nowhere. He's in a rush and has no idea what I'm after. Admittedly my story is suspicious, and in all the excitement of having found the house—or three houses—I realize I don't really have a reason to be here. The best I can do is come up with the Rana story, but that has no currency because he can't remember her. Which raises several questions: Did Rana actually live here? Did I misunderstand her, project meaning onto a situation where there was none? Why did I believe that a Jew and a Palestinian were living together? I am just what Ketter said: an idiot.

I manage to get Abu Dalo to agree to sit down for a few hours when he has more time on his hands. Business is very busy right now, Mary explains on his behalf. I try to ask him what he does for a living, but he rushes off to his silver Mercedes convertible and cruises down the dirt road. Hardly the impoverished Palestinian I had been imagining.

I explain to Mary that I'm interested in Abu Dalo's relationship with Shimon. She starts to laugh.

"What's so funny?" I ask.

She says, "There is no relationship between the two of them."

"Haven't they lived beside each other for years?"

"They never talk."

I have trouble believing this.

Mary smiles, laughs nervously. "What do you care?"

"I'm interested in learning how people live together."

"Shimon," she whispers to me, "he's worse than Hitler."

"Hitler?"

"He's a bad, bad man."

"Has he murdered someone?"

"I don't talk to him," says Mary.

"Why not?"

She giggles nervously and says, "You must come back and talk to Abu Dalo. Friday night is his best night."

Upon leaving the house I feel woozy. I have not drunk any water since nine in the morning. I cross the street and make my way toward Shimon's, stop, hold onto a telephone pole for balance. The sun beats down on my head and I'm not feeling right. I look at old Shimon bent over at work, wiping his left eye. I want to talk to him, but I fear I might pass out. I turn toward the sun, hit the old railway, grass growing between the tracks. Somewhere between the end of Jerusalem and the beginning of Beit Safafa—you can see the mosque and barbed wire piercing the cumuli in the soft blue sky—I crawl into what looks like an abandoned caboose. There are boards with rusted nails, a used syringe and a torn up mattress leans against the wall. Rats likely frequent these parts. But I don't have the energy to worry about the safe and the clean. I sleep here, in between the Arabic and Hebrew slurs and slogans. I dream the words of the caboose, and the graffiti on the walls start to mingle with each other. They become animated, sentient, sun-wobbled. The phrases start to converse—a slander in Arabic is replied to by a prayer in Hebrew, and vice versa. "Go fuck your mother," "God is 7," "2000 years hope," "Jew=Nazi." Prayers and curses in brother languages, sister gestures. Soon the words are coming out of the mouths of two men, their faces clear in my head. Shimon holds an M-16 on his right shoulder and a Bible in his left hand. Abu Dalo rubs sticks of dynamite with his hands as though he were reading Shimon's fortune. Abu Dalo and Shimon. Shimon and Abu Dalo. The two become the words of the caboose, yelling at each other in graffiti language. When I wake up, I see a word in spray-painted black letters on a blue wall. "Blind," it says.

CHAPTER 18

My head hurts, my breath is heavy and my legs are pumping. I'm sweating out yesterday's sunstroke. Feels great to be moving.

The bicycle ride to Bethlehem is a tough climb through the hills of Judea. Minus the eighteen-wheel trucks whisking me into the shoulder, the jets screaming overhead and the signs saying, "Entry Is Forbidden," I feel an extraordinary sense of freedom. The ritual of travel, the euphoria of curiosity. I can't wait to see Jesus. I want to visit his birthplace the way a rock 'n' roll pilgrim heads for Graceland. I'm not meeting Abu Dalo for another couple of days, so I figure this is a good opportunity for some sightseeing. I figure I'll meet with Shimon after I get Abu Dalo's story.

The desert opens its arms to travellers on both sides of the road, marking the miracle of growth—shrubs, cacti and sun-hewn stone. I pass exit roads to Hebron, ancient city of the patriarchs, home to the Kahanite saint Baruch Goldstein. In the distance, a hill rises glorious, and stone houses become silver coins in the sun. Beyond the village, a rainbow points nowhere.

There's a checkpoint farther up the road with no lineup. The Israeli official looks at the small blue and white Israeli flag flapping off the end of the large green mountain bike I've borrowed from Max, who had recommended I see Bethlehem by bicycle. He didn't mention anything about the flag, so I assumed it wouldn't be an issue. The official shows a mixture of suspicion and surprise. He asks me where I'm going. I say to the Church of the Nativity. I show him my passport, he lets me through, and soon enough I discover why there are so few travellers on this road: There's a large concrete wall smack dab in the middle of the highway. A giant blue and white Israeli flag hangs slightly ruffled. The security fence.

"You cannot enter here, brother," a man with prosthetic legs says to me in decent English. He's standing with a friend in front of a kiosk, windows bolted shut. This legless man tries to walk toward me but the prosthetics are too large, they keep wanting to fall out of his hip sockets.

"Welcome to Bethlehem ghetto, Palestine," says his friend, who lifts the Legless Man by the waist so his fake legs dangle in the air. It looks like a cruel ventriloquist act.

"Thank you," I say.

"You are Israeli," says the Ventriloquist.

"I am Canadian."

"Why are you carrying this flag then?" asks the Legless Man.

"It's not my bike."

The two men, Ventriloquist and Ventriliquee, have a heated debate not six inches away from my face. The debate is in Arabic but it's clearly about the flag. The Legless Man shakes the Ventriloquist while the Ventriloquist shouts at him. Suddenly the mood changes. They stop talking. And the silence now spells danger, the premonition of something about to happen.

The Ventriloquist takes control of the bike, his hands pulling on the bars. The next moment I find myself on the ground tasting pebbles. I look up and they're gone, the Legless Man balanced precariously on the bicycle frame, hanging on to the Ventriloquist's neck for support while the two ride off, blue and white flag flapping in the wind. I'm dazed by the fall (did I fall or was I hit?), and before I can decide on a plan of action I find my legs leading the way, sprinting away from the wall up the rough Bethlehem road. The two men turn right up a side street and I chase them all the while yelling, "My bike, my bike!" The army officer, some two hundred metres away, does nothing, his attention focused on a truck trying to enter Israel. I want the soldier to do something: shoot a flare, a warning shot, anything to help a tourist in distress.

The two men have turned onto a rather steep hill, which the Ventriloquist can't manage while doubling his friend. I catch up to them and pant, "Can I have my bike back?"

"I thought it wasn't your bike," says the Legless Man.

"It isn't. It's my friend's."

"An Israeli friend?"

"Yes."

"You can't have the bike back."

"Look, I'm sorry about the flag."

"You are in Palestine now, do you understand what this means?" asks the Legless Man.

"Sure," I say, and while instinct has carried me toward this hill, I wish I hadn't listened to it. After all, it's just a clunky bike. It wouldn't mean the end of the world if I let them have the damn thing. The Ventriloquist puts the Legless Man onto the edge of a rusted garbage can. Beside us is an apartment building with no occupants; blown-out windows, mattresses with bullet holes that might have once acted as shields against military fire. Bullet-ridden glass, rusted rebar and dirty toilet paper litter the edges of the street.

Willing to forsake my friend's bicycle, I start to back away, quietly exiting the situation as best I can. Mr. Ventriloquist mentions in Pictionary language that he has a knife with a large blade on the inside of his leg. I'm not sure if he's bluffing or not. Pulling out a fresh pack of cigarettes, I opt for the Goofball technique.

"You have cigarettes?" asks the Legless Man.

Fortunately I bought two packs this morning. I pull the second out of my pocket and give one pack to each.

"Lucky Strike," says the Ventriloquist. "Now that's a cigarette."

"They toast the tobacco, right?" says the Legless Man.

I tell them I've never watched them being made, but I had heard the same thing as well (that is, I read the package). I ask if I can have a cigarette. The Ventriloquist complies, and the three of us smoke together, silently.

"You are idiotic to ride here with a flag like this," says the Legless Man. "You are asking for trouble."

I tell them I'm not looking for trouble, I was only borrowing the bike.

"If you're going to have a bicycle with an Israeli flag on it, you have to have a Palestinian flag on it as well," explains the Ventriloquist.

"This seems reasonable," I say.

"We are reasonable men," says the Legless Man, who lights a new cigarette off his old one.

"Where do I get this Palestinian flag?" I ask.

The Ventriloquist says, "We will sell you one."

"How much?"

"Fifty dollars."

"Fifty bucks? That's ridiculous."

"Of course it's expensive," says the Legless Man.

"We are in fact ripping you off," says the Ventriloquist.

The Legless Man adds, "But you have to understand, we are in dire circumstances here."

"There are absolutely no tourists visiting."

"Look," I say, not sure about the protocol of haggling in this situation, "I'm sympathetic to your predicament. But I don't have fifty dollars."

"How much do you have?" asks the Ventriloquist.

"Thirty."

"We'll take it."

"But that's all I've got."

"That's more than we have."

"We have nothing."

"We have twenty mouths to feed between the two of us. How many do you have?" asks the Legless Man. The point is well made. I give them my last thirty dollars. "We'll throw in a free tour of the Church of the Nativity too," adds the Ventriloquist.

"From you?"

"No, no, my brother will take you," says the Legless Man.

"Your brother? Where is he?"

"He is at the store, drinking."

"I don't know if I need a tour."

"Isn't that why you came here? To see the tourist sights?"

"I suppose it is," I say.

"You may have this too," the Ventriloquist adds, pulling out a wooden necklace from his shirt pocket.

"I don't need a necklace."

"Please, accept this as a gift."

"I won't wear it."

"Give it to your mother."

A giant wooden cross hangs from the centre. Somehow I know my mother won't appreciate it. I take it anyway. Today is a day to say "yes."

THE VENTRILOQUIST and Legless Man leave me in a Christian gift store not far from the Bethlehem refugee camp. They head off on a journey to find the Palestinian flag and promise to be back within the hour. I'm not sure if what has just occurred falls under the category of robbery, but the fact is I'm alive and they seem to be acting like friends on account of the cigarettes and cash I gave them. The gift store is completely empty of customers and full of Christian tchotchkes: notebooks with Mary painted in watercolour on the cover, iridescent Mary/Baby Jesus postcards, whistle-me-Jesus key chains, God the Board Game, John the Deck of Cards, the three wise men engraved into a backgammon board. Two men, Abdul and Ishmael, one drinking coffee, the other drinking wine, sit and play backgammon. A glass of sweet Bethlehem wine is brought for me.

"I love *shesh besh*," I say.

"How can you love shesh besh?" asks Abdul, brother of the Legless Man.

Abdul strokes his moustache. His focus is completely on the game. He takes a sip of strong coffee. "For two years, we've been doing nothing but playing shesh besh. You win, you lose, it doesn't matter. Shesh besh is waiting. It's the game of the damned."

I watch them play one game after another while my glass continues to be filled with wine. Ishmael drinks with me. He wears dark tinted sunglasses and says nothing. Silence is broken by Abdul to discuss politics.

"This is what they have given us. This is their peace," says Abdul. "For two years, not a fucking tourist comes into this store. Because they're scared. Like any tourist should be. The army likes to shoot at us when they're in the mood to. Terrorist threat. Like hell! You rolled a double six."

"Heh, heh, heh." I realize that Ishmael is blind. Abdul tells Ishmael the roll of the dice, and Ishmael tells Abdul where to move his pieces. This is impressive, for Ishmael has obviously memorized every possible backgammon move, not to mention the shifting positions of pieces on the board. This handicap, I think, would make the game much more interesting than Abdul lets on, but I restrain from voicing this observation. I ask Abdul if he lives in the refugee camp.

"Thank God no. They are the true unfortunates."

I ask him if he'd like to leave.

"Leave? This is my home." He lights a cigarette and looks at me for the first time. "Why? You want to help me get out?"

"How?"

"It doesn't matter. One way or another, there's no escape."

Another drink, another round of shesh besh. I'm starting to feel a little tipsy from the wine, talk and absence of food. Just as I wonder if we're going to make it to the church, the Ventriloquist and Legless Man return with a Palestinian flag. It looks like it's been painted onto a piece of white cloth—the dimensions crude, the lines uneven. The faint colours of Palestine hang off a broom handle. They lend me packing tape so I can stick this makeshift flag onto the back of the bike, then nod their approval as it's larger than the Israeli one. Larger, but doomed to fall, break off, blow away at any moment. I look outside at the darkening skies and surmise that a rainstorm would likely wash out this feeble paint job.

Ishmael starts to laugh infectiously.

"Double sixes again," says Abdul, grimacing the end of his cigarette into the ashtray. "The blind have all the luck in this part of the world."

I give up on the idea of the church, choosing to bike south and east, deeper into the West Bank. Abdul has shown me a map of the road ahead: villages and olive groves, ancient desert palaces. Children run after me, laughing at the two flags flapping in the wind, one trim and taut, the other flailing and huge. Somehow the two flags stay on. The children continue to laugh and point. A man plows his field, two oxen pulling at the earth. He turns at the sight of me, wipes the sweat from his face.

CHAPTER 19

Jacob and Ruthie used to be an item when the three of us studied philosophy at university on the West Coast. Ruthie was a powerhouse postmodern thinker in the early 1990s when feminism was queen of the campus. She was radical in her thoughts, a fan of Beauvoir and Derrida, sexually open and genuinely provocative. Originally from San Francisco, she recently moved to Israel and turned religious. She married a man named Menachem, has a small boy named Herschel and covers her head so only her husband can see her hair (it used to be a gorgeous strawberry blonde). In the twenty-first century she's become one of the *aliyot* crusaders, landing in Israel to receive the word, the message of God, Torah, whatever. The feminist revolution becomes: *We choose to be traditional child-rearing housewives of the Jewish order.*

When Ruthie went through her conversion—or as the Orthodox Jews call it, her *tshuva*, meaning *return*—she wrote Jacob a letter. She asked him to burn all the lust letters she'd written him before. These letters contained words like "Jell-O," "leather" and "take me to Uranus, big boy." I don't know if Jacob complied or not. Ruthie argued that she was "no longer the person she was before." I wonder what kind of a person she is now.

"So I hear you've got a nice Jewish girl," Ruthie says.

It's early the next morning, Friday, and we're at Ruthie's house in West Jerusalem. She pours boiling water into a cup, stirring three spoonfuls of Nescafé into her mug. Instant Nescafé is a tradition

157

Ruthie and I share from university days. We like to drink it with milk warmed up on the stove. Store-bought oatmeal cookies, with or without raisins, dunked into the freeze-dried stuff.

"Her name's Judith."

"Yehudit. She killed Holophernes."

"That's right. She got him drunk, seduced him, then decapitated him. One of my favourite women in the Bible."

Ruthie laughs. "You haven't changed."

"You have."

"Baruch Hashem, all is for the best."

It's been three days since Judith's called and still I haven't called her back. I know that calling her will only take me outside of whatever it is I'm experiencing here. I want to be fully immersed in this world. Need to be.

Ruthie rocks back and forth with her infant son, Herschel, breast-feeding him under a white knitted shawl. A blue woollen hat covers her hair.

I say, "The last time I saw you we were getting stoned and reading Nietzsche." She shifts uncomfortably on the white rocking chair. I look around the room. The bookshelves are full of books about Judaism, Talmud and family. I notice a copy of Spinoza's *Ethics*. "You have a nice house," I add.

"Life is simple here. We don't need too many things."

I take a sip of coffee. It's no Arabic treat, but there is something comforting in this rite, in returning to what we shared ten years ago.

"Tell me about your life in Jerusalem."

"What can I say? Baruch Hashem, it isn't easy, but I have my husband and my health. I study Torah, and I'm curious as I've always been. Judaism demands we ask questions."

"You were doing a Ph.D. in philosophy, last I heard."

"I came here and fell in love with God. He beats the hell out of nothingness."

I don't say anything.

"It wasn't an easy choice and it isn't an easy life. I had to move far away from my family. When my sister died, it was especially difficult to be here. But I chose the path of God, and that involves sacrifices. Avraham Aveinu taught us this when he brought Isaac to Mount Moriah. Faith is never easy."

"Do you question your faith?"

"What is Judaism without doubt?"

Ruthie raises Herschel in the air. His eyes are wide open, brilliant blue. He smiles.

"What about all the suicide bombings?" I ask.

"What about them?"

"How do you feel bringing up your kid in this world?"

"It's dangerous. There's no question about it. But I believe in being here. For two thousand years, our prayers were directed to Jerusalem. Now we have an opportunity, for the first time in millennia, to merge flesh and spirit. This is an incredible time in history."

The chair I'm sitting on is hard. I have the urge to get up and stretch. I ask, "You weren't raised Jewish, were you?"

"We never went to shul, never did Shabbat. But when I got off the airplane, I was transformed."

"How so?"

"I stopped being a skeptic."

I want to say to her, maybe you latched on to this, afraid of the choices life presents us. But that's me imposing this Midrash, my interpretation. There's more to Ruthie's choice than her needing a crutch. After all, the mainstream secular model—to earn, earn, earn so we can buy, buy, buy—is not exactly burgeoning with meaning. That's why Ruthie and I studied Foucault, Marx, whomever. We were young, we challenged the world, and we wanted to find something meaningful in it. In the twenty-first century, Orthodoxy presents itself as a seductive alternative. Judaism has a strong sense of ethics, a close-knit community, and ritual infused in every action—washing the hands, cooking, waking from sleep, making love. Everything is a prayer guided toward right-mindfulness, as Rabbi Spero would say. There's even a tradition of intellectual debate, something that appeals to Ruthie's philosophical mind. I look at the way she holds her child, talking to him in Hebrew, *malachi, olami,* my angel, my world. She believes in both heart and in mind. I have to admit, I'm jealous of her faith.

Ruthie puts down Herschel and dunks another kosher oatmeal cookie into her coffee. She asks, "Why didn't you bring her?"

"Who?"

"Yehudit."

"I'm working. Doing research for a play."

"I heard. You're looking for a story about peace."

"A house," I say.

"Have you found it? Your peace?"

I say, "Of course not. This country is crazy." I crack a cookie in half. Herschel sucks on his fingers. I add, "People are passionate here."

We laugh at that understatement, take back the rest of our coffees at the same time, mirrors of each other.

"How's Jacob?" she asks.

"He's getting married in the fall. So is my brother Aaron." I don't mention that both of them are marrying non-Jewish. I tap my hand on the table. "I don't see Jacob too much. But you know how it is. We've known each other since we were four. We'll always be friends."

"I hear he's a schoolteacher."

"The Lord works in mysterious ways."

We laugh some more. I say, "He was hurt when you asked him to destroy those letters."

"I'm a different person now."

"He cared about you."

"That person he was in love with doesn't exist anymore."

"You can't just erase your past. Doesn't Judaism at least teach us that?"

Ruthie flinches at my response. I don't know why I'm arguing on behalf of Jacob. It's not like I have any stake in their relationship. Ten years ago we ranted, argued and changed the world with our twenty-year-old thoughts. Now we've gone our own ways. I should be fine with that. But somehow Ruthie's conversion to Orthodoxy—her conviction, her belief—is a challenge to my own choices. I don't want to let go of who she was, but I also want to make sure my choices are the right ones. The urge to give in to my faith is strong; to completely immerse myself in ritual, belief, God.

"So you've been staying with my friend Max," Ruthie says, changing the subject.

"He's a great guy. Thanks for setting us up."

"He tells me you went to Ramallah."

"I visited a Palestinian friend."

"I've always admired your curiosity, Jonathan."

"Thanks."

"But you have no idea what life is like here."

My immediate reaction is to tell Ruthie to shut up. I'm starting to get really annoyed with people saying this to me. But in the spirit of maintaining old friendships, I back down. Instead I say, "It must be difficult to live in a country that is constantly under the scrutiny of the entire world."

"God willed it that way," she replies. "We are the moral standard, the measurement by which the rest of the world is compared. We have an incredible responsibility." Ruthie rises. She puts Herschel down in his crib to sleep. She rocks the wooden frame back and forth.

"He's a good kid," I say.

"Will you come for Shabbat tonight?"

"I have plans."

"Then come for the Seder in a few weeks. Please. I insist."

When Ruthie says this, she stares at me, examining my face. Behind her new appearances—the covered shoulders and hair, the lack of sleep from raising a newborn—I can see the old Ruthie, beautiful, feline Ruthie, with blue-green eyes. We're in British Columbia again and she's wearing a black tank top that reveals her bare shoulders, her beauty that made me uneasy. I'm reminded of the day the two of us fell asleep beneath an arbutus tree outside class. She rolled toward me, and I let her rest on my chest. We lay like that, friend to friend, the entire afternoon.

"All right," I say. "I'll come to the Seder."

"You'll meet my husband. You two will get along really well. He has an artistic streak in him."

"So you learned to cook?" I ask.

She grimaces. "Still learning."

I tell her I have to get going. I don't tell her that Abu Dalo is expecting me this evening—on Shabbat—and I need to prepare for the interview. I get up and move to embrace her. She holds out her hands before I come too close. "I can't."

Ruthie, old friend, whose hand I cannot shake.

"Only my husband."

CHAPTER 20

Dusk. An air raid siren wails. The noise scares the hell out of me. I drop my notebook and run outside Max's apartment into the alley expecting the worst. Mothers and fathers sobbing, delirious from grief. ZAKA searching for the remains of bodies to preserve in bags, to bury. Anger and shock, news reporters, soldiers, an old man speaking to no one, to God—*why, why?* Instead I see a few Hasidic men hurrying with their tallis bags. A young girl, skipping happily. An old man, dressed in a white robe, leisurely walking past.

A figure turns into the alley where I stand. It's Max, tallis bag in hand, a smile on his face. "Shabbat shalom!" he exclaims. He sees the panic on my face. "Are you okay?"

"The air raid siren."

Max slaps me on the back. "It's Shabbos. That's what it means."

Relieved, and feeling only somewhat idiotic, I follow Max back inside the apartment. He shows me the drill. We decide which lights to leave on for the Shabbat so he won't have to turn any on or off for twenty-four hours—the bathroom, the front foyer, an upstairs lamp. It's my first time for the Sabbath in a completely observant home since I was a kid.

Max asks me one last time if I'm sure I don't want to join him at Ruthie's for Shabbat dinner. "She really wants you to meet her husband," he says.

"I'd love to come. But I have another commitment."

"Where exactly are you going?"

"Mekor Chayim."

Max rubs his eyes and puts on his glasses. "All right," he says, seeing that everything is in order for the day of rest. He picks up his tallis bag, shakes my hand and says, "Shabbat shalom."

NACHLAOT IS ONE of the most beautiful neighbourhoods in Jerusalem. The walls are soft to the touch; the stone feels like it might crumble if one applies too much pressure. Every corridor, house and square is made of this gentle limestone. One walks through geology here, breathing, living it.

Nachlaot was built in the nineteenth century when Jewish emigration was starting to pick up. There wasn't enough room in the old city so many Jews started to live in what is now called Central Jerusalem. In the 1960s and 1970s it was a real artists' hangout. Now it's becoming more and more religious. There's a synagogue on every corner. Walk through the streets and you'll hear the same prayers sung in myriad ways—the Yemenite wail, the Shlomo Carlbach hippie riff, the Ethiopian chant, the Ashkenaz dirge. The words are mostly the same, but each melody varies so much it's difficult to imagine it being the same prayer. My brain feels like it's being tickled. These voices touch the language and music centres in my head, the blueprint impressed upon me when I was a child. It's as though the neurons firing off in my brain are singing, *Thank you for bringing us to Jerusalem.*

I turn left, walk down a stone alleyway. I don't know where I am. It feels wrong to be playing hooky on my first Shabbat here. I reason there will be other Friday nights during my stay, and I need to take advantage of whenever Abu Dalo will grant me an interview. And besides, I'm *walking* to Mekor Chayim, a good twenty-five-minute endeavour. It's my Shabbat compromise.

I try another courtyard with the hope of finding something familiar. Nachlaot is a series of courtyards, a maze of buildings with few streetlights. Candles from houses illuminate the dark alleys, narrow stone streets. The smell of chicken soup, fresh challah baked in an oven, permeates the air. I'm lost. My initial reaction is panic—but this quickly subsides, and I start to enjoy this confusion. Something about this maze of stone corridors soothes the mind. What keeps me calm is the belief that this unlit path is leading me somewhere. And so these Jerusalem streets are not a maze but a labyrinth. I walk it with the hope of discovering something at its centre.

A man sits at a corner with his hand outstretched, begging for money. I search my pockets to give him something, but I'm not carrying any change because of the Sabbath. A lone car races by on the street below. Familiarity: the road to Rechavya. I turn left, and exit the walls of Nachlaot. Continue the descent toward Abu Dalo's house.

HIS HOME IS TUCKED BEHIND Mary's, hidden by a small yard of olive trees. He lives in a mansion.

Abu Dalo greets me at the door and warmly shakes my hand. His demeanour is completely different tonight; he greets me as though I were an old friend. He takes me through a narrow passageway of his house and up three flights of stairs. There's a wall of photographs that line the hallway. One of the photographs, he tells me, is of Beit Safafa, divided in half during the armistice with Jordan in 1948: Half of the town was Jordan; half was Israel. He lived on the Israeli side, he explains, pointing at the photograph. Divided families reach across a chain-link fence, trying to touch each other.

There is barely enough room to stand in the main third-floor room, crammed as it is with a bizarre array of tourist paraphernalia—paintings of belly dancers from Cairo, wooden dolls from Russia, chopsticks that light up "Beijing" when clicked together. Amid this mess I'm invited to sit on a rather thin and uncomfortable handmade wooden chair that looks to be over a century old—"our best furniture,"

Abu Dalo assures me with a grand hand gesture. Mary's here to help with the translation. Abu Dalo introduces me to his wife, Fathiyah. She is dressed all in black—jeans and a sweater. Cookies and coffee are laid out on the table. Mary sits beside me.

Mary informs me that Abu Dalo remembered Rana after I left the other day. She explains that many people have lived in the house since the mid-1990s, and he apologizes for his abruptness. The apology seems odd, out of character.

"You are a writer," says Abu Dalo. He says this to me in English.

"Yes," I say.

"I am a writer too!" he exclaims.

"You mean publisher," says Mary.

"I am a writer," says Abu Dalo.

"He is a publisher," says Mary. "He has a printing press downstairs."

"You will write big article for newspaper," Abu Dalo says.

"A play," I reply.

Abu Dalo looks at Mary and she provides the necessary translation. He turns to me and clasps his hands. "Theatre!" Abu Dalo rubs his hands together like a child. "Richard Gere," he points to himself.

"I'll try my best," I say, "but the play hasn't been written yet."

Mary tells him this. Abu Dalo is slightly perturbed. "When will the play be written?" she asks.

"Tell Abu Dalo I need to find out the story of the house to write the play."

As soon as this is translated, Abu Dalo leaps to his feet and exits the room. He returns with a stack of photocopies: visas of him and his wife for their pilgrimage to Mecca, pictures of their apartment in Cairo (which Abu Dalo claims they cannot get to because the Israelis won't let them leave the country nor will the Egyptians let them enter theirs), and a bank statement for 1.5 million shekels. This, he claims, is what it cost him to purchase his mansion from the state.

"He would like you to have these documents," says Mary. Abu Dalo smiles profusely.

"For what?" I ask.

"Your research," Mary says.

Abu Dalo joins his hands together at the wrists, miming the universal hand signal for handcuffs. Mary explains, "Mail them to Canada. Don't take them out with you. The customs will arrest you."

I put the items into my bag, figuring I can sort through them later at Max's house and decide which ones I should keep. I notice a photocopied article in Arabic from a newspaper with a picture of Abu Dalo holding up a document. He's offering the camera a large, toothy smile, and I want to know what the article is about. Mary explains, "He won his court case to own the house."

Abu Dalo launches, via Mary's assistance, into the details. "In 1908 my father built the house that Shimon now lives in." At the mention of Shimon's name, Fathiyah spits on the floor. "In 1948, the Nakba occurred." Abu Dalo pauses and listens to Mary's simultaneous translation by staring at her intently, placing his hands firmly on his lap and nodding in agreement with her every word. "The Jewish army told us we had to leave, so we fled to Beit Safafa. After one week we decided to return, only to find Shimon had moved in."

"How old were you?"

"Three. We slept right outside the house, while Shimon slept inside, laughing at us."

"He is worse than Hitler," adds Fathiyah.

"My father made plans. He fought back. He would not let the matter rest."

I say, "He hid himself in the bedroom, right?"

This sends Abu Dalo, Fathiyah and Mary into hysterics. They have a prolonged argument in Arabic, mixed with laughter and much knee-slapping. "This is a story," says Mary, "nobody knows if it's true or not."

"Abu Dalo doesn't remember?"

"Maybe his brothers remember but they don't talk to each other."

"Why not?"

Mary leans over and says in an almost-whisper: "He's suing them for the land."

"He's suing his brothers?"

"*Habibi,*" Abu Dalo says. He's calling me "sweetie." "I have spent so much money on the courts I could have bought a villa in France. What have my brothers done?" One is a professor, the other a doctor. Both are very successful. They live in the house next door.

Mary steers us back to 1948. "After two weeks his father built a hut right next to Shimon."

"Did he talk to Shimon?"

"There was a lot of shouting."

"Did they share any of the house?"

Abu Dalo scratches his head. He doesn't remember. He does remember his father taking the matter to court. In the intervening years, the Abu Dalo family built a new house directly across the street from Shimon. It was a rushed job, and it's where Mary lives today. She explains, "After twelve years of fighting in the courts, the judge decided that Shimon could live in the house."

I remember what Rana had told me. People who happened to be away from their house on a particular day were considered absentees (most absentees fled or were expelled to Jordan, Gaza, Lebanon and Syria). Those who were absent but had stayed within the borders of Israel were considered "present absentees," or internal refugees. Abu Dalo's family would have been considered such a case; they left for a week (or a few), waiting for the war to blow over, but always had the intention of returning. They had left their belongings in the house for this reason. That Shimon was allowed to live there was legal and common at the time. Many Jews moved into the houses vacated by Palestinians.

Mary adds, "The judge did make an unusual decision, though. While Shimon was allowed to live in the house, he decided that Abu Dalo still owned the property."

"So you mean Shimon rents from Abu Dalo?"

"Yes."

"How long is this lease for?"

"A lifetime," says Mary.

Abu Dalo solemnly adds, "My father died because he couldn't live in his house. He died with a broken heart."

Mary continues, "The situation became worse when Azulay's daughter moved in."

"Who's Azulay?"

"Azulay was a Moroccan Jew. He'd shared the house with Shimon since 1948."

Abu Dabo: "We lived across the street in our house, and the Jews lived in theirs."

"Where's Azulay now?"

"He died," says Fathiyah, pouring teaspoons of sugar into her coffee.

"He died," says Mary, "and then his estranged daughter from Tel Aviv moved in. Declared the house her rightful inheritance." Abu Dalo points to the picture in the newspaper. "When Azulay's daughter moved in, Abu Dalo took her to court. The daughter claimed she'd lived there the past six months. If this could be proven, then the house could legally become hers."

Abu Dalo adds, "But the truth is she don't talk to her father for fifteen years. So I say fuck you. I take her to court, and I win the case."

"Then Rana and the other Palestinian moved in—"

"When was this?"

"1997."

"How did Shimon feel about living with Palestinians?"

No one says anything. Mary looks at Abu Dalo and Abu Dalo looks at Fathiyah and Fathiyah rubs at a scratch on the table. Rana told me that life next to Shimon was difficult and unpleasant for the most part, but there were good moments too. She said, "We had good conversations when he was drunk. And he came to my engagement party. He was really happy for me when he found out I was getting married."

Abu Dalo delivers a long monologue in Arabic. Mary and Fathiyah listen attentively, hanging on to his every word. The speech is passionate, a plea that veers between the angry and the tragic. Abu Dalo stands up from his chair and smashes his hand on the table. Then he politely sits down. I'm dying to know what he said. Mary translates. "Look, it was a cheap place to live. Abu Dalo, he gave them a very good price."

"That's what he said?"

Abu Dalo nods.

"So." I adjust my seat. "Are any Arabs living with Shimon now?"

"No," Mary says. Abu Dalo scratches his head.

"And what about Shimon?"

"He pays Abu Dalo rent," says Mary.

"Very little," Abu Dalo says. He adds for good measure, "I wait for him to die."

"What is your relationship like with Shimon?" I ask.

A pause for heated debate. Mary and Abu Dalo argue back and forth. Abu Dalo looks at me with disgust. "We have no relationship," he says, and starts to leave the room.

"No relationship at all?" I ask, following him. "But Rana said you two talk. In Arabic, sometimes."

Abu Dalo stops and says, "I own the land, I own the house and I own him."

THE DISCUSSION with Abu Dalo and Mary about the history of the house is confusing. I try to keep the numbers straight in my head—who lived where and when, what was built, how it was divided—but little of it matches up with what I was told. Rana never mentioned Azulay in any of our discussions. She'd also said that Shimon's occupation began in 1967, not 1948, as Abu Dalo claims. I wonder what Shimon's story will be.

I had thought the house exceptional because Shimon and Abu Dalo shared it peacefully: This is clearly not the case. What is unusual is that the Abu Dalos stayed at all. "This area used to be all Palestinian," Abu Dalo explains. "Very wealthy." He grew up in the only Palestinian family in a sea of Jews. As a boy he went to a Jewish school and was called a dirty Arab by the other students. Several years ago, his children were sent home from school following a suicide bombing one week; the Jewish children had accused his kids of being terrorists. The state made it very difficult for them to stay, Abu Dalo says, forcing them into one court battle after another. He admits that sometimes it was too much; he and his wife left for a number of years to live in another part of the city. And still, he came back to make this his home. Why?

Abu Dalo goes into the other room and returns with an old copper key. He holds it in his palm, won't let me touch it: "My father, Ibrahim, made this. Built this house, too. He lived to be 115 years old. He would not die until he was sure we would stay. He insisted on it: We needed to live on our land." Abu Dalo grimaces. "Bless that stubborn old man."

IT'S DARK OUTSIDE. Across the street in Shimon's house, the lights of candles flicker. Shadows climb faces alive on the walls of the dining room. Shabbat: The end of the week, a night and day of peace. I think about Judith, wonder if she'll be at the Minsk tonight, praying and eating dinner with the old guys. I also think of Rana. She said when she lived in the house with Shimon that only a thin wall separated them. She could hear his family singing Shabbat songs, a warmth not felt the rest of the week. "It let me hear the beauty of the Jews," she said. "It also reminded me of how Jews and Muslims got along for centuries."

I think I can see Shimon rocking back and forth on his chair. His wife is with him, as are his children and grandchildren. I want to knock on his door and ask if I can join them. Shimon reads from his siddur, the children are listening. What message, what prayer is he singing tonight?

CHAPTER 21

Several days later. A phone conversation.

JUDITH: How's the work with Barak going?

ME: I haven't met him yet.

JUDITH: Why not? I figured that's why you didn't call. You were too busy.

ME: I have been busy. But I'm seeing him today.

JUDITH: So what's it like? Did you kiss the earth when you got off the plane?

ME: No, I did not kiss the runway.

JUDITH: Did you go to Yad Vashem?

ME: No.

JUDITH: The Tower of David?

ME: No.

JUDITH: The Wailing Wall?

ME: I haven't done anything touristy. But I've been to the West Bank. And the house. I mean, I found it. Though it isn't quite what I thought it would be. *A beat.* Hello? Judith? Are you there?

Four soldiers frisk me before I enter Mahane Yehuda. This is the shortcut to Yaffo Street, where I plan on catching a collective taxi to Tel Aviv to meet Barak. The security check is normal but the market is strangely quiet today. The usual clamour of merchants haggling oranges, eggplant and hummus is a deadened whisper. The fruit sellers peddle their fruit haphazardly, as though reluctant to do business, and there are very few buyers. There are also at least a dozen more soldiers than usual keeping a close eye on things. They wear aviator shades and bulletproof vests. They carry M-16s, bomb-searching devices and walkie-talkies. Their body language reads, *Don't you fucking bomb me or my people.*

I wonder what's up.

I'm not comfortable in this country, but I'm starting to get used to things. It's not easy. Walking the long aisles of the market I'm reminded of the map Max showed me with all the places bombs have gone off during the second intifada. Max said, "It's the map that turned me from a lefty into a righty. And it's the map that stopped me from loving."

I wanted to know what he meant. I asked one of his friends if he'd lost a girlfriend in a bombing. She said, "Baruch Hashem, Max has been single as long as I've known him. If there's one blessing he's had from the bachelor life, it's that he's had no one to lose." Later Max explained that any time he hears a news report about a suicide bomb he closes off. If he happens to be dating someone, he retreats, avoids her company. "Another person opens you up to the world," he said. "Softens you. Maybe that's okay in America. But not here."

When he said that, I searched for a response to his argument. Wanted to say, who would choose to live in a world like that? I followed the red and blue pushpins he'd stuck into the map of Jerusalem. The borders of west and east took on a new meaning, the ancient holy sites replaced by fear and mourning. I had the urge to remove the pins from the map. Knew there'd only be holes instead.

AT A NEWSPAPER STAND by Mahane Yehuda I look at today's *Herald Tribune.* On the cover is a picture of a man with a long white beard seated in a wheelchair. The paper tells me yesterday morning three Hellfire missiles killed Sheikh Ahmed Yassin, the spiritual leader of Hamas. They were dropped on him while he left a mosque in Gaza.

"Expect retaliation," says Rantissi, the co-founder of Hamas. "Israel will shake at its feet."

The man selling papers wants me to hurry up and take the damn thing or leave it alone. Buy or don't buy, just decide. I buy an apple instead, but don't eat it.

Over there, a man dressed as a Hasid buys cucumbers. He *should* be cool. He has *peyes*, a thin beard. He's young and wears all black, like he walked right out of eighteenth-century Europe. Today he's the ultimate suspect. His long coat fans out over his waist, disguising what might be hidden. And let's called a spade a spade: That supposedly Sephardic Jew has darker skin than an Ashkenazi. His skin colour is a warning, a possibility.

It's the most popular game in the Middle East: Guess the suicide bomber. Today's the day to play it. Up ahead, a wrinkly old woman tries to lift an oversized watermelon but she can't get it off the table. It occurs to me even she's a potential bomber. Hell, the watermelon could be a bomb. Why not? The mind of a terrorist is creative. Anything's possible.

Watermelon Lady turns to me. "Young man, would you mind helping me carry this?"

"No way," I say, and start to walk off. Stop in front of the newspaper and stare.

"This is the moment Yassin dreamed of. Sharon has opened the gates of Hell."

Suddenly Mrs. Blintzkrieg pops into my head. I wonder how she'd deal with this.

When I was twelve, Mrs. Blintzkrieg was my homeroom teacher. She went from being a figure of fear to one of awe. Once she lifted an entire teacher's desk off the floor to retrieve lost papers. It had to weigh a hundred pounds. With one hand she propped up the metal desk, and with the other she rescued the papers from the floor. I was sure the desk would fall on her hand and crush it. But Blintzkrieg didn't think twice, didn't demand help, and she didn't fail. She was fearless and that's what marked the difference between her and me, Israel and Canada. I wanted that strength of belief, to be that strong. To be like Blintzkrieg.

I still want that strength, but her macho-righteous shtick doesn't really apply to today. It's the height of the second intifada, and the co-founder of Hamas has just been assassinated by the IDF. Gaza is enraged. Hamas will strike back. The question, Israelis wonder, is when? Most Jerusalemites are doing what I should be: hiding indoors until the storm passes.

I take a bite of the apple. It tastes wormy and old, so I go for the newspaper instead. Scouring the day-after stats (ten others dead, seventeen injured), I whip the half-devoured fruit into the garbage. It makes a loud thur-plunk. People jump and turn to look in my direction. For the first time since I've arrived in Israel I see that people other than me are afraid. If Blintzkrieg were here—

I feel a nudge at my back. I whirl around and it's the newspaper-man wanting his ten shekels.

I look down at my feet. Rantissi's right. Already I'm shaking. I'm not at ease here. I'm not used to things at all.

YAFFO STREET'S EMPTY. There are only two other people on the minibus to Tel Aviv. One's an Israeli girl near my age wearing a bikini and a towel around her waist. The other is an old man. He smells like sardines and holds a briefcase on his lap.

"Where you heading?" the girl asks.

"Habima Theatre," I say. "You?"

"The beach."

Quite a day to go swimming I want to say, but who am I to say what a good day is for a dip in the sea? With all this security, it's probably one of the safest days to be outside. On the radio, Israeli songs are played to embolden us. Naomi Shemer wails "Jerusalem of Gold," "Yerushalayim shel Zahav," one of my favourites as a kid.

How the cisterns have dried
The marketplace is empty
And no one frequents the Temple Mount
In the Old City

The old man closes his eyes and lets the sun warm his skin. I try to imagine the helicopter pilot who dropped the bomb. Was he nervous? Doubtful. They train them to be this way, raise those special soldiers on a diet of bravery and certainty. *Nerves of steel.* I mull the expression over in my mind. I imagine skin made of iron, bones like the cables that hold up a bridge.

In the mind of the pilot:

My sister or cousin lost her limb or eye or life on a bus, in a stall, in the market. Yassin may be sitting in a wheelchair, but he ordered the death of my people. I should feel badly? For a murderer? For evil himself? To feel guilt doesn't even enter the mind. In Israel, there is only survival.

And when I press the button that drops the fucking missile on that asshole of an animal I do not fall through the Gaza sky. I listen to him die; it's like music.

His words in my head, and the music from the radio...

Yerushalayim shel Zahav
Ve-shel nekhoshet ve-shel or
Ha-lo-le-khol shirayikh ani kinnor

Jerusalem of gold, and of bronze, and of light
Behold I am a violin for all your songs

The old man picks his teeth. He breaks into peels of laughter.

"Are you okay?" I ask.

"Beseder, beseder, hakol besder." Everything's cool.

I'm in awe of the pilot who dropped the bomb. It's not the same Entebbe awe I had as a child. The swoop in and yank out a hundred hostages sort of miracle. Entebbe was awesome, but it was morally clear. We knew what had to be done.

The awe I have for the pilot is different. I'm in awe of the belief he has, the kind that allows you to point laser-guided missiles at a man and not wonder if it's the right thing to do. The pilot has the conviction I lack: He carries out the death sentence from above, believes this trial by rocket is necessary, good and just. For Jews and all of humanity.

I imagine Mrs. Blintzkrieg saying, "What's worse? A dead terrorist, or someone who murders innocent children?"

"Couldn't they have just put him in jail? I mean what about the innocent civilians that were killed by the missiles?" I say.

"Things are much more complicated than that, Shalom. Of course we don't *want* to kill innocent civilians. But how else does one deal with terrorists? Difficult situations demand difficult decisions."

I wouldn't know what to say to Blintzkrieg. Don't know how to judge these acts of violence. I know my morality is squeamish at best, and I have no real understanding of the rules of war. I'm afraid of the suicide bomber, and the Yassins that send them into the world. But I also fear this dialogue of missiles and bombs, what it does to us as people. How a nation becomes hard-wired to believe in violence. Blood in the brain, blood on the land.

"FINALLY, WE MEET."

The director Barak's hand is like a hammer: cold-steel handshake. He's short and younger than I imagined him on the phone, a few years older than I am. He chain-smokes and has teeth like *patates frites*, talks at me, into me, an attack.

"So about this house," he says.

We're sitting in Café Habima. It's elegant and sparse. I'm not sure where to begin, but like most Israelis, Barak doesn't wait for the conversation to warm up. We are, in a manner of speaking, already hot. I tell him what Rana told me in Toronto, and about my meeting with Abu Dalo. I also tell Barak I've dropped by Shimon's twice in the past few days but he wasn't home. The neighbours think he's away visiting his daughter in Tel Aviv.

Barak couldn't care less about the real story. "Tell me the play," he says. His voice is low and gravelly.

I've been running the idea in my head. "It's 2004. A Palestinian comes back to claim the house as his own. The Israeli who's living there says forget about it, but the Palestinian manages to sneak inside and lock himself in his former bedroom. Because they want to avoid the Israeli courts (each for his own reasons), the two negotiate and decide to compromise: They'll share the house."

Barak grimaces. He seems pissed off. "This is not a play for today. This is '48 or '67."

"What do you mean?"

"In the twenty-first century we don't talk to each other. We're no longer human in this country. Why are these characters, Shimon and Abu Dalo, negotiating? One can just as easily shoot the other dead."

He has a point. "That wouldn't be much of a play."

"Let's look at what happened yesterday. Yassin is a terrorist. There's no disputing that. But this is not about killing a dangerous man. It's about messages, and a Hellfire missile is a very strong message. Sharon will pull out of Gaza. But he doesn't want to be perceived as weak."

"So what's going to happen?"

"There will be retaliation. If not next week, one month from now. If not one month from now, a year, a decade. We are breeding an entire generation of Hamas. That's what our 'security' will bring."

Barak squashes his cigarette in the ashtray. "Now back to this house. What you're telling me is not a usual situation. For an Arab to live in West Jerusalem—this is rare. Is that the point then—Abu Dalo's stubborn? What do you want to say?"

I tell him when I first arrived in Israel I saw the house as a strong metaphor for the historical problem: two people trying to live on the same disputed land. I also thought the fact they shared it—in spite of their contradictory claims to rightful ownership—would make it a good story about peace. Saying this now, I see how naive it is. Why should they share a house?

Barak asks, "Why do you care so much about peace?"

The question surprises me. "Isn't that what everyone wants?"

"Is it?" He waves at the waitress to bring him another espresso. "All right. So write about peace. Why not the peace between your government and the Indians? Why not write about land disputes in wherever it is you live?"

"What goes on here matters to me."

"Do you want to live here?"

"No."

"Then why do you care about this house?"

I don't say anything because I don't have an answer. I thought I came here to write a play. But Barak's question points to the heart of things: Why peace? And is it peace I'm actually searching for?

Barak changes tack. "Abu Dalo is waiting for Shimon to die. If we're to extend this metaphor to the whole country, it means the Palestinians are waiting for us to die so they can come back and take our homes. This is not going to happen. We're here, they're here—that's the reality. We both know it. Only the fanatics don't acknowledge this. Yes, your story is unusual. A Palestinian living in a Jewish part of Jerusalem is not the norm. But in another sense, it's the same old story: two people disputing history, fighting over land. It's interesting, but where do you go from there?"

He rubs his cracked lips with his thumb, turns to look out the window. "You're a writer. If you ask me, you want to go to the heart of the problem: occupation." The security guard at the front door sits in his chair. We're the only people in the café. Outside, the city is stone silent. "The question isn't how do we achieve peace. Leave that for the politicians, the land carvers, the Churchills and the Roosevelts. The question is, what has this occupation done to our moral fabric? What has it done to us as human beings? I'm not like you North Americans who go to the parliament with your petitions and say, 'War is bad.' Not all war is. It's aggression and occupation that's the problem. In 1967 we became responsible for over a million Palestinians, many of whom are refugees. At the time we thought we weren't going to be like the Europeans; we could be a light onto nations, and there would be a blending of cultures, an enlightened occupation." Beneath Barak's real-talk is a voice of hope. But this is quickly covered up. "The idea was idiotic. In the end, occupation is simply occupation. They don't want to be ruled by us, and who can blame them? Today we see the culmination of this problem, whether we were reluctant occupiers or not. And I will argue we were not so terribly reluctant." Barak taps his spoon against a saucer. "I directed *Saved* by Edward Bond in England a few years ago. There's a famous scene when the mother forgets her child in its pram. The father's there with his buddies, but instead of taking care of the baby, they stone it to death. He hates the kid, the burden of it, doesn't want it to exist. In a way, as occupiers, we become like those parents. We wish the Palestinians did not exist. We want the problem to simply go away. What does that say about us?"

Barak lets the question hang in the air. The answer, unsaid, stands before me: denial. In this country and myself.

I think about all those years I wouldn't read articles about Israel. I was fourteen when the first intifada began, my first year of public high school. I'd been out of Bialik four months and wasn't doing too well with it. I didn't understand the rules or the language at Forest Hill Collegiate.

On the cover of the front section of *The Globe and Mail* that October was a picture of a young boy with a stone in his hand, south-paw, gearing to whip it at an Israeli tank (a teenage Sandy Koufax, my first thought). Half-asleep, I tried to absorb the details. So-and-so was leading a demonstration on a university campus in the West Bank. The army came in, the students got rowdy. Shots were fired, eight were killed, many more injured.

The news surprised me. Stones are not bullets, and a protest is not a war. At that age, I understood that much. What do they want? I wanted to know. I stared at the picture on the front of the paper, hoping for an answer to the question. Heard the voice of Mrs. Blintzkrieg in my head: "They want us dead, Shalom. Be grateful we have tanks to defend us, not just our prayers."

Mrs. Blintzkrieg's words comforted me. I missed Bialik, and her voice brought me back to those dark and stuffy halls. It evoked the Israel I wanted to remember, the Israel of adolescence: a country of heroes, of fearless Blintzkriegs, Arnons, Dayans and Ben-Gurions. That October morning, I stopped reading the article. The words *right of return, checkpoint* and *refugee* were easy to ignore in the face of Jewish history. The old lesson returned: The Jews are doomed to be victims forever. And so the map of the West Bank—a black and white bulge in the shape of a fetus—remained foreign to me. Unwanted. Unknown.

Barak: "While you and I sit around and drink Italian espresso, only a few kilometres away the Israeli army is dropping missiles on Gaza." He says the word *Gaza* like he's grinding a peg into the ground. "You'll see, in a few days, Tel Aviv will forget Yassin. People will be out partying their heads off as though nothing happened. To live in this country requires absolute denial. Which is why I'm moving to Berlin."

Berlin? Is this some kind of joke? "When did you decide this?"

"I've been thinking about it for some time. Look, I want to direct theatre. Here it's pathetic entertainment. *Fiddler on the Fucking Roof. On Golden Pond.*"

"What about working on my play?"

"What have you written?"

"Nothing. I was going to try to write something in Tel Aviv."

He bangs his cigarette pack against the table.

"Look, I can help if you want. We can meet here for coffee and discuss. I won't be leaving for a couple more months."

"What about working with actors?"

"We can get some. But you have to write the play first."

It seems as though a residency in Israel is different from one in Canada. Or maybe I made up this idea of a residency in the first place? Barak goes on to say that he no longer has anywhere for me to stay in Tel Aviv. I'd been welcome at his flat, but since he and his girlfriend are in a bit of a "situation," he can't take in any guests. I hear his words, but I'm not listening. I ask the waitress for some water. She looks at me, says I'm already holding a glass. I drink. Better? No.

"Barak, I'm not qualified to write this. I'm an idiot. Just like everyone tells me."

He looks at me. Does he see how scared I am of life and art? I'm terrified to walk on the street, get on a bus, eat falafel, let alone write this play. I think about Shimon and how reluctant I was to even knock on his door. I lamely tapped my hand on the cold wood. Didn't want him to answer. Didn't want to hear his story that would only confuse things even more.

Barak changes his tone. He's reassuring for the first time. "Maybe you are trying to understand peace. After all, peace requires a kind of innocence."

"I'm an outsider. How can I understand anything?"

"It might take someone from outside to make sense of this mess."

A loud bang suddenly echoes from outside the café. We drop spoons and cigarettes, stand up and look. A taxi is wrapped around a metal post, and the driver screams at his smashed-in bumper. We sit down and breathe again. Barak takes out his last two cigarettes and hands one to me. For some reason, I'm no longer nervous.

"An accident can be a blessing," says Barak, "only in a country like this."

CHAPTER 22

The beach is empty. The heat of Tel Aviv gets to me. Shirtless, I lie back in the sand and close my eyes. I've been in Israel for two weeks now. For the first time I feel alone, unbearably so.

When I fall asleep I dream of the book *Madrigals*. I hear Judith's voice reading to me, and my body rises off the sand, feet first into the air. I look toward the west. The sun is mirrored in the rough waters; a graveyard of fire in the swelling sea.

"Easy, easy," says Judith. Her hand rests on my shoulder, but I can't see her. She smells like vanilla.

The fishing boats struggle to return to Jaffa. A sky of angry clouds gallops toward me. One cloud reaches down, yanks me into the air, into darkness.

"I'm losing myself."

The words in my head, like the sound of the sea.

CHAPTER 23

Day five of "Yassin Week" and the streets are still dead. People don't go anywhere unnecessary. Shopping malls are a definite no-no. Restaurants, galleries, nightclubs—forget about it. As falafel stands are favourite places for terrorists to attack, I stand back a good four feet from the woman ahead in line. One has to pick and choose exposure to risk, assess the ratio of benefit and cost. I'm almost willing to lose a limb for my favourite Tel Aviv sandwich, the *sabeech*—grilled eggplant, boiled egg and hummus in a pita.

The main avenue, Shenkin Street, has an abundance of funky cafés and clothing shops. The surrounding streets are lined with white buildings erected in the 1920s and '30s. The downtown core is a renaissance of Bauhaus architecture—the largest concentration anywhere in the world, thanks to Jewish-German architects fleeing Europe. Curved balconies, flat roofs and smooth, Modernist facades without adornment provide evidence of a New Berlin rising from the Mediterranean. Eighty years later these doors and balconies barely hang on. Struggle to persist.

Shenkin is not hopping. This week it's a ghost town. Fear is white. I make my way to Café Habima where two security guards stand outside. I have to confine the terror to a room at the back of my mind with the other unwanteds: frustration, confusion and the sense that whatever I do is fraudulent.

I write, put words on the page.

"What'll it be, Shakespeare?" asks the waitress.

"Beer, please."

I draw an outline of my hand on the page.

Nothing inside the lines.

EVERY DAY for the past five days I've met with Barak. In the morning I come to this café and try to write something in my notebook, then email him whatever notes or sketches of scenes in the afternoon. We meet in the evenings to discuss my ideas. It has not gone well.

Since my plan to stay with Barak fell through, I've been crashing on Rivka's couch. She's a visual artist with a downtown loft, a cousin of a friend of mine from Toronto. Rivka says whatever's on her mind, smells like cream cheese gone bad and wears terrible eighties clothes (shoulder pads, silk smocks, fat Olivia Newton-John sweatbands on wrists and head).

Rivka does a ridiculous form of yoga with ropes attached to the walls. After a fitful night's sleep I wake up on the couch to see her hanging a few feet away from me. Amidst the clutter of palettes, paint stains and stained coffee cups, her arms are hooked through two ropes; she hangs before me like a deranged mermaid on a bowsprit.

"Your girlfriend called when you were out."

"Thanks."

"Sounded annoyed. What you do?"

Outside the apartment window an old man washes windows, standing precariously on a wooden platform. He wears what looks to be a loose harness. Rivka dips her head down, yanks herself up. Her mouth hangs open, and drool froths from behind her crooked teeth. I don't answer the question.

"My last boyfriend was a traveller like you. He ended up in Sinai. Ten years later, he's still there wandering. Maybe you aren't meant to be in a relationship. Some people prefer to be unattached; to people, places, things. I have a book about it. It's about people who can't live with nouns. You can read it if you want."

"Thanks."

The window washer steps off the end of the platform into the air. His brush clanks against the window of the apartment. He spins several feet below the window.

"You want to go to an art opening today?"

I consider my options: Call back Judith, to whom I have nothing to say. Try to write another shit-ass scene and endure Barak's "What are you getting at?" questions. Or go back to Jerusalem and interview Shimon, the man otherwise known as "Hitler."

The window washer is incredibly relaxed. Twisting in his harness seventeen storeys above the city, he lights a friggin' cigarette. He doesn't seem to be in any rush to get back to work.

I sit up from the couch and scratch my head. "Sure, an art opening sounds great."

WE'RE SPUTTERING ALONG in Rivka's clunky brown Volvo on our way to the art opening at Ein Harod Kibbutz in the Galilee. I will call Judith back, but it's difficult. The one conversation we had last week felt very not right. I imagine talking to her now:

> JUDITH: How is it there?
>   ME: I don't know.
> JUDITH: What do you mean you don't know?
>   ME: It's not anything like I imagined.
> JUDITH: Is it beautiful?
> *A cabbie cuts us off.*
>   RIVKA: Go fuck your whore of a mother!
> TAXI DRIVER: I'd rather fuck you, ugly!
>   RIVKA: May your firstborn get a vasectomy instead of a bris!
> *A beat.*
>   ME: Yes Judith. It's beautiful.

Rivka and I drive north out of Tel Aviv and into the Galilee. The quick metronome of sprinklers punctuates the lush green fields. A flock of whatever glides above the arc of highway. At a turnoff we pass signs for Jenin, take a right, then head north. Enter the kibbutz marked "Ein Harod."

CHAPTER 24

Mrs. Blintzkrieg: "Is anyone perfect? Please raise your hand if you are."

Blintzkrieg is baiting us, fishing for something. Fingerbaum and Engelblott whisper to one another.

"Yes, Motti Engelblott, you are close. But perfect in physics and geometry is not everything. It does not mean you know how to live. The calculus of morals is an inexact science, and believe you me, I will cherish the day when we can all raise our hands and say, 'We are perfectly good people. We have banished evil from our lives.'"

What the hell is she on about? We're silent, waiting for the hook. Blintzkrieg marches back and forth in front of the blackboard. Our gazes fixed on her every move.

"On the kibbutz where I grew up, we were fine-tuning our souls. We were raised to be better people. It was not us versus them; it was us and us. There was no them."

Ah, the kibbutz again. I breathe a sigh of relief. Blintzkrieg loves, more than anything, to talk about her ideal childhood. I like it too. For one thing, it keeps her nice. For another, it's the dream. I don't want my stupid thirteen-year-old concerns. (Why do I have so many zits? How am I gonna write all those bar mitzvah thank-you cards?) I want the kibbutznik's strength, the physical and moral muscle that says you can help build a better world.

"When we picked oranges in the groves, we felt the sun in our hands. When we planted wheat in the fields, we communed with

the earth. When we argued at all hours of the night about a decision
that needed to be made, we were arguing from our souls. My children. Look at the eighteen of you. You're the only ones in Grade
Eight. No fewer than 125 of your peers dropped out along the way.
They couldn't do it. But your bodies and minds were strong enough.
Smart enough. You're the brave *halutzim* who drained the swamps
of malaria." I can't help but feel a rush of pride. It's like I'm being
knighted for surviving the rigours of Bialik.

Blintzkrieg stops pacing and clasps her hands. "In two months, you
will graduate from Bialik. For your graduation, you will put on a play
about life on the kibbutz."

A play?

"You will be actors and singers. Great and brave performers! But it
will not be enough to simply learn your lines. You must *be* the
kibbutz. Community. Cooperation. Coexistence."

I look around at my fellow classmates. What do we know about life
on a kibbutz? Okay, we've read some books. Written a paper or two.
But to act as though we live on one?

Mrs. Blintzkrieg pulls out a large garbage bag from underneath her
desk. She removes nineteen white Zionist *Gilligan's Island* hats and
passes out eighteen of them. The nineteenth she holds over her head
like a crown, as though anointing herself. When she finally lets the
hat fall onto her head, she nods at us, and we know we must do the
same. She passes them around. I put it on. The hat feels ridiculous.

"Now clear your desks and push them to the side of the room. We
need a field! A community hall! A cafeteria! Who wants to play the
tractor driver?"

Sheepishly, Fingerbaum raises his hand.

"Wonderful. Now let's begin."

On the grey tile floor, I bend down and start to dig. I'm planting
the seeds. I'm singing sorrowful songs, longing for a land I do not
know. But I do know it. I do.

RIVKA AND I drive up a long dirt road. Pass an old barn with tall black Hebrew writing emblazoned on the side—letters several feet high. Mount Gilboa is visible to our right. Little wooden complexes dot the fields. I'm reminded of Camp Shalom, the wooden cabins sprinkled in the Muskoka forest. Three kids emerge from the bushes, their faces scratched.

"Socialism. It's just another way to glorify incest," Rivka announces. She rolls down her window. "You're too young to fuck!" She turns to me, shrugs her shoulders and says, "Well, don't you think there's something weird about it?"

Rivka parks the car.

"Do people still not own anything?" I ask.

"Lunacy," she says.

"What is?"

"That such a place exists."

THE GALLERY Mishkan le-Omanut (Abode for Art) in Ein Harod is impressive. At first glance it seems garishly large, foreboding in the way it dominates the view of the valley of Jezreel. It sits on a large series of boulders and announces its presence loudly. Light enters the gallery laterally through small windows in the upper sections of the walls. The effect is sublime: natural light that does not damage the work, but softly illuminates it. Today they are showing an exhibit of a young Israeli artist who died in her early thirties. Her work is colourful and vibrant. The gallery is crammed with artists from Tel Aviv.

The year this building was constructed amazes me. 1948. It was the first art museum built in Israel and was erected at a time when the country was struggling to be a nation. It also goes against what I had imagined a kibbutz to be—a kind of collective farm modelled on the Soviet kolkhoz. Housed far from an urban centre, the kibbutz leaders of the time were proposing they grow art, cultivate culture. For the founders of the museum, art was as important as having enough food to eat, or sufficient housing for the hordes of Jewish immigrants coming from North Africa, Eastern Europe and the Arab nations. Like Tel Aviv and its Bauhaus architects, the founders of Ein Harod wanted to create a European aesthetic in the Palestine wilderness.

Rivka introduces me to the gallery curator, Helene, a petite redhead in her late fifties. She wears an emerald-green suit. She speaks French and English with an elegant German accent that coats her words in the proper and precise.

"What do you think of the paintings?" she asks.

"I like them," I say. "I'm also curious about the photographs." There's a series of desert shots. The stone is desolate and the sun a blur of grey.

"You must meet the photographer. She's from Paris." Helene escorts me to a woman leaning against a post in the centre of the courtyard. "Aimee, meet Jonathan. He adores your work."

I shake Aimee's cold and limp hand. She does not look at me and I can barely make out what she says.

"I hate this shit," she mutters, ashing her cigarette in a eucalyptus plant.

Helene interrupts our riveting conversation. "Jonathan, you must join us for lunch. We're going to an Arab village and you have to try their hummus. It's the best in all of Israel."

An Arab village? For lunch? Helene turns her attention to the other guests.

"I didn't know Israelis were friends with Palestinians," I say to Aimee.

She watches a crow land on the roof of the gallery. Doesn't say a thing.

MARC, THE FRENCH CULTURAL ATTACHÉ in Israel, drives Aimee and me through the farmland of Galilee. Jews hanging out with Arabs? What kind of people live on this kibbutz? We pull into a gas station on the side of the highway. Marc parks the car and gets out. I stay seated until he knocks on my window.

"We're here," he says.

"This is a gas station," I say.

He drums on the car roof. "Le restaurant, Monsieur."

I get out of the car. Behind the gas pumps is a diner.

"I thought we were going to an Arab village," I quietly say to Aimee as we walk toward the restaurant door.

She says, "If you want to see the actual village, you have to go five hundred metres the other way."

"Will we go there?"

She stops and glares at me. "They will not set foot in an Arab village. But they will say we are in one now."

IT'S A FAMILY-RUN RESTAURANT—nothing fancy. Truckers gorge on fava beans and slurp strong Arabic coffee. Families on their way to Mount Gilboa or the Sea of Galilee stop for a quick bite. Ten of us are gathered around a large table. The topic is art, and the voices are loud.

"She wouldn't be as highly regarded if she hadn't died so young." Rivka spits flecks of feta and yogourt across the table.

Leah, a potter, responds: "That's mean."

"If honest is mean, then I'm mean," says Rivka. "Just look at her composition. It's simplistic." She spoons a lump of tabbouleh onto her plate.

"The composition is brilliant," interrupts Helene. "You're just jealous of the fact she has an entire exhibit to herself."

"Of course I'm jealous," says Rivka. "It's been ten years since you've shown my work, Helene. Ten years. Instead you show this sentimental crap. It makes me furious."

Nobody knows what to say, so we eat really loud.

Helene turns to me and asks the inevitable question, "What are you doing here in Israel?"

Everybody turns to listen. I tell them a bit about my upbringing, and I tell them the story of the house—that I've come to find it. Many of them nod their heads. Rivka, who has already heard it, stays focused on her food.

"That's an unusual story," Leah says.

A man named Nachman adds, "I've never heard of such a thing. An Arab in West Jerusalem?"

"His name is Abu Dalo."

"He talked to you?"

"Yes, he invited me into his house for coffee."

"And he knew you were Jewish?"

"I didn't advertise."

This seems to bring relief to the table.

"If it was an Israeli going to visit, it's another story altogether," says Leah.

"Still, he met with him," Nachman says to her.

"Is that unusual? Do none of you interact with Palestinians?" I ask.

"Of course we do," says Leah.

"We're eating in an Arab restaurant, aren't we?" says Nachman. I look around the room. Seems like it's mostly Palestinians serving Jewish patrons.

"I was in Ramallah," says a woman at the far end of the table. "In the 1990s."

"Things were very different then," says Leah.

"But what about here in Israel? Do you know Palestinians?" I ask.

"Sure, we talk to them. If there's an occasion for talking."

"Do you put their art up in the gallery, Helene?"

"We tried to do an exhibition with Palestinians from Nablus. But it fell through. My worry was we would be perceived as too patriarchal, too controlling of the work. It needs to be an equal affair."

The artists at the table nod their heads in agreement. "It's not right if it's only on our terms," Leah says.

"They have already suffered so much," adds Nachman.

The restaurant owner massages his right elbow with his left hand. He doesn't seem to be listening.

Rivka says, "It's not so unusual, this house." She's rolling a falafel ball on her plate with her hand. "We took their land and their houses. So what if one Arab stays a bit longer? Eventually we'll take that too."

"And that's okay?" asks Leah.

"Not at all. It's a real problem we have here. For real."

Nachman asks, "So what's to be done?"

"What's to be done?" asks Rivka. She shrugs her shoulders. "Who am I? Gandhi?" She rests her forehead on her palm. "I do little things. I refuse to go to the occupied territories."

"None of us support the occupation," adds Leah.

"We can agree on that," Helene says.

"But within Israel," I say. "Do you spend time with Palestinians? Do you have Palestinian friends?"

Nobody answers. Nachman and Leah seem to flinch when I use the word Palestinian instead of Arab. This is starting to irritate me. I remember when Rana complained about the government branding her as Israeli-Arab. It Israelified her, made her what she isn't. It occurs to me that the term also serves to ease our conscience; it erases an entire history. When Israel was created in 1948, so was the identity of the Israeli-Arab. The Palestinians are the ones in the territories, the ones-not-here—a moral and social problem that began four decades ago on account of some overzealous military decisions. It's easier to protest the West Bank and Gaza, and the implications are simpler too: Withdraw now. Give them a state. But what does one do about the inequalities here in Israel? When the Palestinians here have full citizenship and supposedly equal rights?

Eventually Rivka says, "It's a difficult situation. We're their neighbours, but they think we're their enemies. Really, we like them. We wish them no harm."

"Can they live on the kibbutz if they wanted to?" I ask.

"Arabs? Living on a kibbutz? Are you joking?"

I realize the question is somewhat ridiculous. After all, kibbutzim were essential Jewish outposts for the original settlement of Palestine. They helped defend against Arab attacks from the early twentieth century up until the Six Day War. And while only a small percentage of the country lived on them, the kibbutzim constituted a moral and spiritual backbone for the secular Zionist movement: They housed (and raised) the strong and brave Israelis working the land. They also produced the best soldiers. But looked at from another perspective, from the idea of what a kibbutz is (what Blintzkrieg taught me), maybe my question is not so crazy. Blintzkrieg would say during rehearsals, "There isn't a single decision made at a kibbutz that wasn't discussed for hours in the mess hall by the entire community. It is the ultimate social democracy." She'd fire us up, make us swell with moral pride: "The kibbutz is a living example of equality, not only in terms of distribution of wealth, but human rights. Everyone is to be treated equally." What if a Palestinian, who feels a similar tie to the land and yearns for this kind of socialist and artistic community, wants to live at Ein Harod? Would the kibbutz members deny a Palestinian's application to live among them as equals because of his or her background? If the answer is yes, then what is this kibbutz democracy? What is this democracy of the chosen?

"We have good relations with Palestinians," Helene says quietly. "Some of them work for us in the dairy."

Then it occurs to me to ask a question I hadn't considered: "What used to be on the land before the kibbutz?"

"An Arab village, of course."

"So is that why you don't let them live with you?"

"We let them visit whenever they want," Helene says.

Nachman says, "Look, they live in their community, we live in ours. That's the way things are here. It's better that way. For everyone."

The owner's son, a boy of ten, comes to the table. He asks us if we want anything more. For a moment, we're silent.

"Coffee," says Aimee. "I'd love an Arabic coffee."

I'm not sure why, but I'm relieved that she's talked.

"Now that's a nice idea," says Leah. "I'll have one too."

"Arabic coffee for everybody," says Helene, indicating with a measured wave of her hand. "Who doesn't like sugar?"

The owner does not need to be told our order. Unprompted, he moves slowly to the scum-lined sink and turns on the cold water. He lets it dribble into the brass pot and places it on a rusted plate on the old stove. A blue flame sears the damp metal base.

I'M THINKING ABOUT RANA. It is only now, looking into the grinds of coffee at the bottom of my cup, that her story shifts into focus. And I'm seeing that there are layers to listening, an archaeology to understanding. Rana told me the facts, her facts, but I did not fully comprehend them. Did not want to. It's only now I remember her telling me she was not allowed to study contemporary Palestinian poets like Mahmoud Darwish at school. She wasn't taught the history of her people and culture. These subjects are banned for Palestinians living in Israel, Rana explained to me in Toronto. Teaching the Nakba can lose a teacher his or her job. So what did Rana learn? The War of Independence. Hebrew literature and grammar. Tanakh. Hatikva. What my parents paid for me to study at Bialik.

I didn't fully believe her at the time. As with the JNF, I told myself, I'll check on that later, there's always another side to the story, and I need to find it. But I haven't searched for those stories. Perhaps I'm afraid if I do I'll find out uncomfortable, unwanted truths. The stuff that would make my Baba roll in her grave. I'm looking at you, Rivka, Helene, Nachman. You're the artists, the left-wingers from the kibbutz and sane Tel Aviv. Are you aware of what goes on beside us? Or are you like me, would you prefer not to hear this story?

I'm shaking here, do you see my hands, and it's not just the caffeine from this kick-in-the-ass coffee. My mind is unravelling, this home on unstable ground. There is so much I would rather not know.

THE NEXT MORNING I'm sitting on the front porch of a kibbutz cabin, drinking coffee trying to wake up. Rivka went back to Tel Aviv yesterday, and I stayed here the night. I'm trying to decide if I should take up Marc's offer to join him and Aimee on a trip to the Golan Heights in the north. I can feel it, I want to get lost. I'm supposed to be in Tel Aviv, working with Barak. He's probably trying to get in touch with me, wondering where the next scenes of the play are. We were supposed to get together this afternoon. I barely slept last night on the couch in the visitor's dorm. I lay awake in a panic: What the hell am I going to write? I should be in Jerusalem. I should be talking to Shimon. I should be doing something.

When I couldn't sleep I sat outside hoping to see the kibbutz workers doing their early morning thing in the fields. Instead there were three children dancing to hip hop on concrete. They weren't bad, especially the little nine year old with Converse high-tops. He seems to be Ein Harod's number one breakdancing prospect. This country confuses the hell out of me. If I didn't have any expectations, if I didn't have years—decades, centuries—of ideas crammed inside my head, what the hell would this country look like? I wish at Ben-Gurion Airport there was a guy with a phaser gun ready to blank out your mind before you set foot into the country. So one could see things, if not as they are, at least a little more clearly.

Then again, Yonni tried his best, didn't he?

While I debate what I should do with myself, an old man walks toward me. He's hauling an old plow and he's dirty from work. I look at him closely.

"Zaida Ben? Is that you?"

He pulls out a handkerchief from his pocket and wipes his brow.

Zaida says, "The thing about work is it keeps you honest and clean. Procrastination is the disease of modern man."

It's true what he says. I happen to be one of the great delayers of my generation. Zaida drops the plow to the ground with a *SHUD* and rubs his hands. A cloud of dust forms.

"You were good when you went to Bialik. You worked hard. Every day you did homework until midnight. Remember when I taught you about the Manitoba Urban Kibbutz?"

"Of course. You showed me the plans."

"The abolition of money. A communal kitchen run by the clinically insane. Solar-panelled recyculing. All to be housed in downtown Winnipeg within eight geodesic domes made of glass. So we could see things. Everything must be transparent." He points to my chest. "There's something wrong with you."

"I have a question I'd like to ask."

"You ask too many questions and don't do enough. I created the Manitoba Kibbutz because I believed in the future. I wanted to build a better world." He firmly plants his hand on my shoulder.

"Would you let a Palestinian into your kibbutz?"

"I don't want to talk about Arabs. I want to talk about your work. What do *you* want to build?"

"I don't know."

"Where's your focus?"

"I've lost it."

He pauses, looks at me. "What happened to you? Why aren't you doing what you came here to do?"

"Zaida, the truth is, I'm afraid of going back to the house. That I'm going to leave the house with nothing. I'm afraid I'm not going to understand, and I'll have nothing to write."

Zaida digs his fingers into my back, roughly rubbing the bones. "You need to give something to the house," he says. "An offering. Then maybe things won't be so confusing."

Zaida picks up his plow. He walks slowly toward the dry stony field behind the cabins. My shoulder aches. It's likely my grandfather's right. I need to reach out farther, dig deeper, before I'm ready to go back to Shimon. If I ask the right questions, learn the right things, do the work, then the house will be something, provide me with some kind of answer.

CHAPTER 25

Tensions are high in East Jerusalem. In three days it'll be Passover. That, combined with the fear of post-Yassin retaliation, means extra, extra-tight security (this fear was absent at Ein Harod; the problems of Jerusalem an idea, illusion). On every corner a soldier asks me for ID or an undercover officer approaches asking questions. The stress makes me dizzy. I wait at the local Palestinian bus stop. The graffiti is in Arabic, the smell is sour and the lives are grim. When I called Samer to meet me I told him I didn't want a fancy ride this time around. I want something closer to the earth. The people waiting at the bus stop look at me. Their faces a warning: *Poverty is contagious. Come too close and you'll get hit with it, die from shame slowly.*

The bus has no shocks and nobody speaks. A superhuman effort is required to shift from first to second. Beneath her black shawl, a Palestinian woman breastfeeds her child. I get off the bus with the others. People carry huge canvas bags holding blankets, pots and bulbs of garlic. I help an old woman walk her belongings to the checkpoint. Samer's waiting for me in his TV-tank Land Rover. He opens the door and we take off for the hills.

The first time we met, Samer told me about his 105-year-old grandfather, Zuhdi. Yesterday morning at the kibbutz I opted out of the Golan trip. Instead I called up Samer and said, "I need to talk to your grandfather." My hope was he'd have some perspective on things. He's lived through the entire twentieth century and is probably one of the oldest people living in the West Bank. As long as the guy's not completely demented, he has to know *something*.

We drive on a different road from last time, end up at another checkpoint few people use. After some negotiation the soldiers let us through. A few kilometres later we pull over and Samer points out a few settlements, as well as the forbidding military base on the hill. It looks like a giant white helmet. As he steps out of the car, his mobile rings. He talks to the other person in Hebrew. "Of course, everything's fine," he says, and hangs up. "A lieutenant from the army," he says to me. "He wanted to know what we were doing. I told him I was taking a Canadian on a tour."

"Are they following us?"

"No, they're watching." He points to the military base and smiles as though posing for a photograph. He waves nonchalantly. "Don't worry, we have a good relationship."

We continue our drive, following the contours of the narrow highway.

MAZRA 'AL SHRQYA, West Bank. It's the birthplace of Samer and the home of Zuhdi Shalabi. He sits on a boulder in the sun, wears a brown wool toque and a dark grey suit. He leans on a black cane and does not seem to notice Samer and me when we slam the metal doors of the armoured TV tank. We walk halfway up the path toward the house.

"Parking brake," Zuhdi suddenly says.

Samer looks at me then runs back to the truck. Sure enough, the brake isn't in place.

"Idiot," Zuhdi mutters under his breath.

He rises slowly and walks toward his house.

WE'RE TRAVELLING at grandparent speed. Each step demands a pause to inhale the fresh spring air. Zuhdi leans on his cane to ponder a shrub, comprehend stone. On the rocky hillsides the roots of olive trees cling to the earth. Their gnarled and tough branches look like hands trying to hold up the sky. Zuhdi's face is worn leather, cracked stone. Behind us is the Israeli military base perched on the hilltop. There is something arrogant about it; it sees, means to be seen.

Samer's sister brings out a tray of *manakiesh*—what Samer calls "Arabic pizza"—a thin oven-baked crust spiced with *zaatar*. We dip the pizza in homemade olive oil. Samer and I devour it. Zuhdi does not eat—he eats once at sunrise, and once at dusk. This is the secret to his health, he says. Like my grandfather.

Right away, Samer tells Zuhdi I'm a Jew. He nods. "I owned a bakery with a Jew once," he says. "Jerusalem in the 1920s. Man's name was Joseph." He sits forward on the couch. Samer translates: "You have to understand, Jews and Arabs, we got along then. There were problems, but they were nothing compared to now. We found ways to live together. Everything changed and I blame that on the British. They played us like a poker game."

"What do you mean by that?"

"They bluffed both sides, promised the same land to us both. And in the end, they pulled out when things were too risky. They pushed us into civil war."

Samer's sister brings out the requisite coffee. Zuhdi drinks a tall glass of water. I look at him, try to figure out where he's coming from. Okay, so the British have a role in this mess. But they're not coming back to fix things. And why did Zuhdi immediately tell me he used to work with a Jew? Does he really not put any blame on us for this situation? After all, Israel is occupying his land. This should bug the shit out of him. Is he just telling me what I want to hear?

The problem is, the story of Zuhdi and Joseph *is* what I want to hear. It's the narrative I'm looking for, the possibility for coexistence. When I was a philosophy student I was a fan of the Hasidic philosopher Martin Buber. He used to argue that the success of a Jewish state depended on the quality of its relations with its Arab neighbours, and the future of the region depended on neither nation's exerting its will over the other. Zuhdi's story makes me wonder how many other Bubers there were back then. Or more practically speaking, how many Zuhdis and Josephs existed.

But Zuhdi doesn't want to talk this angle of history. "The twentieth century," he says, clearing his throat. "I suppose I don't know any other time. Things changed too much." He strikes lint off his suit jacket. "I was the first man in the West Bank to own a truck. I bought it in 1936. It was beige and it made a loud THWANK when I tried to take it up a hill. People would jump onto the side and hold on for dear life. I was a good driver, known for it. The British employed me for some time. When they left, we were conquered by the Jordanians."

"What was life under Jordan like?"

"We were still occupied, but they let us be for the most part. Now the Israelis not only occupy the land, they want to occupy your head. They humiliate you. Then they want you to say, 'Thank you for making my life better than it was under the Arabs.'" Zuhdi gazes out the window at a bird perched on the hood of Samer's truck. "Sometimes I think that beneath all that, they're just as afraid as we are. Maybe even more." He turns to look at me. "In the end, any occupation is bad. A man needs his freedom. It's like driving."

"Like what?" I say.

"He's talking cars," says Samer.

"Oh."

"I used to drive a bus from Amman to Ramallah to Damascus. After '67, the bus went to Jerusalem and Tel Aviv. I love to drive. It lets me think about the world at the right speed." Zuhdi stares at his field of olive trees. "Staying still keeps the thoughts still. Dead, really."

Samer takes a sip of coffee. "He's bitter. We took his driver's licence away ten years ago."

Zuhdi turns and points at Samer: "The thing I loved the most. And you took it away."

"He was ninety-five," Samer explains.

I say to Zuhdi, "I totally understand. My grandfather had the same thing happen to him. His daughters took away his licence and it made him really mad."

This intrigues Zuhdi. "What is there for a man, other than to drive?" He points to Samer's Land Rover as though to say, what would you do if I took that away from you? Samer shrugs in response.

Imagine my grandfather sitting with us on this veranda in Palestine. I'd like him to hear Zuhdi's story about the driver's licence. I'm hoping it would surprise Zaida. Taken aback by the similiarities between them, he might feel compelled to take Zuhdi through the ins and outs of Churchill and the Manitoba Kibbutz. Zuhdi would listen, curious about this strange man from Canada. Then Zuhdi would tell Zaida Ben about the trucks he drove, and the buses too. And things wouldn't be bad. They wouldn't be so different.

Zuhdi continues to reminisce. "I know driving, and I know my neighbours. 1982. It was five in the morning, still dark out, and I was driving an empty bus. All of a sudden I heard a loud bang on the road. I'd blown a tire; I must've run over something sharp, I thought. I got out of the bus, crouched down to look and noticed there were little holes in the side of the vehicle. I was confused. Who put those there? I felt something skim my back. That's when I realized the flat wasn't from running over something. I was being shot at. By settlers." Zuhdi taps his fingers on the table and waits for Samer to finish translating. "I pretended to be dead. And when the bullets stopped, I got up and walked back to town."

"Did you ever try and get back at them? Retaliate?"

"No, though later on, some of their homes were burned down. I didn't do that. I don't know who did."

I pull my chair in closer toward Zuhdi. "Do you have resentment or anger toward Jews for doing things like this?"

"Of course not. I can hate one person, or two. But not an entire people."

"How did you feel when the Jews started coming to Palestine?" I ask.

Zuhdi leans toward me. "When they arrived in the twenties and thirties on all those boats, it was frightening. Where were they going to live? What did these strangers want? None of them knew anything about living here. Of course we were afraid. Then they said the country belonged to them. Well, the country belongs to no one, if you really get down to it. Land is land, and people live on it. It's what we all need. Water. Good earth. A home. It's not so complicated. It's just that nobody wants to have to share. Who doesn't want to be the master of their own house?"

"Do you wish the Jews had never come here at all?"

Zuhdi raises his right eyebrow, strokes his chin.

"I can't answer that question."

"Why not?"

"Because you came, didn't you?"

AT THE END of the day, Samer and I pull in to a line of traffic at the Qalandia checkpoint. "Thank you for listening. Really, we need people to hear our stories. Understand it is not only for your sake I bring you to my village." The windows are down and we can hear the mess of traffic waiting to get into Israel. "I have another friend from Canada, she's from Vancouver. She married a man from Tel Aviv. I said to her, you must bring your husband to visit me. He wouldn't come. She insisted and said to him, 'I'm your wife, aren't you interested in my friends?'"

Not far from us is the wall; a group of Palestinian construction workers are starting to build it. One man works to uncoil dozens of metres of barbed wire. "I met them at the checkpoint," Samer says.

"He was pale, wouldn't speak, couldn't look me in the eyes. I drove and gave him my West Bank tour. When we went for lunch, I was sure he didn't go to the bathroom because he was afraid there'd only be a hole in the ground. Later we walked the streets of Ramallah and passed a CD store. Finally he spoke. 'Can we go in?' Why not, I said. He asked me what CD he should buy. I thought, I have no fucking idea what you should buy. But I didn't say this. I recommended, I don't know what, Fayruz, probably. Then he said, 'I had no idea that you people live like this.' 'Like what?' I said. 'Like normal.' I didn't say anything. It's ridiculous to have to convince people we are human beings. But such is the situation."

"Samer." I want to say something profound without sounding idiotic or sentimental. Instead, all I say is, "Thanks."

He slaps my left thigh and says, "Thank God for meeting you. God has brought us together."

I'M BACK in East Jerusalem when I stop to watch four soldiers. It's early evening and they're leaning against a wall in the old city chatting among themselves. A teenager walks by and they ask him for his ID. They shine their flashlights on the card, then his face. Now two of the soldiers hold the kid against the wall. He's frisked by a third. Quickly this turns into punching. The chest and stomach, but not the face. The fourth soldier, who's keeping an eye on things from the corner, catches me watching. He approaches me, points his Uzi and asks to see my ID. I comply.

The boy is eighteen or nineteen years old. "What the hell do you want?" the soldier asks.

"Nothing."

"Then go. NOW."

The soldier's yelling, but he's trembling too. The funny thing is, I'm also shaking. The other three continue to punch the Palestinian. Again the young soldier tells me to leave, but he won't return my passport. Won't take his eyes off me. He stands frozen, blue-eyed, helmet too big. What's he thinking?

ME: You know, you don't need to go back there.
SOLDIER: I have a job to do.
ME: Job or no job, ask yourself the question: Do you really need to beat the shit out of that kid?

But I do not speak these words. Finally the soldier says, "This is a dangerous area. Leave. Please." He returns my passport and joins the others. They've stopped pummelling the young man. He leans on his legs, tries to catch his breath.

I'M LOST AGAIN. Damn this city.

Searching for the road back to Nachlaot where Max lives, I see an old man with a *kippah* turn the corner of an old cobblestone road. I look at the street sign. This is near to where Zuhdi and Joseph ran their bakery. I follow the old man. He disappears into an alley. "Joseph," I yell out. I turn down the alley, but he's disappeared. Where am I? In front of me there's an old stone building with a light inside. The storefront windows are filled with postcards. In the window a lamp illuminates a framed poster, the stone painted gold and orange. The Dome of the Rock is cast in shadow. And at the bottom, in bold print: VISIT PALESTINE. Zaida Ben's poster.

As a child I believed in this poster: city of gardens, cool stone houses, lush trees under a blazing sun. It is simple and beautiful. The world the Zionist artist presents is a Jerusalem devoid of people slaughtering each other in the name of an idea, God or greed. I still cling to this beauty. Want to believe that the building I stand before is the bakery where Zuhdi and Joseph baked their bread, 4 A.M. hands pounding dough in rhythm with each other. I know this story is made up, or at least long past. This city is not orange with heat. This holy stone is smeared with bird shit and human blood, and the alleys are filled with soldiers pummelling the guts of men.

The door is locked. I can see someone behind the desk. It's eight in the evening and dark out. I need to get in there. I knock on the door, the man opens it and I ask him, "Can I buy the poster?" He complies, rolls the print carefully so he can fit it in a cardboard tube. There's something satisfying in the way the man scrolls the poster, as though it were an ancient, holy text. As though this tourist souvenir could save me.

I think about Judith. What she said before I left: "You're always leaving. Why don't you stay and try to work things out? Things never fix themselves." She's right. I would rather dive into the problems of another place. Like my grandfather, I'd rather try to solve something else before I figure out my relations, myself. But I'm not completely deluded. Perhaps there is an end to the search. Somewhere, at the centre of the Israel-Palestine labyrinth, lies some sort of answer, an insight into how the myths of my past and the realities of the present can live together. Peace. Not only between nations, but with myself.

CHAPTER 26

Last night I passed out on Max's couch, drunk on raki. Before I fell asleep, I imagined Shimon in the room with me.

He sat down next to me and said, "You really are an idiot."

"Thanks."

"Meeting a couple of Palestinians means nothing. They'll tell you what you want to hear. They're Arabs, remember? It's just like your grandfather said: They smile when they kill you."

I wake up with a bad taste in my mouth and a strong urge to call Judith. I feel a need to connect to her, to talk to someone not part of the world here.

Judith sent me an email asking if everything was okay. She has that sixth sense lovers develop: the where-the-hell-have-you-been sense. It's been four weeks since I've been away and we've only talked once. I feel stupid for being so absent. It's the Passover Seder tomorrow and I want to wish her well. Outside the Damascus Gate I'm buying a phone card when an old man hobbles toward me.

"Holy Day? Did I hear someone say Holy Day?" He speaks in a Jersey accent. I look around to see who he's talking to. It's me, I think. "Every day is holy in Jerusalem, didn't you know?" He fishes around in his worn green suit-jacket, pulls out a crumpled cigarette, lights it up and inhales half the thing in four or five breaths. "Don't tell me you're here on vacation." He has nine fingers. The whites of his eyes are yellow. "You're better off in California or New Mexico. Hell, try

Milwaukee. Even Winnipeg isn't so bad." He guffaws, coughs tobacco and phlegm. "Name's Charlie."

He holds out his hand. The skin looks like it's barely hanging on. He tells me he has cancer of the foot, the leg, the mouth. His right leg is a prosthetic he bought second-hand. He says, "I'm a friggin' puzzle. Every morning I have to put myself together and hope the pieces fit. What's your story?"

"I need to call my girlfriend in Canada."

"O Palestine, our home and native land," he croaks. He sounds like he's going to keel over. "Come with me and I'll give you a hand."

CHARLIE SMOKES one cigarette after another. We're onto number three since we've met. "Cancer is a pain in the ass. And the foot. All over, really. But what's pain, other than a little jolt to remind you of prison?" I'm not sure what he's talking about. We find a rusted old phone in East Jerusalem. I call Judith, but she isn't home. I leave a short message wishing her Happy Pesach, don't worry, I'm fine, I'll call again soon. Her message on the machine reminds me of her, all of her: the serious-ness at the beginning, the slight, playful rise toward the middle of the phrase, and the way she says "goodbye," with a slight curl of the "good." But her voice also cracks when she says "bye." As though she cannot quite hold it together. Cannot endure these terms of departure.

"Don't be blue, kid," Charlie says. "Sadness doesn't suit you. Say. I have just the thing that'll cheer you up." Charlie's bottom teeth show a neat row of silver caps. "Qalandia."

"What?"

"The refugee camp."

I hesitate. "How's a refugee camp supposed to cheer me up?"

"When you see it, you'll thank fucking God you don't live there."

WE WALK TOWARD the decrepit Palestinian bus station in East Jerusalem. I help Charlie onto the bus. Think, I have nothing to lose.

And Shimon can wait, right? It's not like he's going anywhere. If anything, maybe I'll find an interesting character or two, finally write an interesting scene for the play. I'd like to impress Barak. Transcend the stupid tourist in me.

Behind the bus station the daily lineup for Palestinian work permits in Jerusalem snakes around the block. Charlie shows off pictures of his grandkids—three in Minnesota, two in Milwaukee.

"I lived there for twenty years. Then they kicked me out."

He had a job doing cruises to the Caymans playing piano. She was a bartender, ten years his junior. They met on the boat and got married in a drive-thru in Vegas, moved to Milwaukee.

"I can't say I miss playing the fucking 'Entertainer' five hundred times a day. But the pay was good. And a river of whisky, to keep the fingers moving."

"What'd you do in America?"

"Got into trouble," says Charlie, looking wistfully out the window. Piles of people are getting onto the bus. "She divorced me. It was after September 11, everyone was paranoid. Government, neighbours, my wife. It was quite the scene, pipsqueak. I come home one day, and all of my stuff is out on the front lawn. Fortunately I didn't have much." In the station outside a bunch of kids are hacking apart a rocking chair with a sledgehammer.

"Now?"

"I live in Beit Hanina with my wife."

"You remarried?"

"Between you and me kid, I was married to them both at the same time." He slaps my back forcefully. It surprises me. "Survival, my friend. That's what love is."

He does one of his cough-guffaw numbers, and I'm not sure if he's going to last this round or not. "It's the only thing I have left, pipsqueak: my will to love."

Now I laugh. But Charlie's serious.

"The key to peace isn't negotiations. It's sex. If Israeli men learned to go down on Palestinian women, and Palestinian men went down on Israeli women, don't you think peace would be possible? The Cunnilingus Revolution, kid. Orgasms. Not walls."

This time Charlie laughs so hard I think this is it, he's gone for sure. But instead of him dying I hear the bus door close and the engine starting. We're moving.

"So you are coming with," he says. "I thought you might back out. Really. You'll love Qalandia."

WE FOLLOW the now-familiar route to the checkpoint. The bus stops and the passengers pile out. He points ahead. "Just walk through there and head straight up the road. The refugee camp's on the right."

"Where are you going?"

"I live back there." That is, not the West Bank. He can see the look of apprehension on my face. This time, there's no Samer waiting for me.

"Don't worry kid. What do you think? They're gonna eat you?" The thought crosses my mind. What if I was just lucky those other times? "If there's a problem, give me a call." He writes his number on the back of a pack of matches. "Why don't you come by for some lunch later?"

Charlie and I shake hands. He limps west toward his apartment complex. I adjust the cap on my head. Look into the bus window at my reflection. I look like Tevye the Milkman. Slowly, I walk toward the West Bank.

"EXCUSE ME, where's Qalandia refugee camp?" I ask a cab driver stuck in traffic. He points at a collection of dilapidated buildings sloped on a hill some one hundred metres away. It's to the right of the road leading to Ramallah. "Over there," the cabbie's finger says. He does not look at me. As though looking will take him there, make him one of the permanently displaced.

The traffic waiting to get into Israel winds several kilometres up the road. At a bend I turn right, away from the blaring horns, the faces red with sweat and agitation. I head up a concrete street. The hill is incredibly steep and I have to pause halfway to catch my breath. At the end of the street stands the minaret of a mosque. The refugee camp is not a bunch of tents as I'd imagined. Charlie corrected that notion on the bus. "Sure, when it was first set up there were tents. Plenty of 'em. It was 1949 and we all thought this was gonna blow over quick, soon we'd go home. But more and more people came. And time made things solid: The camp is not temporary. Qalandia," he said, and paused on that word. But the pause was not a resting place, nor was it quiet. It was acrid, the smell of burnt bread. "It's one of the oldest camps in the West Bank."

I HAVE NO BEARINGS here. I'd assumed Charlie was going to take me on a tour, not abandon me at the checkpoint. Next to the prefab grey houses, the mosque is bright white. Like it's been recently polished, obsessive hand, neat-freak God.

I turn left at the top of the hill. Three bearded men stand at the doorway to the mosque. They eye me suspiciously and I quickly walk past. I'm looking for something to take me in. Up a ways is a site of unfinished buildings. Long fingers of rebar poke out through blocks of concrete, pointing toward the sky. A set of stairs leads nowhere. A skeleton without flesh, a house without walls.

The folly of my journey: I have to decode the objects before me, create meaning out of what I do not know. But the decoding is of a world still unfolding in the present tense. In the fields of bent rebar, children play with empty shells and shrapnel. A boy no more than eight stands on a balcony and screams at a rooster. A foundation has been dug, but nothing fills the gaping hole.

When the children see me they scurry, lead me farther up a road. I'm off the concrete street onto a dirt path. Mothers and grandmothers hang their laundry, slam shutters as I approach. The boys whip junk at each other, hard as they can, pelting each other with rusted carburetors, a cracked oil cylinder. A hubcap is thrown at me like a Frisbee. I scurry out of its way, then pick it up. One of the kids, toothless, spits in my direction. The hubcab is sharp as a razor. Somebody has taken the time to file the edges.

It's a warm, dry day. I take a sip of water and turn back toward the mosque. The familiar blue and white flag of the United Nations hangs from a short, flat building—a school. Charlie taught me more on the bus: Following the '48 War, the United Nations Relief and Works Agency (UNRWA) was established to carry out relief and aid programs for the seven hundred thousand–plus Palestinian refugees. Today the UNRWA is still here, providing education and health care in nearly sixty camps in Lebanon, Syria, Jordan, the West Bank and Gaza. Over a million refugees and their descendants live in these camps, and there are over four million Palestinians registered as refugees in total.* It's the largest and longest-standing refugee crisis in the world.

I enter the school grounds, hoping I might meet someone who can speak English and show me around. What kind of curriculum do the students have? Do they study what Rana studied (or did not study)? Then again, how many kids are actually in school?

The entranceway is in decent-enough shape. A stone walkway leads to a white room. Inside the ceiling is low. I try to tiptoe down a narrow set of stairs, but it's too steep and my feet clank loudly on the steps. At the bottom stands a man with a black beard. He speaks to me in Arabic, sounds agitated. What do you want?

I pull out my notepad and mime, "I'm a writer."

Without saying a word, he leaves the room and slams the door. I stand in darkness. I try to open the door but the handle is locked.

---

* Source: UNRWA website: http://www.un.org/unrwa/publications/index.html.

I jiggle it back and forth, but nothing happens. Now what? I breathe in the darkness. I should've told the bearded man, "Some crazy near-dead man sent me here. Thought I'd find it educational." I wonder if the children of Qalandia have ever met a Jew who isn't in the army. I decide I'd better not speak Hebrew, just in case. The door opens and the bearded man has returned with three boys twelve years of age. He mutters something to them. One is tall. One shakes two stones like dice in his right hand. The other chews bubble gum, makes pink bubbles the size of his face.

"Come with me," says the tall boy in English. He wears a red sweater with a big X knitted on the front.

"Malcolm X," I say.

The tall boy says nothing, cracks his knuckles. They lead me down a set of stairs. The darkness is stifling. When they open a door onto an alleyway, I've been reborn. Watch a boy hit a cat with a stick. Remember where I am.

THIS IS BECKHAM. He's the joker of the bunch. Calls himself Beckham because of his British hero on the soccer field, even though he's too small to make it beyond the position of water boy. He's got a shadow of a moustache. This is Ibrahim. He's the shortest of the bunch, talks with a snarl, tells dirty jokes in Arabic. X has broad shoulders and speaks a pinch of English. They lead me to a concrete soccer field and Beckham runs in circles, kicking imaginary balls. Ibrahim spits on the field. I wonder if they long for grass the way Jacob and I did, if this concern even makes it into their litany of worries.

The kids are in junior high and they've been ordered by the bearded man, their teacher, to take me on a tour. Qalandia refugee camp: village of cinder block, dry, cracked roads. Men play shesh besh in the cafés. Corner stores sell cigarettes and news. There are frequent power failures and water shortages, say the kids. The roads smell like sewage. At the highest point of the camp, X points across the valley to a settlement on a hill. The houses are fists pounding the air, saying *Get out of here*. But how do you get rid of a city of ten thousand refugees? Beckham climbs into what once was a shed and explains with his hands that the army launched a missile that blew it up. "There were cows," X says. Ibrahim re-enacts the missile with *Star Wars* sound effects, and Beckham improvises modern-dance moves to demonstrate cow brain flooding the valley.

The boys take me down another street. They point out broken windows, gun-splattered from a recent army raid. A kid approaches us. They greet him warmly, call him "Crazy Boy," and he stands sullen before us, rocking back and forth on his feet. I reach into my pocket for a piece of chocolate and he knocks it into the air. They chide him for being so rude to their guest, turn to me: *orphan, no school, no respect.* Ibrahim gestures like he's wobbling on a surfboard. *Crazy Boy, he's unsure in the head,* says his body language. X and Beckham laugh; they're anxious. Crazy Boy stands stone still. I reach into my backpack and hand him an orange pencil. He smells it, trying to decide whether there's poison in it. He looks like he hasn't eaten in days, wears a rusted key around his neck.

"Where's the key from?" I ask.

"Home," he says. And he points past the hills of the settlement, toward Jerusalem. Without warning he throws the pencil back at me, breaks into a sprint, stops, squats at the street corner and collects rocks. An animal gathering scraps of food.

I want to invite Crazy Boy to come with us but the boys say no. They lead me into the graveyard. We're standing by their best friend's grave. Beckham takes off his black and grey toque and holds it by his chest. X weeps softly. Ibrahim looks away, kicking at dust. I think back to what Barak said about his one hope for peace: "We'll grow tired of killing each other, of seeing our children's blood. This is the only way the violence will end." The realist's prayer.

We leave the graveyard and start our descent back toward the school. I ask how their friend died. X says, "He was carrying coffee." Ibrahim mimes a heavy sack. Beckham adds: "To his mother's." They thought he was carting explosives. He was eleven years old.

Back at the school the bearded man is friendly and less abrupt.

"Good tour?" he asks. His English is only slightly better than X's.

"Yes," I say gratefully.

On the bearded man's desk is a box of textbooks. I ask if I can look through them. They're mathematics. I want to ask him about the Palestinian education. What do they read in the West Bank? Amichai or Darwish? In one of our conversations in Toronto, Rana told me about the controversy in the Israeli Knesset surrounding Mahmoud Darwish's poetry. It was 2000, and then–prime minister Ehud Barak's education minister, Yossi Sarid, wanted to have five of Darwish's poems as an optional part of a multicultural school curriculum in Israel. The proposed curriculum change provoked outrage from the political right and a vote of no confidence against Ehud Barak. He survived the no-confidence vote but closed the issue when he announced that Israel is "not ready for Darwish." "Nearly twenty percent of the people in Israel are Palestinians," said Rana. "What is Israel not ready for? Reality?"

"Darwish?" I ask the teacher, pointing at the books.

The bearded man says, "Of course." He shows me the school texts written in Arabic; they're still on a Jordan curriculum. He opens the lowest desk drawer and pulls out a tattered book. He mouths the word, "Darwish." A whisper.

Children from the school come into the room hollering. They're excited to have a visitor. I pull out my camera and they adopt their favourite poses. The eleven-year-old girls bat their eyelashes, put on imagined lipstick. The boys shoot with rulers and hurl chalk like grenades. The teacher invites me to a class party tomorrow but I tell him I can't make it. I don't tell him it's the first night of Passover, and I'll be busy with Ruthie and her friends.

X volunteers to escort me to the checkpoint. A mob of children, twelve, thirteen of them, follow me down the stairs of the school. They reach for me, tear into my pockets, grab at my backpack. They want to know what I'm carrying. I pull out a blue spiral notebook and tear out pieces of paper. Potential airplanes, hats, sailboats, love poems. They snatch them hungrily.

X parts a path through the mob and we push our way down the stairs. Just outside the door, Crazy Boy is there, a collection of stones in a small leather satchel. He puts down the bag, picks up a broom and marches with it, back and forth, a guard on duty. I joke, salute him as though he were a soldier. Crazy Boy doesn't find this funny. He comes at me with the broom and whacks me in the neck. I try to grab the broom from him and he swings for the bleachers, connects fully with my chest. I keel over, winded.

"Darwish," I think I hear someone whisper.

"Fuck off," yells X at Crazy Boy, who grabs his satchel of stones and runs.

THE CHECKPOINT is abuzz with activity. It's late in the day—only an hour of sunlight left. According to a taxi driver the car lineup into Israel is three and a half hours. X leads me to the foot-passenger lineup. It will only take a few minutes to get through. Before I leave X insists I meet Sam. He's fifty years old and he speaks near-fluent English. He spends his days by the wall-in-progress, tending fire, burning scraps of paper and garbage against the chain-link fence. X tells him I want to learn about Palestine, and Sam's willing to give me a history lesson. When he starts to speak, gunfire erupts. I whirl around and see it's coming from near the camp. There's an Israeli army vehicle on the other side of the fence, stopped at a point on a hill some one hundred metres away.

People walk to the checkpoint a little more quickly. X is nowhere to be seen, he's taken off. "What's going on?" I ask Sam, but he's into the history.

"Now this field, on the other side of the fence, you wouldn't have thought such a thing, considering the—"

BLANG BLAM BLAM

"1936 for example, there was a sudden mix of forces, east and west, nobody could predict this, contradiction, confusion—"

More gunshots. X runs through the crowd toward me. He's carrying a bottle of Orange Crush.

"What the fuck?" I say.

X says, "Drink this. Be calm."

"Why are they shooting?"

"Crazy Boy." And he mimes a stone being thrown.

Is it me or does Sam not make sense? He has a look in his eyes, the whites glazed over, but he's calmer than I am for sure. I'm wondering what I have to do to understand him. He's counting years, the usual ones: "'48, '67, '73, '56." But there are other numbers as well: "22, 58, 33, 91." What's he on about?

BLAM BLANG BLAM

"What do you do?" Sam asks. The question is suddenly coherent, sensible.

"I'm a writer," I say.

"A writer has the power. To hear. Be heard."

More bullets. Three soldiers chase Crazy Boy up the road. He's hurling stones and I swear I can hear them plonk off the jeep. My chest aches from where he hit me with the broom. Sam bends down and reaches into his pile of "to be burned" magazines.

He picks one up and tears out a page, presents it to me. Sam says, "Bring this to the people of Canada." It's a Western Union ad, only it's written in Arabic. On the page is a studious-looking woman counting American dollar bills. "Show them what is going on here," he says.

The soldiers are back in the jeep. The vehicle leaves its position on the hill and approaches us. I'm frozen, stuck on the spot, Orange Crush in hand. I try to open the soda but I can't twist the cap. My hands, feet, nothing wants to give.

Sam adjusts his red trucker hat and admires his trash-fire. I want to write Sam off as crazy. But there's something about his conviction, the way he said, "A writer has power," that glues me to where I stand. I stare at the familiar colours of the Western Union logo, the words that mean nothing to me. "Bring this to the people of Canada," he said. I want to write something as important as Sam's conviction. But I can't even read the ad. More bullets are fired. Where's Crazy Boy? I look back. Dozens of people are running down the hill. "Go." Sam's last word. Bullets spray through us. I stuff the ad down my pants and sprint to the checkpoint. DO NOT say goodbye. DO NOT turn around. DO NOT turn into a pillar of salt. A soldier looks at my passport, then at me. He says nothing, asks nothing. I pass through the metal detector into Israel.

WALK THE HIGHWAY through Charlie's town. I do not call Charlie, do not know what to do. I hail a taxi but I realize I have only four dollars. "Driver, where can you take me?" We drive to Jerusalem. He drops me off in a neighbourhood I have not been to. A sign in front of the houses:

WOMEN DRESSED IMMODESTLY
TOURISTS AND GROUPS
STRICTLY FORBIDDEN …
DO NOT IRRITATE OUR FEELINGS!!!

The streets are quiet but for the few men rushing with bags stuffed with bread. It's the night before Passover and they're carrying their *chametz* to be burned before sunset. Pesach: to mark our passage from slavery to freedom. Starting tomorrow we eat matzo, bread without yeast. And so Jews burn what we hold in excess: arrogance, ego, our puffed-up thoughts.

I recognize this neighbourhood from films I've seen. I'm in Mea Shearim, the most Orthodox section of Jerusalem. On metal grates the chametz is burnt, an altar of yeast and smoke. Farther up the street I take out my camera. A woman hangs laundry whites from her balcony window. A stone lands at my feet. Another hits my elbow.

"Go away," a voice says.

It's a young boy, ten or eleven years old. He has black peyes, wears a black kippah and black suit.

"Go where?" I ask.

His father appears from a doorway and yanks him by the hand. The boy turns around and sticks his tongue out at me. His father leads him away, speedily, carrying bread and prayer books to burn away the year.

CHAPTER 27

It's the next day, the afternoon before Ruthie's Seder, and I'm coming to Shimon with shit-all. I have nothing to give, know nothing. In fact, I know less than when I first came here.

I want to say to Shimon, "You were a refugee on the boats from Europe. Your parents' house was probably taken over by a Pole or a Russian at the end of the war. How could you move into a house that belongs to someone else? How can you be okay knowing that?"

The house is narrower than Mary's bungalow, and I have to pass under a canopy of jasmine to get onto the property. The design is Arabic in style—several columns on the porch support the flat roof. I knock hard on the door and nobody answers. I go into the backyard to take some photographs. A few toys lie scattered on the lawn. A line of laundry hangs innocently above. Shimon appears with an armful of groceries, bags filled with matzo and wine.

"What are you doing here?" he asks in Hebrew.

"Forgive me for intruding," I reply, careful to speak with a strong accent. "I wanted to ask you a few questions about this house."

"Who are you?" Shimon asks, putting down the groceries.

"I'm from Canada."

"Who do you work for?"

"Nobody."

"What the hell do you want?"

"I want to know the story of this house."

"Why?"

"Because I want to write about it."

"Go away."

"Now Shimon—"

"How do you know my name?"

"Abu Dalo and Rana—"

"You see these two hands? They built this house. Every brick, column and plank. Then that asshole came and stole it from me."

"Really?"

"Now if you don't leave my property, these two hands will make you leave."

"But Shimon—"

"Leave! Or I'll call the police."

My feet won't listen. They're saying *not yet, there is so much more to find out.* "Shimon," I want to say, "tell me *your* story." But the look in his black eyes, the almost-prophetic pointing of his finger to the canopied gate, all tell me to leave. And I do.

On the other side of the house Abu Dalo waters Shimon's lawn. He playfully sprays his five-year-old grandson.

"What are you doing here, Mr. Writer?" asks Abu Dalo.

"I was asking Shimon some questions," I reply.

This response makes Abu Dalo very angry. "Do not ever talk to that man about this house. Do you understand me?"

I tell Abu Dalo there's no need to get mad. That Shimon wouldn't talk anyway.

"Just by bringing it up you create problems for us," he says. His grandson hides behind Abu Dalo's right leg. Angrily he adds, "Leave us alone. Leave us in peace."

CHAPTER 28

I'm tired and frazzled. Yesterday's gunfire and today's encounter with Shimon have done me in. I feel like I'm coming down with something nasty. I've been sweating since I walked in the door of Ruthie's house. I'm introduced to her husband, Menachem, who's leading tonight's Seder. He's American and he made aliyah four years ago. He speaks Jersey-Jewish with the sagacity of an eighty-four-year-old man at the JCC shvitz.

"So, Jonathan, what have you seen of Israel?" Opening his palms to the sky, he tries to make his question sound like a proverb.

I need to be careful with what I say. I might not feel completely myself, but I have not abandoned my sense of diplomacy. *Don't talk about the West Bank.* I tell him I've been in Jerusalem, Tel Aviv and the Galilee. The others at the table—Chana, Leah, Rivka, Rainbow—all groan when I say Tel Aviv.

Rainbow says, "Tel Aviv. It's Babylon."

"I liked the architecture," I say.

Nobody can understand why I would go anywhere in Israel other than the holy sites; after all, what is Israel about? When I mention Ein Harod, the reply is an even more oyish groan.

"I can't stand the kibbutzniks," says Rainbow.

"Now, now," says Menachem. "It's Pesach. Let's not insult other Jews."

"They're not Jews," says Rainbow. "They're Communist morons."

226

"Didn't they help build this country?" I ask.

This is not the right thing to say. "God built this country," Rainbow says, pointing her finger at me like I'm one of *them*. "And it's only the ones who pray to Him, who remain dedicated to His commands, that keep this country going."

I sink back into my chair. Don't say a damn thing.

MENACHEM STARTS the ceremony. "We begin by reciting the order for the night. Why, on the festival of freedom, do we pay such close attention to order?"

"Because only through structure can we know freedom. It's a paradox," says Ruthie. "We need to roam freely but we also need a house." She looks at me when she says this.

There are eleven of us. Nine have moved from North America in the last five years. Like Ruthie, they've renounced their former lives and become ultra-religious. Leah used to go to arts school, Chanah was a dancer and Rainbow followed the Grateful Dead, selling acid in parking lots for five bucks a hit. In a way, Judaism is not so different from the Grateful Dead. The Hebrews are that old desert cult, the original hippies dancing by Mount Sinai, praying for a hit of the good stuff, a miracle, deliverance.

Ruthie makes the blessing on the candles to welcome the holidays. Menachem holds his son, Herschel, at the waist, raises him to the light. We watch Herschel's little feet dance.

Later in the Seder we count out the ten plagues. Blood, frogs, lice, boils. Menachem says, "We're spilling wine on our plate because Hashem does not like it when any of His creatures are killed."

There's a healthy amount of violence in the Passover Haggadah. I always noticed it as a kid, but it never bothered me. In fact, I used to take pride in the vengeance God carried out in our name. After all those years of slavery we deserved to be on top. And besides, Pesach isn't only about God's strength. It shows His humour too. The frog plague has to be one of his best routines, hands down. Tonight, however, the Seder gets to me. From the slaughter of the first born to the paschal sacrifice, this country, this belief, steeped in blood.

Moses parted the Red Sea to allow the Hebrews to cross, but all I can I think of is the thousands of Egyptians who drowned as they followed. We don't ask why God inflicted so many plagues on our behalf. The debate at the table is over the number of them. "How many did God actually inflict? Not 10, not 200, but 250 plagues." That he kicked the shit out of the Egyptians is a sign of His incredible devotion and love. Like a parent protecting its kid from the school bully, we thank Hashem for defending us, we who are constantly picked on.

Ruthie points to the Seder plate in the middle of the table: the boiled egg, the bitter herb, matzo, parsley, *charoset*. We're encouraged to ask, what does it mean? As a kid I loved this ritual. I'd compose lists of questions to ask my father, for it's part of the holiday to provoke discussion.

Each time we do a blessing on the wine, we're required to drink an entire glass. We just did number two. I'm ahead by one, sneaking in gulps whenever I get the chance. I'm tipsy. The crappy wine eases the nerves, and soon enough it doesn't taste half-bad. And it opens the floodgates. Memories of other Passovers.

The Seder was a time for family. My father sat at the head of the table, my mom next to the swinging door that opened onto the kitchen. She spent days preparing Baba's famous gefilte fish. Chicken soup with matzo balls, brisket and mandelbroit. An entire symphony of food. As per the commandments of the sages, my father reclined in his tall chair on a stack of pillows. He sang off-key, but there was always something reassuring in the way he sang. It was unapologetic, familiar.

We knew all the songs from Bialik. Joseph sang the four questions, Aaron did his famous backup harmonies, and I'd propose alternative melodies. It was one of the only times we sang together as a family. My dad raised the wine glass for Halachma and recited the ancient Aramaic prayer that invites anyone in need of food, Jew or Gentile, to the table. He would tell bad jokes, my mom would laugh. My father would kiss my mother on the forehead and say, "The food is delicious," and my mom would blush, feign humility.

The last Seder I had with my whole family was three years ago. My father had moved out four months before. He'd called it a temporary separation but we all knew he wasn't coming back. Two days before that Pesach, my Baba Jesse died. The entire family went to Winnipeg for the funeral. Jewish tradition commands that a shiva be held for seven days after a death. The only time this isn't completed is when a major Jewish holiday falls on the days of mourning. Fulfilling the mitzvah of celebrating the Pesach trumped the shiva for my grandmother.

We returned from Winnipeg drained from the funeral. We had to do the Seder as best we could. My father led it for his last time in that house. He was rushed, uneasy. There were no jokes, and my mother apologized for the food catered by Perl's; she had no time to prepare. The gefilte fish tasted too sweet, and the roast beef was dry. At the end of the Seder, we sang "Chad Gadya." My father took his coat and kissed my mother on the cheek and left.

"I'll stay if you want," I said to her. I didn't want to stay, not in that house, not that night. She knew it.

"You go," she said. "I'm too tired anyway."

I should've stayed, but I didn't. I didn't want to sleep with all that pain in the air. I said, "Shall we have a drink before I go?"

"If I drink," my mother said, "I might start crying. If I cry, I'm not going to stop."

WE EAT MATZOS, bitter herbs, separately, then together with charoset. A thin string binds me to my faith. The people at the table—they nod sincerely, bow their heads, agree with the prayers, eat devoutly. I'm making it all up. I'm a sham, holding on to my past: Bialik. My parents. The house I grew up in. Judith. To believe in God means to have a relationship with Him. I have to blot out ninety percent of what I know to make our relationship work. Why am I doing this? What is this marriage, other than a lie?

Ruthie argues passionately for following God's commandments. "He led us to freedom. He will lead us again and again." Amen, say the others.

I want to ask, "What is this freedom?" Instead I pour myself another glass of wine. I cannot make the ancient stuff relevant in the present. I cannot do this at all.

DINNER ARRIVES in clay pots. A feast of chicken, roast beef and *kugel.* Martin sits next to me. He's the only one here who's fought in the army, and has lived in Israel since the late 1980s. I ask Martin, "What was your worst and best experience in the army?"

Martin says, "The worst was Gaza. I was sent in with a Bedouin unit. We'd get orders to shoot, and they'd lie back on the tanks and smoke cigarettes. It was pathetic. I know I shouldn't make generalizations," he says, leaning toward me, "but the Bedouin are worse than sloths. Laziness is in their nature."

"What was your best experience?"

"For three years, me and three buddies are dispatched to Ramallah. We're told to occupy the third floor of a Palestinian home for four days. We stay up all night shooting the shit, eating pizza, sleeping in shifts, wearing infrared goggles. And we shoot any suspected terrorists. It's a lot of fun."

The wine is tasting better and better. I've decided to embrace the Passover celebration as best I can by being the "simple son" in the Haggadah, the one who asks the most straightforward and innocent questions. After all, I'm a foreigner, a tourist. An idiot.

"What would happen if a Jew walked across the Qalandia checkpoint and into the refugee camp?"

"He'd be torn apart limb for limb," Martin says. "Without a doubt."

I point my fork at Martin. I'm not sure why but I feel a need to tell him. Maybe I just need to talk to someone. "I did that. And you know what? Nobody tore me apart."

"You were lucky. You heard what happened to those reservists."

"I wasn't a complete moron. It's not like I was wearing a kippah on my head, chanting, *"Am Yisrael Chai."* I walked into the refugee camp. And the Palestinians were very hospitable."

I realize that everyone at the table is listening. "What did you do there?" asks Ruthie.

"I was taken on a tour by three schoolchildren."

"Were you frightened?" asks Chana.

"Yes," I say, pouring myself another glass of wine. I should shut up now. But I want these people to know I was frightened. I nearly shit my pants when the Israeli soldiers opened fire. And Crazy Boy, he scared the hell out of me too. I wasn't sure who was going to kill me, them or us. I look at my wineglass. It's already empty. So is the bottle nearest to me.

Rainbow speaks up: "You're lucky. They're animals, really."

"Who?" I say.

"What she means is, Arab hatred for Jews is immutable," says Martin.

Rainbow: "He's right. When Ariel Sharon went up to Al-Aqsa mosque, the Muslims went nuts. Arabs get hysterical when it comes to religious issues."

I can't hold back my tongue. "We're right and the Arabs are wrong. Even the secular Zionists are morons. Listen to you. What kind of God is this with his band of elite bullies?"

"Your problem is you're a self-hating Jew."

"That's not true, Rainbow. I love Judaism. I love Friday-night dinners and the blessing over the wine. I love the songs, the ethics, the literature. Hell, I love the people." I look around the room. Do I love these people? Not exactly. "What I don't love is being brainwashed to believe we're constantly under attack." I'm standing up now. I have to piss like hell. I hold on to the table for support.

"Let me ask you something," Rainbow says. She calmly brushes back her dreadlocks. "When a Palestinian woman enters Dizengoff Mall and blows herself up, who's under attack? I lost my fiancé because of a suicide bomber. What have you lost?"

"Look, I'm sorry about your fiancé. It's terrible. But that doesn't mean it's okay for us to occupy another people and pretend we have the right to."

"Life here is a lot more complicated than your lame North American ideals."

"Rainbow, building a wall isn't going to make the bombs stop."

"Then what will?"

I take a breath. "I don't know."

Menachem says, "I think we should move to dessert. Ruthie? What do you say?"

"I'll get the cake."

I leave the room, head to the bathroom but it's locked. Ruthie's in the hall.

"What are you doing, Jonathan? Why do you have to talk like this?"

"It just came out."

"All you do is criticize."

"I just wanted to ask some questions."

"Not those. Not tonight."

I scratch my head. "I went into a store in the old city yesterday. There was a model of the third temple. It was huge. I said, 'How are you going to build this?' The Haredi said, 'When the third temple falls out of the sky and lands on Al-Aqsa mosque, then you'll see how it will be built.' Do you believe this shit?"

"Of course not. Not everyone's a fantatic, Jonathan. You're too polarized."

I'm polarized? "Nobody asks questions. Everyone's just waiting for God to deliver the magic answer. It's like faith is this sacred thing we can't touch."

"You're not a believer. That's all."

"I don't believe the claim to land as defined in a book several thousand years old should not be questioned."

"Jonathan, it's Pesach. Don't you have other things to worry about? How's Judith?"

"I don't want to talk about Judith. I want to talk about the occupation."

"Why are you so concerned about this occupation?" Ruthie rubs her right wrist with her left hand.

"Because. I feel like I'm occupied."

"By what?"

The thought is ridiculous, but I say it anyway. "My faith."

CHAPTER 29

And it does not leave me. I can't erase my faith. The voice of Baba in my head: How will you continue the line of belief?

I leave Ruthie's. Walk quickly, something's chasing me, can't get rid of it. I head to the old city. Lose myself in the stone corridors. Don't want to know where I am but I know exactly where I'm going. I'm in the Jewish Quarter staring at the Kotel from above. There's no avoiding it anymore; I have to go down. Frisked by security, I walk through the metal detectors and I'm free. My lips pressed against the ancient Western Wall. Soldiers with their guns bent at prayer. Their gesture a question: *How far would you go for your faith?*

For two thousand years we've chanted our prayers east, directed here, to the foot of this stone. The wall, the only one: remnant of the holy temple. And the power, when confronted by it, is undeniable. The question, "Do you believe in the sacred?" shrivels up and dies. Judith wants to get married here for good reason. It is *the* place of places. When I was working on the Jerusalem Project I'd get a drunk feeling gazing at the poster in class. I'd stare at the cracks in the ancient rocks and the black tufts of moss growing between them. The image haunted me. I was sure God was on the other side. Now, here I am, face to face with the breathing, living, holy awesomeness of it.

This place has layers of complexities beyond my Jewish ideas about faith. The land around the Kotel has not always belonged to us, still crosses boundaries, borders, a crossroads. At Max's I read about those

who lived here, between the ancient and the modern, a neighbourhood of a thousand. After '67 they were shipped off to Jordan or
wherever on buses. Their houses razed by bulldozers. So I could pray
here. In peace.

When I wrote the Jerusalem Project, I imagined the prayers people
scribbled then scrolled inside the wall. They were removed nightly by
an angel, the small pieces of paper placed in a large pile. A mountain
of yearning rests behind this wall. God reads the notes to keep Him
company. I take out my pen, feel a tap on my shoulder. I turn around.

"Dad?"

He's dressed the way he used to when we went to shul and I was
just a kid: a boxy eighties grey suit with a navy striped tie. Thick
black glasses, and a black kippah on his head. "You seem a little
unbalanced," he says.

"I feel funny." The sweat that began at Ruthie's has now evolved
into a full-body chill. "I might be having a low blood sugar."

My father has always amazed me with his own sense of balance,
conviction and intelligence in the face of adversity. He's there when
you need him, and he also manages to have the right remedy in times
of crisis. He reaches into my coat pocket and pulls out a pack of red
LifeSavers. How did he know I had them, when I didn't know myself?
I pop one in my mouth. I feel a bit better. "You remember Joseph's bar
mitzvah?" he asks. He rests his hand on my shoulder. "You led the
congregation. Me, I could never sing. But you were a chazzan, you
were always on key." He lifts his hand, taps the wall with his fingers.
"To be on key is to be centred. You had a certain *gravitas* then."

"I was sixteen years old."

"You need to find that again."

"How?"

"Pray."

He adjusts the black kippah on his head. The chanting from the
men, a wail, swells around us.

"I don't like these prayers."

"You were thinking to write God a note. A personal prayer. I like that idea, go with it."

My father puts his other hand on my shoulder. I have the urge to say something meaningful. But all I can say is, "Why did you never send me to Israel when I was a kid?"

"Because I can't stand this place," he says. And my father walks away from me toward the circle of men praying.

I pop another LifeSaver, follow his path, but I can't find him. I'm lost in a thicket of black beards and white tallises.

Rabbi in your white kittel, bless me
Twirl with your Torah and bless me
For you must be learned and wise

I need the balance my father's talking about, a bolt of something to make me stand straighter. I look at the wall as though it could provide some sort of answer. But the wall doesn't talk. God doesn't either.

I write: "Why do I question You?" Tear out the sheet and scroll it into the wall.

I want to stay here in Jerusalem. But there's no stone in my blood. I'm too soft in the head, apologetic in the heart. I do not belong here. Do not know where to go. I listen for a voice. My ear pressed against the wall. I hear the voice of Barak.

"When you're confused, go to the Sinai. There's clarity in the desert."

CHAPTER 30

I'm on a bus in the Negev en route to the Sinai. My head pounds from bad wine and bad thoughts. I have the urge for something holy, something to clear away the mess of last night's Seder.

At our last meeting two weeks ago in Tel Aviv, I expressed to Barak my growing confusion. "This country is not right and left having a discussion," I said. "It's a thousand different opinions screaming at once." Barak replied, "You go to Sinai, and all of this becomes quiet, unimportant." He waved his arm magically in the café and I believed him. Instead of rubber bullets, Tel Aviv traffic and Jerusalem fanatics, I saw desert, sea and sun. All in the sweep of Barak's arm.

We pull over in the middle of nowhere. Two young soldiers board the bus and walk down the centre aisle. They stop and ask the woman in front of me for her ID. She and her two kids are the only ones carded—they're Palestinian. The young soldier commands the three of them to get off the bus. I figure the soldiers are simply going through their belongings in a more private environment—the mother carries two small cotton shoulder bags—but they never get back on. Nobody else on the bus seems to notice or mind. The driver smoothly shifts the bus forward; the tinted windows keep out the bright sun. I look back and try to catch a glimpse of the family's fate. See Bedouin living in tin shacks, shantytowns carved between road and rock.

I'M OCCUPIED by my faith.

The statement replays itself over and over again in my mind like a bad pop song. Sing it loud, repeat as chorus. It's catchy, but what does it mean?

To be occupied by one's faith. It's like saying I've been born into a prison. I can still see Ruthie's face, her shocked eyes, after I said it.

"You're crazy," her eyes said. "You're completely insane."

I'm hungover. I feel like puking.

AT BIALIK, my Bible and Mishnah teacher Alon Eloni was a relief from the rigours of Blintzkrieg. Alon's voice seduced me, sometimes into listening, other times to sleep. He was a teacher I could talk to, and I'd go to him after class. I listened to him muse on literature, philosophy and art. Hints of a world outside the one I was familiar with.

In class he once intoned that while the Greeks were chosen for their art and philosophy, the Arabs for mathematics and poetry, the Romans for law and government, the Jews were chosen for their ethics. Thus each and every one of you, and I mean you, too, Shalom Garfinkel, yes, you may wake up now from your nap, thank you very much for listening, your duty is to strive to be good and righteous. There is no choice in the matter. God has chosen us to fulfil his mitzvoth.

At the age of thirteen, I did not pay much attention to Alon's statement. I struggled to stay awake in class. But I'm kicking myself now for not picking up on it, for here someone was trying to answer the question I've carried with me my entire life: Why have I been chosen? For what? Alon's answer, in retrospect, was dissatisfying, annoyingly textbookish. I should have pushed the matter further.

The bus stops in the middle of nowhere. A man with a black fedora and black sunglasses gets on. Slightly hunched, he sits down next to me. When he removes his sunglasses, I see that it's Alon, an older, greyer version of him.

"So Shalom. You finally made it to Israel."

"I wasn't ready until now."

"You were procrastinating. A skill you were well versed in when you were my student."

"Can I ask you a question?"

"Only if you pay attention to the quality of the question. There is an art to that, you know. Heidegger said that."

I clear my throat. The question is ridiculous, but I have to ask it. "Why must Jews strive to be good?"

"If no one tried to be good, we'd live in chaos. Remember your Hobbes: Without the moral law we're barbarians, living in terror and fear."

"I know, I know," I say. "But why us more than anyone else?"

Alon adjusts his fedora. "When God gave Moses the Torah at Sinai, He gave us 613 laws to follow. We were to teach the world by example." From a blue travel bag the older Alon pulls out a chopped-egg sandwich and takes a bite.

"Isn't it strange that God should have a favourite people?" I ask.

"God has no favourites. We're all His children."

"But He chose us," I say.

"Choosing a people to follow the Law doesn't mean we're better than anyone else. It only means we have a certain duty to carry out. And we fail—time and again, we fall short. It's the striving, that's what makes us Jewish." Alon rubs his hands slowly as though to warm himself. His sandwich in wax paper rests on his lap. "Though it's true, people who hate Jews will point to our election to say how arrogant we are. They'll say we think we're superior to other nations. Of course we're not. Jews are stupidly human."

Alon puts away the sandwich. He takes a jar of hand cream from his travel bag and rubs some onto his palms.

"If only you'd have been this conscientious a student twenty years ago we might've had some real debates in class. You really were a mediocre student," he says, patting my knee. The bus stops and he gets up. "Resisting your chosenness is very Jewish, Shalom. You're like the Children of Israel, lost in the desert, wavering between faith and doubt. There is perhaps nothing more Jewish than that."

I GET OFF the bus in Eilat. From there I take a taxi to the Egyptian border. As soon as I walk through customs, I'm in another universe. Ten Bedouin men sit crouched by the side of the road smoking cigarettes. I ask if I can catch a ride to Ras Hasatan or Neweba but nobody answers. I ask again; not a peep from any of them. Exasperated, I say I'm willing to pay whatever it takes, just get me there, the sooner the better. A tall man offers me a cigarette. I grab it hastily from his hand, annoyed that nobody is saying anything. An Israeli tourist leaning against a pole says, "Take a load off, brother. We're on Sinai time." So I play copycat to the Israeli, sit down and surrender to the surroundings: flies on the face, smoke in the air. Soon enough I'm following that smoke up the dusty, empty road toward Sharm el Sheikh, Cairo, the pyramids, Alexandria.

The voice of Barak in my head: "You get off at Ras Hasatan and rent a cabana and look at the sea. Let it take you in. Eat, drink. There'll be no need for thought. The rush of security, the paranoia— all vanishes in Sinai. The water," he said, "is good for the body and the soul."

AFTER TWO MONTHS in Israel I'm watching fishing boats bob up and down on the sea. As though that's all that matters—the water's movement, the balance of boats, the food men gather.

A beautiful young Israeli couple sits on their veranda smoking a joint. They invite me to join them, Chayim and Tamara, from Tel Aviv. Chayim's hairless chest is bronzed from the sun and he has the strongest back I've ever seen, posture solid as a chair. Tamara has infinity tattooed onto her right ankle and wears her black dreadlocked hair in a simple yet elegant ponytail. "We're here to get away from Pesach," Chayim explains, stroking his girl's left hand as he passes me the joint. They're thrilled to be skipping out on Passover, eating all the *treyf* they want without a single ounce of guilt.

"We celebrated Pesach with a quarter ounce mushrooms and a bottle of JD," Tamara says as I pass her the joint back. I tell them about my Passover, and Tamara shakes her head. "They think Judaism is something you have to follow, a bunch of rules like on a driver's test. Really, it's in here." She points to her chest and inhales deeply on the joint. Too deep. She hacks up a lung of smoke.

I like Tamara and Chayim. They seem incredibly sane, and they know where they stand with their faith. I lie back on the beach and look out at the sea. It's so quiet I feel like screaming, a happy kind of howl. I look at Tamara and Chayim. They speak only when they have to.

What am I doing on this stoner beach? I suppose I want to be like Tamara and Chayim: guiltless and free. I want to escape the thoughts of Ruthie's Seder. I want whatever Barak promised.

The joint is out. A row of cumuli marches toward us. Chayim pulls out a backgammon board. He and Tamara start to play; they're in rhythm with each other and the sea is a metronome for their moves. They've been together five, six years at least, this is a good thing they have going. She touches his thin wrist when he rolls a double five. He looks at the cut above her right eyebrow when she leans toward him. From behind their tanned shoulders, at the other end of the beach, a short old Bedouin man emerges from behind a dune. He shouts at a camel while leading it on a long tattered rope. He approaches us and Chayim lets out a groan.

"I don't want to buy anything," he says to the Bedouin.

"I don't want to sell," the Bedouin says in a mix of Hebrew and Arabic. His name is Kabina and he spits a fleck of licorice root he's chewing in his mouth. "You," he says in a language I can't fully understand. "I take you to the desert."

I look to Tamara and Chayim for guidance, but they're sucked into each other and the game. Why not? I say to the Bedouin. What have I got to lose?

KABINA IS NOT the Bedouin I imagined as a boy. He wears a blue Gore-Tex bag around his shoulder. His sandals are plastic flip-flops—not the handmade rope ones you see in pictures. Kabina walks, a limp in his stride, head covered in a white headscarf. He wears long grey robes dirtied from the desert.

I give him eighty Egyptian pounds so he can buy groceries. Kabina disappears and I spend the afternoon walking along the beach not thinking about whatever it was I was so concerned about before. I swim in the ocean. Doze on the sand. My skin loves the salt and sun. I eat Bedouin food under a wide-open tent, drink a couple of watery Egyptian beers. Smoke apple tobacco and drink coffee. The life.

Dusk comes and Kabina hasn't returned from shopping. I ask if anyone knows him and the tourists shrug their shoulders. Nobody cares about anything and there's something to this not caring. I figure the money I gave Kabina's gone and that's okay, maybe it's better I stay here on the beach. But the next morning I hear a tap on my cabana door. It's not yet 6 A.M. and there's Kabina with cans of Spam, corned beef and corn niblets. A sack of dark flour, three skins of water. I help him tie the leather bags with our supplies onto the side of the camel. Then he helps me up with a boost. It's a long stretch to the top, even though the camel's kneeling. Two wool blankets are tied on behind where I sit. Already my crotch hurts like hell.

We start at Ras Hasatan, trekking alongside the sea for the first half-hour in near darkness. The stars are spectacular. Light sneaks in from the east. Hundreds of Israelis (Germans, Australians too) come here to smoke pot, eat Bedouin food and snorkel. To lose themselves in beauty. And it is beautiful, there's no denying. We cross the highway as the sun rises. The road is a long yawn. The mountains slope into the sea. A Bedouin crouches by the side of the road, waiting for a ride or the wind to change or just taking it all in. We turn from the sea and follow a hollowed-out riverbed. Round a corner, then another and that's it. Nothing but Kabina, me, the camel, an eternity of stone.

KABINA DOESN'T TALK to me. He argues with the camel, telling her what a shit she is, how lazy she is and so on. The camel endures his complaints with a smarmy grin. She chews whatever a camel chews, and this makes her seem even more arrogant. I ask Kabina if he wants a break from walking, if he'd like a turn on the camel. He responds by beating the camel's legs with a stick. He says he never sits on a camel, it's bad for his back.

It must be eleven now. The sun is hot on the head. The white kaffiyeh I'm wearing does nothing to protect me. The camel and I take a rest while Kabina goes off to check out another trail, a possible change of direction. I take a sip of water. The sun is relentless, inescapable. Beside me is a low pile of rocks. I kick at them to pass the time. The pile falls over and I think it's just another stone beneath the rubble, but I see him, peacefully sleeping. Herschel, Ruthie's baby, lies in a white bundle on the rocky desert floor. He's wrapped in a little white robe, as though he's been abandoned and I've been left to take care of him. Then I think, what if the kid's dead? I lean over to check him out. A tiny hand reaches out and slaps me in the face.

"Wake up, Garfinkel," he says.

"What?" I say.

"You heard me." Herschel pulls himself up. He sits in lotus on a rock. He wraps the white robe around his head. He looks like a baby Gandhi. My cheek stings from his surprisingly hard slap.

"I was thinking about what you said to my mom at the Seder. It's not completely absurd to say you're occupied. Really, any religion is a kind of prison." Herschel puts down his bottle of kosher-for-Pesach infant formula. "The birthing angel doesn't ask when you pass through the birth canal, 'So what'll it be? Monotheism? Paganism? Non-belief?'"

"Doesn't that bug you?" I ask. I'm amazed by how eloquently Herschel speaks.

He has an oversized head and puffy red baby lips.

"Not at all." He looks at the camel inquisitively. The camel turns her head away and stares at the horizon.

"But look at your parents. They at least got to choose their meshuggeneh life. You're born into yours."

"Don't be so angry at your faith."

"I'm not angry. I'm questioning it."

Herschel pensively sucks on his right hand, four-finger sandwich in his toothless mouth. "Does the Palestinian starving in a refugee camp question his faith when Hamas feeds him and builds the schools he sends his children to? Yours is a problem of privilege."

"Why shouldn't I question my faith? And why shouldn't the Palestinian in the refugee camp question his? Isn't that so much of the problem here?" I'm so damn hot I waste some of the precious drinking water by pouring a thin stream onto my head. "It's infuriating, really. We're taught things as kids we can't shake as adults. And I have this ridiculous nostalgia for a religion whose rules I don't even follow. How can anyone be expected to develop a clear opinion about anything?"

"Creativity," Herschel says. "One must be creative in the interpretation of one's faith. Then you know where you stand." And he actually tries to stand up on the rock. He props himself up by placing his hands on me.

"What do you believe?" I ask.

"Nuh-uh, Garfinkel," Herschel says. "The question is, 'What do *you* believe?'"

I'M THIRSTY as hell. I've finished the small skin of water and am looking for another when Kabina returns. He grabs me some and I guzzle it back. Woozy from the heat, I leave him and the camel and enter a maze of stone to take a piss. Red walls, turn right, then left. My ears become attuned to minute details: a slight wind, the sun in my hair. The commentary ceases. The rush of silence—it seems to come from the rock itself—is almost too much to bear. It pummels me, makes me dizzy. I feel like I might fall over.

When I return Kabina looks concerned. He says, "We look for oasis. You must rest Jewish man, you have had too much sun."

THE OASIS is in a narrow valley with a few palm trees. Kabina unloads the camel and I lie in the shade gulping water. He finds some dry palm leaves and starts up a fire. He pours water into a blue plastic bowl and adds flour. He mixes the dough with his hands, pounding and rolling it. The fire burns quickly down to coals, and he takes the flattened dough and sticks it in. After a few minutes he flips it over with a stick and buries it beneath the coals and ash. When the pita is ready, we tear into the fresh hot bread with our hands. It tastes ashy but good. Three vultures circle above.

The climb out of the oasis is steep. The camel is old and stubborn. She likes to eat any hint of shrub or vegetation poking out of stone. Stare at the rock long enough, you think you can make sense of it: faces, hieroglyphs, letters. Cities of alphabet, carved by an unknown hand. At the top of the canyon the desert opens up. Two acacia lean toward the earth away from the sun. We follow the dried-up riverbeds. Contours of sand, places where waters once ran. Sinai is not sand. It is rough stone, carved in boxes and slabs.

THE NEXT OASIS is at the base of a wide canyon. We place our gear down for the night. Kabina lights a fire and I walk into the valley where it opens up into a field of immense boulders. A feeling pulls on me, a magnet in this rock—I could keep walking and never turn back. Follow a trail, which one, that one, to the north and the west. Something bigger than anything I've ever imagined calls me farther, commands me forward. A voice so wild and ancient I don't even have to speak. I turn down a narrow walkway of stone. The fire of the camp is lost from view. Silence dwarfs me. I want to bow down, surrender to this quiet.

It's hunger that drives me back to the camp. When I see Kabina and the fire, the question returns, different now: Would you rather not have been occupied? It's absurd this question. It's like asking, would you rather not have been born? I look back toward the sea of boulders I just walked through. There's something rich in these contours, stone and its layers of meaning. Something still flows in these dried-out riverbeds. I don't know what. Maybe that's what religion or prayer originally tried to do. Name these nameless places. To take us back here. Where God begins.

WHEN I WAS A BOY of ten I fell in love with Moses. He was where Jesus and Jacob met: Moses was kind and accepting, but tough when the situation demanded it. He was different from the other heroes of my childhood: Groucho Marx, Laika, Sandy Koufax. I loved Moses' lack of confidence: "Who am I to lead a people from slavery to freedom?" And yet when it came to the task he was presented, Moses always got the job done. I was impressed by his will and his ability to sweet-talk God, but most of all I admired his patience. "Don't forget," Alon taught us, "Moses had to lead the ultimate kvetchers in the world through the desert." The Children of Israel always had one thing or another to complain about. The seemingly insurmountable Red Sea, a lack of food and water, Moses gone too long to receive the word of God. For forty years, Moses put up with their shit. God's shit too. Moses continued to believe amidst his throng of doubters. And he never made it to the Promised Land.

Tonight I imagine a different Moses. His patience has been pushed to the limit. I see him pounding his hands against this stone. I hear him cry out to heaven: "Okay God, what is this promise? You freed us from slavery—now where are we going? And what do we do when we get there?"

AT DINNER Kabina talks about the Six Day War.

"We didn't care who we were with or against. We were loyal to no one but ourselves. We fought for this."

He does not look up from the can on the fire. He stirs it, corned beef on hot coals.

"The desert has changed over the years. Now there are tourists, government regulations. But in the end, land is land. This is still home."

I ask Kabina, "What does home mean to you?"

He does not look up from the fire. Does not answer the question. As though to say, you do not ask that question.

KABINA AND I smoke more, drink more coffee. At another camp in the distance, a bunch of German tourists join Bedouin in song.

Kabina gives me a wool blanket to sleep on. He clears away stones and lies on the rough desert floor. Within minutes he's snoring. I'm rolled up in the blanket and I'm cold. The wind has picked up since dusk. The stone retains nothing of heat. The sky is full of constellations I've never seen before. Shooting stars. Tall walls of stone mock me. I'm wide awake.

MY THOUGHTS TURN toward the house in Jerusalem. In my mind the house where Shimon lives is empty. There's no furniture, the walls are white, the windows are high and wide. I don't know the story of the house, or the story of the people inside it. It's no wonder I haven't been able to write. I'm stuck, at a dead end, in the journey and in myself. The only way to escape this cul-de-sac is invention. Shimon's, Abu Dalo's and mine.

I see the heavy stone door of the house and enter it. I close the door only to see another one open on the other side of the room. I follow it and enter this labyrinth. I go from room to room, see nothing. When I stop walking, stop demanding *forward,* I hear the sound of weeping. Is it in me, or is it out there in that darkness? No matter: beneath the confusion of faith, the clamour of nationalisms, of I-was-here-first decrees, this cry, this human longing for the sacred. A constant prayer.

I'd like to think God has left us with a choice. That we are free insofar as we can choose whether or not to act morally. In doing so we reinterpret the laws of Sinai in our current lives. We're free when we examine our actions, ask hard questions, search for the personal connection to the ancient. And this freedom is not for the sake of some ecstatic feeling, nor is it a test to see how well one follows the laws. Rather, our choice lies in the attempt to become better people, to do better unto others. And so even the people of Jerusalem must sing at the Seder:

Next Year in Jerusalem
Next year may we be free

MOSES' FORTY-YEAR WALK was a prayer, unanswered in his lifetime. In the days, he heard the cry of his people. At night, what did he hear? I hear music. A language I can almost make out. Faint, in the distance. Under the rising moon—full, Nisan—I pull out my diary. I have the urge to write in Hebrew—the first time since I was a child. *Shin.* I put my pen to the page, and it feels like the first time I've written honestly since I've been in this part of the world. *Lamed.* I don't believe in most of the synagogue prayers anymore. Don't follow the rituals. *Vav.* So what does this writing mean? It's my connection to this place. *Mem-sophit.* Binds me through the dark flames of its ancient characters. *Shalom.* The word, both a greeting and a departing, bring me peace.

IT IS ONLY NOW as an adult I begin to understand the significance of Chayim Nachman Bialik, for whom my school was named. Bialik was a poet from Odessa who moved to Tel Aviv during British Mandate Palestine. He was one of the first poets to write in modern Hebrew. He challenged the Orthodox of his time who said Hebrew was only meant for prayer. He took on his faith at the very root, the language itself. Alon Eloni would say wistfully, "How wonderful it must have been to discover the language of Jews again. To create the words that an entire nation would speak, write, read and dream in." Bialik wrote the ancient language of Moses, but he also wrote it anew.

My hand aches. I can't read what I write. But the language moves me to write more. I can just make out the lute's melody, a few faces by the fire across the way. Light flickers against the shadows. A sea of stones shimmers in the moonlight.

I put down my pen, consider what I have left to do. Will I ever really get to talk to Shimon? I close my eyes, hoping I will sleep. I do not see Jerusalem stone, nor do I see the red stone of Sinai. I smell pine forest. Feel fresh water on my skin and hair. I see Muskoka. Algonquin. Killarney. Highways cutting through Precambrian Shield. Toronto. The graffitied alleys of Kensington Market. Judith. Her pale face, pressed against the apartment window. A question.

Will you come home?

LANDING

"Exile is more than a geographical concept.
You can be an exile in your homeland, in your own house, in a room.
It's not simply a Palestinian question. Can I say I'm addicted to exile?
Maybe."

—MAHMOUD DARWISH, *A POET'S PALESTINE AS METAPHOR*

CHAPTER 31

The return to Canada is not a neat and orderly affair. I call Judith from a payphone at the Toronto airport and she promptly dumps me. Tells me she doesn't want to speak to me, I'm a drag on her spirit, an anchor stuck in her whatever. "I have to get rid of the extra weight, you know, this baggage?" she says over the phone. I'm waiting for my bags to come around on the carousel in international arrivals. "Why didn't you call for four weeks?" she asks. Before I can answer, she tells me she's tired of my questions, this search for something or other, my constant ambivalence. She waits for my response, but I don't say anything. And she hangs up the phone.

The next day I'm riding my mother's bicycle in downtown Toronto. I'm staying with her until I get back on my feet and figure out what I'm doing. I've returned without a plan, a girlfriend or a place to live. That should make me anxious, but it doesn't. As I turn west onto Dundas, I have an enormous feeling of relief when I think of the end of Judith and me, the finality. I'm also more or less thankful for the outcome of the trip: I didn't die in Qalandia refugee camp. I didn't have a Qassam land on my head, didn't meet a suicide bomber at a falafel stand. I survived Israel and Palestine.

And it feels good—to be moving my body, riding a bicycle. Spring in Toronto. I think to call Rana and tell her about the trip, but I don't know what to say. Just what did I learn over there? It's the question the traveller has upon return: Has anything actually changed?

I'm thinking this when a blue Toyota Tercel tries to overtake me and pass a streetcar on Dundas. I'm thinking this when the blue car hits my left hip and I take flight over the handlebars toward the sidewalk. I'm thinking—as time slows down, as I brace myself, helmetless, as the Chinese grocer rubs an apple on his apron—Jesus Christ, I'm going to die.

JUDITH COMES TO VISIT ME in hospital. She brings me goat-milk soap and honey-vanilla hand cream. She stands by the window while I lie in bed with a plastic bedpan, high on morphine, a broken femur pinned together by three metal screws. We say nothing, avoid each other's eyes. The ghosts of ourselves start to talk.

JUDITH: I wanted you to die.
    ME: Really?
JUDITH: Well no. I wanted you to almost die. Then for you to
           come back and say, "I love you. Let's get married and have
           a child." But you didn't. You won't.

The two ghosts stand looking at the dull Toronto sky, holding hands and mourning the end of things. Her ghost leans on my ghost's shoulder and cries. The real Jonathan and Judith: silent.

WE DO NOT GET MARRIED. We do not stand beneath a *chuppah* in the Minsk synagogue and say, yes, yes, yes. We do not sign a *ketuvah*, the rabbi watching over our shoulders, our names and families inscribed in Hebrew black ink. We do not listen to the pleas of the rabbi to continue the lineage with honour, love and commitment. There are no good wishes from the family, no *Sheva Brachot* from friends. The arguments between cousins don't exist, nor the question of who will sit at what table. There is no clinking of the glasses, no fights over what colour linen, should the wine be kosher, chicken or fish, what should the guests wear, formal, semi-formal, separate or mixed, how modern, how Orthodox—we do not negotiate these issues. I do not stand on a glass and feel it shatter beneath my foot on the Minsk's red carpet. The rabbi does not shake my hand and say, "Now you're a man." Morris doesn't arrive with schnapps and a kiss on the cheek. We are not held aloft on chairs above circling horas, our hands are not joined by a white handkerchief. There is no child in the belly, our future is not bound to the womb. We will not give birth to a nation, there's no hope for a messiah in our midst, no prophet in the house. And now, no peace between us, no dialogue, no words, not for some years at least.

IT'S FRIDAY, Mincha, and I'm back in the Minsk synagogue. I was supposed to wait for the doctors to okay my leaving the hospital, but I got restless, needed to get out of bed for an hour even. I hobbled the six or seven blocks from the Toronto Western on my brand-new aluminum crutches. Sitting at the back, I get a good look at the men.

Nothing has changed: They sing out of tune, struggle to make their prayers meaningful. I suppose I'm here to say a kind of Kaddish, to mark the passing of things. But it's more than not marrying Judith. It's my faith that's gone, or what I thought I believed that's changed.

The rabbi nods hello but doesn't approach. Is it written on my face? My trip to Israel has been a betrayal to everyone in this shul. Yankl, the Engineer, the rabbi, his kids. And to those not here: Mrs. Blintzkrieg, my grandparents, Judith. I lean back in my seat. I can feel the three new pins in my femur press against my skin. It's as though the violence hasn't left me. I'm alone at the back of the Minsk, but I'm still at the Qalandia checkpoint, pain in my ribs from where Crazy Boy whacked me. Yakov sings "Shma Yisrael, Adonai Eloheinu, Adonai Echad" and I can hear the spray of rubber bullets.

I leave the sanctuary and slowly climb down the fourteen synagogue steps. A taxi backs into a truck. The sound of metal crushing metal nearly makes me lose my footing. Anything can happen anywhere, any time. So proclaimeth the world. On the long trek through Kensington Market I think about Sam. The Arabic Western Union ad. I can still see the glossy page with the studious-looking woman counting American money.

Sam's voice: "A writer has power. You listen and make people listen."

I know I can't discover the key to peace in Israel and Palestine. But I want to do justice of some kind, and to make—or find—something of value, of which I will not be unspeakably ashamed. I want to write, and I want the writing not to be a lie.

Back in the hospital, I open up my notebook.

CHAPTER 32

Three months later and it's the day of my brother Aaron's wedding. The wedding is a Toronto-Newfoundland, Jewish-Catholic affair. It's being held an hour north of Toronto at a spiritual retreat called "Mysthaven." Young pines and birch decorate the sides of the long driveway. At the end is a twenty-metre-tall corrugated iron statue of a woman with a fetus in her belly. The fetus resembles a giant metallic porcupine. It's late-August humid, and the guests are starting to arrive. The groom is wearing an Indian prince outfit he had designed in Little India, Toronto. His robes are made of gold and white silk and come down to his ankles. His feet are adorned in traditional pointed Indian shoes, with all the glitter and sparkle fit for a king. I figure Aaron has decided to dress like an Indian prince because this is an elegance truer to his character; fuck the tux, he's saying, I want to be king for a day.

See him walk around the pond flanked by nephews and nieces, scattering pink roses at his feet. He arrives before his beloved Anne, who's dressed in an emerald-green dress splattered with silver sequins. She wears small fairy-wings on the back, a slender crown on the head. A Baptist minister conducts the ceremony. Neither Anne nor Aaron is a Baptist, but the minister is open to both their faiths, and that's what the two want: inclusion, openness, a celebration of who they are. A chuppah covers the about-to-be-weds. Beside them is a table with a giant silver cross and a silver goblet full of red wine. On it is engraved in Hebrew: *Borei pri hagafen. Blessed is the fruit of the vine.*

Vows are exchanged, speeches are made, poems and prayers recited from a hodgepodge of religions: Buddhist, Jewish, Cree, Hindu, Catholic. As the guests scatter toward the celebrations in the large field, Baba Jesse appears next to me wearing a yellow sundress and pink lipstick.

She says, "Some wedding, isn't it?"

I lean on my cane for support, having only recently started walking again. I can see she's serious. "You mean you approve?"

"Nu, they're happy with each other."

"Are you trying to tell me you don't care anymore?"

She sighs. She smells like she always does at formal occasions—strong and cheap rose-scented perfume. "Of course I care. They're in love. That's more than I could say for me and my Jewish husband." She opens her purse and offers me a piece of homemade mandelbroit wrapped in paper towel. "That's so you don't go hungry."

"Thanks Baba."

"Those Catholics don't know a thing about eating. But she's a nice girl. And he's happy. Granted, they'll have their challenges. Where will they send the kids to school? Will the son have a bris? Will the daughter have a bat mitzvah? *Genug*. These are questions for another day. Let's enjoy the simcha."

AUNTIE RACHEL won't speak to my dad, and my mother awkwardly dodges the looks of my father's girlfriend. All things considered, we seem to be getting along fairly well. Anne's family is a lot of fun. They've brought cases of Screech with them, that infamous Newfoundland rum, and shots are passed around in honour of the newlyweds. In the field a Celtic-Klezmer band strikes up; they open with "Greensleeves" and move into "Rozinkes mit Mandeln." An announcement is made inviting everyone to gather for a hora in the middle of the field.

Jacob's here with his fiancée, Claudia, and I hang with them, drinking sangria by the Ode to the Pregnant Woman statue. I haven't seen Jacob in months.

"So how was Israel?" Jacob asks.

"It was good," I say.

"I hear you were in the territories."

"Yup."

The hora—uneven circle, broken in places—spins round and round. People are having a good time. It promises to be a fun night. Shrimp cocktails on the deck, Hasidic dancing in the field.

"I saw Ruthie," I say.

"How's she doing?"

"She has a kid."

"Good for her."

The band moves into a rousing rendition of "Sunrise, Sunset." The whole thing makes the head spin. The heat, the blending cultures, the sweet sangria.

"Meet any Palestinians?"

The day is hot, the wine goes straight to the head. Jacob and I are on to our third and fourth glasses.

"I had some good experiences."

Jacob: "I don't get why the whole world sympathizes with them. I might if there was actually peaceful intent. But there's no Palestinian leader with a vision."

We're in uncomfortable territory. To be honest, I don't exactly know where Jacob stands on these issues. We never talk Israel.

Diplomatically I say, "For sure. Arafat's a corrupt bastard."

We drink to that.

Jacob says, "My question is, where are the Palestinian Gandhis?"

It's the question I asked Samer when we first met: Where are the peaceful demonstrations? But for some reason I feel compelled to not agree with Jacob. I feel the need to choose a side, so I say, "If there was a Gandhi in Palestine, the IDF would probably drop a missile on him."

Jacob flinches at my response. Another round of sangria. Jacob says, "You should read Alan Dershowitz, *The Case for Israel.* The guy has some good things to say."

"Like what?"

"Like most criticism of Israel is anti-Semitic. Sure, the country has its problems, like anywhere. But why are its actions constantly under the scrutiny of Europe and the media? Why not focus on the human rights abuses in China or Darfur? Why are so many UN resolutions taken out against Israel? Deep down, most non-Jews don't like the idea of a Jewish state."

He has a point. The boundaries between anti-Zionism and anti-Semitism are easily blurred. But does the legacy of anti-Semitism mean one shouldn't be critical at all? Does the threat of attack—real or imagined—demand absolute patriotism, unquestioned loyalty? "Look, I think it's important to be truthful. Sometimes criticism is warranted," I say.

"Your problem isn't Israel. It's Bialik. And I don't blame you. We went to an insane school. But you shouldn't let it influence your political beliefs. You resent your education," Jacob says.

"I do not."

"You're trying to get back at them."

"It's more complicated than that. You were locked in a fucking closet and you probably believe in targeted missile assassinations."

"I was not locked in a closet."

"Sure you were. Mrs. Blintzkrieg. Grade Five."

"We weren't even in the same class that year."

"Of course we were."

"I *liked* Bialik."

"You hated it. You dropped out when you were twelve."

"I found it challenging."

"You were a hyperactive shit who couldn't sit still and read."

"What's your point?" he says.

I pause for a sip of wine. I don't know where I'm going with this. I look around to see if anyone's listening. I'd actually forgotten I was at my brother's wedding. Fortunately, nobody's paying attention. "My point is there's more to it than Bialik. Sure, it screwed with the way we look at things. But what school doesn't fuck with kids' heads? What I mean is, we're guilty too."

"Of what?"

"Of not asking questions."

Jacob shifts on his feet. It's strange. We spent God knows how many hours studying the country, but not once have we voiced our thoughts to each other on the matter. "I believe in giving the Palestinians a state," he says, "but they have to earn it."

"You don't earn a right to exist."

"They're never willing to make peace."

"Neither are we."

"From the beginning they hated us."

"We came to their country and said, 'This is our land.' Did you expect them to put down their guns and hug us?"

"Are you saying you don't think there should be an Israel?"

"I'm not saying that. But get out of the territories. Give them their own country. Otherwise it's going to turn into South Africa."

"Give me a break."

"Ghettos. Townships."

"Shut the fuck up."

"Maybe when Israelis start building concentration camps we can say the Palestinians have earned their right to a country."

I have no control over what I'm saying. The words no longer belong to me. But the argument goes no further. Jacob lands a jab on my shoulder and I lay into his body. We're in Grade Five again, boxing in the basement of my parents' house. All the booze and strangeness of the day is mixing in with our punches. Jacob releases hard and heavy on me. Joseph and Claudia are there to break us up.

"Don't say that shit, man," Jacob says.

"You're an idiot," I say.

Joseph separates us, makes us shake hands. Claudia insists there'll be no more talk about the Middle East for the rest of the night. I look at Jacob sheepishly. We're out of breath the same way we are after a game of one-on-one. In a way I was better off before I went to Israel. I was more diplomatic, willing to hold my tongue.

Fortunately Jacob and I are able to move on. After a couple of drinks, we're swapping jokes again. Stories about what other friends from university are up to. Remembering the time we were caught stoned in Jacob's mother's living room, the time we locked Mr. Silverberg in a closet, when Mr. Heathcliffe came to class drunk and flirted with the fourteen-year-old girls. Jacob and I have so much history together that we're able to resist getting locked into one way of talking. In a way it's just like when we were kids: We can forget the fighting and move on as though nothing happened. Or else we know better now, the argument goes nowhere, so why not shut up?

I look out to the field. In the centre of the hora, Anne's stepfather is leading the Newfoundland tradition of "kissing the cod." People are told to kiss a fish, then given a shot of Screech to complete the ritual. Outside the cod kissing, people continue to dance the hora. Another shot, another drink. The music is sounding better and better.

"What song is that?" I ask.

"Oyfn pripitchik."

"Right. My baba used to sing that to me to put me to sleep."

Jacob says, "That's the one about the rabbi teaching his kids the *Aleph-Bet*."

"And whacking them on the head with a stick when they don't get it right," I add.

"Shit, going to Bialik was like living on another planet."

"Sometimes I still feel like I live there."

"That sounds like hell."

"No," I say. "It's just who I am. I mean, I'm glad I went there."

Jacob looks at me, incredulous. "You're confusing as shit."

"And you're a bloody schoolteacher."

Jacob slaps me playfully on the shoulder, like he's ready for another round of ball.

"Let's dance," I say.

"With your hip?"

"We'll go slow."

Jacob takes me by the elbow and guides me to the circle. He grabs my free hand and the circle sweeps us up. The violinist riffs a number, the clarinet follows not far behind and the accordion moves us along. What's that song? It's on the tip of my memory.

CHAPTER 33

It's been four years since Rana and I first met. Now she's here in my flat, considering it for a sublet. I live in the Portuguese part of Toronto and I want to visit Israel again, among other places. Rana needs a place to live while she's in school.

Rana surveys the space. The "Visit Palestine" poster hangs framed in the centre of the living room. I have an extensive collection of literature from the Middle East: Yehuda Amichai, Mahmoud Darwish, David Grossman, Samih al-Qasim. She flips through the Edward Said reader.

"It would be nice to live here, just to read the books," she says.

I finally ask Rana a question that's been bugging me for years: "Why don't you wear a hijab anymore?"

"I never wore one."

"When I met you at the film you did."

"That was my friend Mary."

"Are you sure?" She looks at me like I'm crazy. "Didn't your husband make you?"

Rana laughs. "Of course not. He was orthodox, but he let me do what I wanted. He was cool like that."

I could've sworn she had one at the film. Then again, she does look different from when we first met. Less of a cliché, no longer the exotic from the Orient. She's become a friend.

We move to the kitchen and I put on water for tea. She tells me about her recent separation. It hasn't been easy; her ex is a lawyer, and he's throwing the book at her. In the meantime, she has plans. She's finishing her bachelor of social work and has a summer placement in Ghana. She'd been offered to work in the West Bank but chose Africa instead. She doesn't have a need to go back to Palestine, she says; she wants to create a new life. Rana also confesses she's told her mother about the split, but hasn't told her father yet. "He's become more and more religious since the second intifada and he isn't going to like it. We had a very traditional wedding, you know. The whole village came."

We sit down at the kitchen table and wait for the water to boil.

"I'd like to see your village," I say.

"Why? It's ugly. There's nothing there."

"I'd like to see where you come from. My work in Israel isn't finished."

Rana seems to wince when I say the word "Israel." There are still many things we do not talk about. The fact she calls the country she comes from "Palestine," and I insist on calling it "Israel." Why it says on her passport under country of origin, "Jerusalem." What our core beliefs are.

"Sorry," I say.

"For what?"

"The mess."

It's embarrassing. Dishes are piled high in the sink; pyramids of clothes in my bedroom; archipelagos of books and papers in the hallway and living room.

She says, "I don't mind it too much. You seem relaxed. In a domestic sort of way."

The kettle whistles. I take out a bag of loose mint tea and dump a spoonful in a cast iron teapot. Rana is down the hallway scanning the bookshelves.

"Can you afford it?" I ask.

"With a student loan, anything's possible."

She picks out a book. It's Alan Dershowitz, *The Case for Israel.* She flips through it.

"Do you like this?" she asks.

"Not exactly," I say. I had decided, following my fight with Jacob at the wedding, to buy a copy of the book and at least see what he was talking about.

"It's funny, I actually have no idea what you think about Palestine. You've always been very quiet about it," Rana says.

"That's because I haven't known enough to say anything."

"And now?"

"I know a bit more."

I pour Rana a small glass of mint tea.

"So when are you going back?" she asks.

"December."

Rana pulls out a pack of cigarettes and offers me one. I decline. Since the accident, doctors have made sure I stay far away from the stuff. "Should I smoke outside?"

"It's fine," I say.

"You shouldn't let me."

"I like second-hand smoke. It reminds me of Jerusalem."

She lights up. We quietly sip our tea. "What will you do there?"

"I want to find people who build."

"You mean houses?"

"No, I mean better relations with each other."

"Radicals, you mean." We both laugh.

"There's also someone I need to talk to. An interview I didn't get to finish the last time."

Rana puts out the cigarette halfway through. She isn't enjoying it. "You know, it's bullshit what I said. I should go back, even just for a visit. I need to see my parents again. I really miss my family. And it might be kind of interesting to see some of the country with you. It could be part of this building, as you say."

I've made plans for my return trip in the coming months. Recently I contacted Zochrot and the Oasis of Peace, two groups in Israel focused on reconciliation and peace. Rana tells me that no friends of hers in Canada have ever expressed interest in seeing where she came from. And no Jews—Israeli or otherwise—have visited her town either. They were all too afraid. I'd like to think I'm not.

RETURN

"Forget your perfect offering."
—LEONARD COHEN, "ANTHEM"

CHAPTER 34

The old Palestinian railroad tracks run toward Beit Safafa. My feet clank against the rusted tracks, the rhythm of my thoughts. It occurs to me again and again: This obsession is ridiculous. I've travelled six thousand miles to talk to some crotchety old man who kicked me off his property three years ago. Why do I give a shit? Why do I cling to this idea of the house? These strangers, their lives, a land that isn't mine.

The truth is, I don't really want to be back here. But after the accident I made a promise to myself that I'd return and try to fix things. My fight with Jacob at the wedding confirmed this need. I can't help but think my first trip to Israel and Palestine was a failure. I got angry, became polarized, knocked off-balance. Qalandia, Crazy Boy, the gunfire—it turned me adolescent, blind with anger at this country, with my teachers too.

To return is to yearn for something hopeful, not to give in to the despair I left with the last time. In the interim years I have not gone and dissed my Jewish faith (I can't get rid of God). I cling to the belief that Judaism has some good to fulfill in the world. The ancient notion of the Jew acting as moral witness and priest is more and more relevant given the current fucked-upness of the twenty-first century. What's left of my Jewishness is grounded in the message of the Zohar, tikkun olam: *Let us work to mend our brokenness, hallelujah.*

In the years since I was last in Israel, I wrote the play, but the story of that house was a fiction, my invention. I've come back to Jerusalem in part because I want to hear the full story, add Shimon's version to what I already know.

AS FAR AS I CAN TELL, little has changed, though the landscape isn't quite as I remember it. The shopping mall seems closer now. And the road that goes by the house is paved—wasn't it gravel last time? There's trash on both sides of the tracks: rusted mattresses, empty bottles, useless chairs. Still, there's something unusual about the surroundings. Open space juxtaposed with a roughness to things. Stones, silence, lawns filled with rubble. Behind the house of Mary there's a small cluster of olive trees. A dog sleeps tied to a metal post. I've written Shimon a letter to ask him to meet with me, prepare him. I clutch the letter in my pocket. The plan is to put it inside Shimon's mailbox, which hangs unfortunately close to his front door, meaning I'll have to unlatch the gate and go inside.

Shimon sits on the front porch. His face is smooth and he smokes a cigarette. He seems less frail than I remember, rests his elbows on his lap, draws his free hand through a full head of white hair. I try to hang back behind the jasmine trees but it's too late. He's seen me.

"Can I help you?" he says.

"Who, me?"

"No, I'm talking to the lamppost. But since the lamppost isn't answering my questions, maybe you can tell me, what the hell do you want?"

"Do you live here?" I ask.

"Yes, Einstein. I live here."

"Well ... I'm working on something about houses in Jerusalem." I can barely catch my breath, let alone get any words out of my mouth. "Your house. It's very beautiful."

"My house? It's nothing."

"It's old, isn't it?" I come out from behind the jasmine and into full view of the porch. "What year would you say it was built?"

He rises, smoke streaming up his face. He wears a white apron blackened from oil and grease. There are different vegetables—faded carrots and eggplant—printed into the cloth. He wipes his hands and points at the columns. "This was probably built in the early 1900s."

"Do you know who built it?" I ask.

"Who else? An Arab," he says, flicking the stone with his finger.

An Arab? So he agrees with Abu Dalo?

"Sure, an Arab built it. You can tell by the columns. I'd say they're the nicest thing about the house. Minus the seashells." He points to the front porch where rows of shells have been inlaid into the stone. Shimon winks at me. "I did that myself. The shells are from Morocco. So, you want to come up for a coffee?" He asks this like we're old friends.

"Sure," I say. "That'd be great."

I open the latch of the gate, walk up the stairs and sit next to Shimon.

He smokes Time cigarettes and offers me one. I say yes. Somehow it feels appropriate in spite of the doctor's orders. I'm willing to sacrifice my diabetes and left hip for this conversation.

"Shimon Dayan's the name."

"Are you related to Moshe?"

"No!" He calls me *motik*, Hebrew for sweetie. "Moshe, he had one eye," he says, and makes his hand like a patch. "Shimon, he has two." Poof. He can see. He laughs, his cackle hoarse from years of smoking.

"How long have you lived here?"

"What do you want to know this for?"

"Like I said, I'm interested—"

"He's interested, of course, everyone's interested. First, go to *Ulpan* class and brush up on your Hebrew. Where did you study?"

I tell him.

"I have a cousin in Montreal. Do you know him?"

"What's his name?"

"Cheap-son-of-a-bitch. When I went to visit him, he insisted I get a hotel. Paid for it myself!" And he holds his hands up to the sky like a prayer. The prayer turns into a question—open palms to show he has no money. "What can you do? A man dies, rich or poor. You like to drink?"

"You mean—booze?"

"Shhh!" He looks left and right to make sure no one's listening. "Homemade juice," he says with a wink. "Grapes from Hebron. It's not French, but it's not toilet water either."

He leads me slowly through his garden, pointing out the ceiba, the eucalyptus and the jasmine. We disappear into the shed where I first saw him three years ago. Inside is a clutter of tools, wires and glass. A single light bulb dangles from the ceiling. He holds two wires together and asks me to touch the metal they're connected to. Heat rises from the surface. I can feel the current going through me, I think.

"Electricity. It's beautiful, isn't it?" he says. "I'm building a hot plate. For Shabbat."

He can turn it on, Sabbath eve, and leave it on until the next evening without having to break any laws. From the corner he removes a large glass carboy, murky inside and dusty on the edges. He pours purple into two small glasses. The wine is sweet, too sweet, but I drink it anyway.

I ask, "Do you like living in Jerusalem?"

"Nah, I hate this place."

"Really?"

"Paris. Now that's a city."

"So you speak French?"

"I'm from Morocco, motik. Meknes. I was born French."

We leave the shed with our wine and step into the warm December day. Shimon insists we shift to the greater language, and by the second or third glass, it's possible, it's not too bad; I make do with my Grade Ten French.

"So how did you end up here?" I ask.

"I'm a Jew, what can I say? I ended up here. Came in '48. There wasn't anything. No electricity, no water. Nothing but this house." He points at the apartment buildings of Qatamon in the distance, resting on low hills, and the houses around us. He tells me that the area behind us toward David Ketter's house was a huge refugee camp. "Fifty thousand Jews lived in tents waiting for somewhere to live. It was terrible."

"Did you live in the camp?"

"Why do you want to talk about the camp? Drink your wine, please, and stop asking questions."

It's all I can do to get a straight answer out of Shimon. He'd rather drink wine and smoke cigarettes than talk about the past. Meanwhile, I'm starting to get tipsy. It's not even noon. We move back to the porch and sit in the sun.

"What do you know about that house?" I say, pointing across the street to the door where Mary greeted me three years ago, the second house owned by the Abu Dalos.

"It's owned by an Arab."

"What's his name?"

"Who cares what his name is? He owns the house." He lights a cigarette off his last one. Pours a healthy glass of wine and drains half of it in a single gulp. "In Meknes, we lived in a palace until my father died. Why did we come to Israel? Because the Jewish Agency promised there'd be work here. A home, too. 'The Promised Land,' they said. Never have I heard such a backward phrase. Not a day goes by I don't miss that place, motik. The Arabs in Morocco," he says, and frames this idea in his hands, "are good. Do you know what a good Arab in Israel is?"

"No."

"A dead one. Motik, don't look surprised. Of course, I used to be friends with Ibrahim Abu Dalo, that old mutt. He loved me. He'd sit down right here like you are now. We were friends."

"What happened?"

Shimon tells me the Abu Dalos left for Beit Safafa during the '48 War. While Abu Dalo told me they were away for only a week, Shimon presents a slightly different story: It was well over a year before the Abu Dalos returned to find Shimon and three other Jewish families living in the house (Shimon himself didn't move in until March 1949. He lived there with his mother and two sisters). The families were immigrants from Morocco; the Jewish Agency had rented them the house.

"One family in each room," he says. "We were cramped as hell."

"Where did Ibrahim live?"

He points across to Mary's. "When they returned, they built that house."

"And he built this one too?"

"Yes, he was a good builder."

"And you got along—even though you were living in his house?"

"Sure, why not? We won the war, the Arabs fled and we took their houses. That's history, right?"

"Right."

"Only Ibrahim returned. He was a stubborn man. Every month he'd go to the military and tell them this was his," Shimon says, pointing at the earth beneath his feet. "Then, one day, after five or six years, the state said, okay, you can have the land back. And they gave the house back to him."

"Did that bother you?"

"Why should it bother me? I pay rent to the state or I pay rent to Ibrahim. I don't want a war. I want a house."

Ibrahim went from being a good friend to a dog in the 1970s, when he decided he wanted to kick Shimon out and turn the house into a medical clinic for his doctor son. Shimon said he was willing to leave if they provided him with another home. They found one for him, a dive of a place in nearby Qatamon, but Shimon wouldn't take it. He demanded the house be as nice as the one he lived in. Ibrahim took him to court, but Shimon won since he was considered a protected tenant. After all, he'd been living there for twenty-five years.

"Ibrahim was pissed. Oh, was he mad! Then that Arab dog wouldn't take rent from me anymore. Fine, see if I care. I'm happy not to pay."

"But why wouldn't he take your rent? He owned the house."

Shimon's eyes suddenly darken. The early morning booze, the unusually warm December day, the memories—they all mix together, drive him to anger. "I built the kitchen. The garden. The shed. Sixty years I lived here. Tell me. Is this his?"

I don't know what to say. I didn't mean to piss Shimon off. I just assumed it was understood—didn't he just say that Ibrahim built the house himself and the state gave it back to him?

"You're him now! You're Ibrahim!"

Shimon stares at me menacingly. My first instinct is to flee, but I do my best to meet his gaze. Part of me believes Shimon should've said, "No, I will not take the house of a refugee. It's not right." Shimon did not do this. On the other hand, he was likely not told the whole story by the Jewish Agency. He might've let himself believe their mantra as I did: "The Arabs fled, they don't want to come back." It's not as simple as his coming here and kicking out the Abu Dalo family. He was brought to Israel by a government hungry to populate its land with Jews, to fulfill an ideology he didn't even believe in. Now Shimon's lived here for over half a century. Does he not have some legitimate claim on the house?

Shimon takes two cigarettes from his pack and offers me one. I gladly accept. He lights us both and the look in his eyes vanishes.

"Why are we talking Arabs? I want to talk Paris." He clinks my glass, winks at me, takes back another gulp of sweet wine. "When

I came here, I hated it," he says. "There wasn't anything to eat—no meat, no fruit, no vegetables—only olive oil. I hate olive oil. So I left. 1951. I moved to Montmartre."

"Montmartre?"

"Three years, motik. Best time of my life."

"Why'd you come back?"

Shimon drops his head to his chest and slumps back in his chair. He seems to be slightly drunk. "My mother was alone with my two sisters," he says, holding up three fingers. "We weren't Zionists. She just wanted a home. A chance to live. And I had to help her. You want to know what a house in Jerusalem is? I'll show you."

He gets up and shows me small holes in the house: bullets here. And here. And here. From 1948. Evidence in the metal shutters, the outer brick too.

"Who shot the bullets?" I ask.

"The guns did, my child," he says, offering me another cigarette. "Who do you think, motik? We all did. It was a war." He draws his hand tenderly across the pockmarked brick.

THE BOOZE HITS ME hard. It spikes me, blood sugar high. I have to piss like hell. I tell Shimon I have to go inside the house to use the toilet. I knock on the front door to make sure I'm not disturbing anyone, and the door swings open, welcomes me in.

The first thing I notice is the floor. It's straight and smooth, the surface original. A pale green arabesque spirals around the centre. Yellow squares punctuate the outside of the circle. I feel like I'm being hypnotized by the floor pattern. This house is from another time and it takes me there, somewhere else, a history I don't know. The ceiling is high and the walls are cold stone. A large oak table stands in the centre of the room, spread with a white tablecloth. Two candlesticks, a challah and a silver goblet are laid out for tonight's Shabbat dinner.

I've had too much to drink, and I can taste the stale tobacco on my breath. I touch my cheeks, stare at my image in the mirror.

"So what do you think?" I hear a woman's voice say from behind. I turn around but no one's there.

"What do I think about what?" I say to no one.

"About me, idiot. What do you think about me?"

"Who?" I step out of the bathroom. A cheesy wall hanging depicts a scene from Renaissance Italy. Beside that, pictures from Shimon's life. A child in Morocco. A young man in the army. At forty, he wears a black suit and loose tie, stumbling party-drunk.

"You're staring at me," says the voice.

"I'm looking at a wall."

"The wall, the floor, the pretty archways."

"You mean the house."

"Bing-o."

"I'm talking to ... *the* house?"

"Yup."

"That's weird."

"I'd say it's normal. Shimon speaks to me. Abu Dalo does too."

"Oh." I scratch my head. I really don't know what to say. After all, I hadn't even expected to talk to Shimon today. I certainly didn't imagine I'd be talking to a house. I scramble through my brain as though it was a desk full of papers and I'm searching for the right one.

"I want to know what you think about me," she says.

"You're, um, unusual."

"So?"

"The unusual gives me hope. I mean, Barak was wrong. You are peace."

"Go on."

"Okay, it's not perfect here. Abu Dalo and Shimon hate each other. They both think the other is evil and wrong. But peace isn't love, nor is it happiness. It means not killing your fucking neighbour."

I put down my half-empty glass of wine, pour myself some water instead. I'm kind of wishing the house would take over and say something—who she really belongs to, who she prefers—a clue, anything. But the house doesn't give answers. She only asks questions.

"What do you want from me?" she asks.

I say this without thinking, "I want you to speak to Mrs. Blintzkrieg. I need you to make her shut up."

It sounds ridiculous, but in the years since I was in Israel, Mrs. Blintzkrieg's voice has been pestering me. The more I question what I learned as a child, the louder Blintzkrieg's commentary becomes. Sometimes I even think I see her: at the theatre, a jazz concert, a café.

"Blintzkrieg can't be shut up," says the house. "You have to figure out how to talk to her."

The house is likely right. But how do I talk to Blintzkrieg? I'm thirty-three years old and still I'm terrified of her twenty years after the fact. She's always there to remind me, taunt me, ridicule me for all I don't know. Suddenly I'm incredibly tired. I sit down on the couch. It feels as if the house sits next to me, as if a house could stand and sit. Something pats me on the head. It's soothing, and I feel more restful than I have in years. I lie back and fall fast asleep.

I WAKE UP to the sound of voices. Looking at the clock, I try to remember what time it was when I came in to use the toilet. I step onto the front porch and Shimon's there with his wife, Dina, and daughter Niri. They make fun of me, ask if I've had a good nap. Shimon talks to me like a zaida; he invites me to join him for Shabbat services in the shul. Dina insists I stay for dinner, there'll be couscous, figs and lamb—delicious. I thank them, tell them I have plans to meet a friend in Tel Aviv, but it's not without regret: I like Shimon. I'd like to spend the Sabbath in his home.

"Come back any time," he says.

Before I leave the area, I drop by Abu Dalo's house. I buzz him from outside the gate and his wife answers. "Is Abu Dalo there?"

"Go away," she says. She doesn't even ask who it is. I figure I'll try my luck another day. But the gate opens, and it's him, Hassan Abu Dalo, hands covered in glue.

"What do you want?" he asks.

"Do you remember me?"

"Do you have it?"

"Have what?"

"Richard Gere."

I tell him yes, the play's almost finished, but I have a few more questions first.

"Come back another time. I'm working." I try to press him for a date, a time, something. "Call me," he says, and he slams the iron gate shut. I don't have his phone number.

ON THE MICROBUS to Tel Aviv I try to make sense of things, sober up. Staring out at the highway, I see a river of cars rushing to get home before nightfall. Their hum and throttle lull me into thought. What is the house? On the one hand, it's completely normal. People live there, try to make the most of what they have. Shimon is old, cranky (and slightly drunk). He squabbles with his wife of sixty years. He has his pictures, bottles of hidden booze, a treasure chest with artifacts valuable only to himself.

But the house is also an exception. It's a blip in Israel's history. Abu Dalo, Ketter and Shimon actually agree: They all said that not one other Palestinian family remains in the area of Qatamon and Mekor Chayim. The Abu Dalos fled to Beit Safafa and returned—and the government gave them their land back. Why? Has this happened elsewhere in Israel? I'd like to find out.

This question takes me to Tel Aviv, to Eytan Bronstein, Israeli Jew, leader of the group Zochrot, "remembering." I'd been in touch with him by email before I set out on this trip. He's one of those "builders" I wanted to talk to before I left. I want to ask him about his work, to hear his vision for peace. I'm also hoping he might help me make sense of this house.

CHAPTER 35

The story of Eytan starts in Canada Park; he made a sign that said, "Welcome to the Village Centre." He laminated it and posted it where the village of Yalu once was. The sign provided details of Yalu's population, the number of mosques and schools that had been there, and where the people live now. Eytan then put up two other signs to commemorate Yalu and Imwas cemeteries. He left some pamphlets behind with his phone number too.

A few days later the signs were torn down, and Eytan received a phone call from someone at the JNF. The man asked Eytan why he had put up the signs. Eytan explained that he was trying to tell people what had been there. The man told Eytan the signs were illegal. Eytan said, "So what? They're only signs." The JNF man was concerned because Eytan's signs were political, and the JNF does not like to get involved in political matters. Eytan wondered how putting benches, hiking trails and water fountains on top of the ruins of a former Palestinian village was not considered political, whereas a sign explaining where a cemetery used to be was. The JNF man said that if Eytan wanted to put up a sign, he'd have to get permission.

Eytan did just that. Eventually his request ended up in the Supreme Court. After a year of proceedings Eytan won the case, and the JNF agreed to put up a sign in Canada Park saying: "Two thousand people lived in the village of Imwas and one thousand seven hundred in Yalu. Today they live in Jordan and Ramallah." There was no mention that in the Six Day War, under the command of Yitzhak Rabin, the Israeli army demolished three Palestinian villages at that location, even though the villagers had not put up any resistance. There wasn't a peep about the villagers marched off at gunpoint, pointed to Ramallah and beyond. And there wasn't a word about the fact that on top of the razed villages, using money from wealthy Canadian donors, mostly from Toronto, the JNF planted Canada Park. Still. Eytan felt vindicated: He'd won the right to put up the sign legally. And he didn't stop there. With his new-found organization, Zochrot, he put up signs wherever Palestinian villages had been destroyed, disappeared.

NOT FAR from Yitzhak Rabin Square in Tel Aviv is the small and cramped Zochrot office. Eytan reminds me of Jacob. His handshake is firm and he looks me in the eyes. He's broad shouldered and has a buzz cut; he's more like a soldier than the waif of a peacenik I was expecting.

Our conversation begins formally. I feel like I'm getting the Zochrot website spiel except for a new detail: Of the two signs the high court ordered the JNF to put up—bolted into the ground, Eytan says—one of them was mysteriously removed. The other was spray-painted over where it mentions the names of the Palestinian villages. (The sign also mentions that the site was the location of Ottoman, Roman and Byzantine villages. These details were not blacked out.) Eytan says, "You see how this history is very relevant to many Jews in Israel. It *affects* people. These signs are powerful."

When Eytan asks me why I'm interested, I tell him I remember Canada Park from when I was a child. This catches him off guard. "What do you mean?" he asks. I explain to him Canada Park was the pride of Bialik. *Look at what your money can do,* was the message from the teachers. *It can turn desert into a lovely picnic spot. The calm of Canada in the wildness of Eretz Yisrael.*

Eytan is surprised. "You mean you actually know this place?"

"I've never been. But I saw pictures."

"So you're ... wow. You remember this from school?"

He looks at me with a kind of shock, as though to say, "We have a kind of relationship, you and I, don't we?" Or: "You exist—you Diaspora Jews—and you have a role in this story too, do you understand?" Instead he says: "This is very interesting. Perhaps, after we talk, you can help me with something."

THE ONGOING DEBATE surrounding Canada Park takes Eytan into the why of his story: what made him want to start Zochrot in the first place. Eytan had an education similar to mine. He was taught that 1948 was a miraculous victory, seven Arab countries attacked Israel and Israel somehow emerged victorious. While there is truth in that narrative, the other side of the story is absent: the refugees. If they're even mentioned, Palestinians fled because neighbouring Arab leaders told them to leave the country in preparation for their onslaught of the Jewish people. In other words, Israel had no role in the Palestinian exile, the dispossession and exodus of over seven hundred thousand people. Eytan says, "The Nakba is the other side of the coin. The death of Palestine is as much the truth as the birth of Israel. And we Israelis played a big role in that death. In this way it is an essential part of Israeli and Jewish consciousness today."

Eytan's vision is more than laying blame. He wants to change what Israelis and Jews learn. Bialik ingrained stereotypes, made me fear what I didn't know. But Eytan is arguing for another possibility. He's saying that education can reach across barriers, encourage us to see another point of view. Empathy.

Eytan says that Zochrot's mandate is not only to re-educate Israelis. "I'm interested in the construction of landscape. Canada Park is interesting because it is one of the most violent examples of how we alter the landscape here. Today many Israelis visit the park.

It's a very beautiful place, they barbecue there and so on. But it's not only a recreation place. There are many signs telling the different histories. You have impressive plaques telling the Jewish, Roman or Byzantine history, but there is nothing about the hundreds of years of Palestinian life. If you look a bit beneath the surface, you'll see the ruins in the forest. There's a cemetery with graves marked in Arabic." For Eytan, putting up that first sign was a way of resisting the historical narrative he was taught.

I wonder how many people in Israel support this. Really, who wants to deal with the ugly legacies of his or her country? Are there signs all over North America saying which indigenous people used to live where? It's much more convenient to say, "The past is the past. Let it rest. Today is hard enough." The problem in Israel becomes even more complicated since the history itself is disputed. There is no consensus on the Israeli role in the Nakba. While "New Historians" like Benny Morris and Ilan Pappe have written extensively about Israel's role in massacres like Deir Yassin and Dawayima, many Israelis and Jews have a hard time seeing themselves as anything but victims. History has ingrained it in our heads: Hatred of the Chosen exists forever in the Gentile psyche.

Eytan tells me it's still a big taboo for Israelis to talk about the Nakba. And yet people are deeply moved by it. How else to explain the erasing of the plaque at Canada Park? He also tells me that more and more Israelis are coming out to Zochrot events. "They don't go with us all the way ideologically, but they are very much interested in knowing what happened. Just like you didn't know, and are interested in knowing, many of us don't know what happened here." He points out his window to the north. "Not five hundred metres away, you can walk and see the ruins of a Palestinian village. It's off Ibn Gvirol on the corner of Arlozorov street. It's called Sumol. You go up a staircase, above the sidewalk, and you find yourself suddenly in a village. You know it's not a modern city with buildings like these. But who knows this? The Zionist attitude has been to erase this history. Zochrot is a way to start something new here—through stories—through memories. For Palestinians and for Israelis. I think this process is important. We become better people, and we promote peace."

I agree that saying "Yes, Israel helped cause a refugee problem" is important in terms of creating an understanding between Israelis and Palestinians. But it doesn't exactly settle the score. There are real land issues here. Hundreds and thousands of people were displaced from their homes and they and their descendants want them back. The yearning hasn't disappeared; it's blazing inside the refugee camps of Qalandia, Jabalya and Jenin. "What do you do about that?" I ask.

Eytan says, "They need to be able to move back to their homes."

"But there's over four million refugees. You're living in their houses."

"They won't all come back. But they should have the right to. Isn't that the just thing?" In other words, Eytan believes Palestinians should have the right to return.

The right of return is based on UN Resolution 194, which declares that any Palestinian refugee and his or her descendants has the right to return to land they lost in the 1948 War. The resolution also states that if their land's been destroyed, they have the right to be recompensed. The right of return is one of the major obstacles to peace in the Middle East; it's one of the main reasons Arafat turned down Ehud Barak's offer in 2000. For most Israelis, letting the Palestinians come back to their homes isn't an option. Not for Eytan.

"When we began Zochrot, we said our position was we want to know the Nakba, to speak about it, and we want to have a good debate about the refugee issue. But once we heard the stories from the refugees themselves it became very difficult not to develop a stronger stance. Especially in the case of internal refugees." Eytan reminds me that internal refugees remained within the borders of Israel after its founding, and are thus considered Israeli citizens, but they were considered absent by the state. They were, in the doublespeak of the day, "present absentees." Their land, like that of other absentees, was taken by the state. Today twenty-five percent of Palestinians living in Israel are internal refugees. Eytan argues: "What's the problem of their return if they're already in the country? This whole idea—that letting Palestinians return is a mistake because they will drive us into the sea—is a myth. Why not let them return to their land if they're already here?"

It's clear to me why Palestinians can't return. It's the line I've always heard and believed in: Israel will lose its Jewish character if there aren't mostly Jews living in it. It makes sense. Tired of being a persecuted minority, nearly exterminated time and again, we wanted our own country, to be the masters of our fate. But Eytan does have a strong point. Importing Jews from Siberia and Assam to combat a rising Palestinian birth rate seems, well, completely bizarre and unnatural. While millions of people are in refugee camps literally dying to get back to their homes, I can get full Israeli citizenship—even get a one-way ticket from Canada paid for—with the drop of a hat.

"Has anyone ever been allowed to return?" I ask.

"Over fifty years ago, in Ikrit and Biram [two towns in the Galilee], the courts said the residents could go back to their properties. But the military never allowed them to for 'reasons of security.' Today the government still won't let them back. But everyone knows the court's afraid of setting a legal precedent. If they're let back, then what about the others?"

"So no one has successfully returned?"

"Not as far as I know," Eytan says.

I shift in my seat. Now's as good a time as any to tell him. "I think I might know of one case," I say.

And I tell him the story of Abu Dalo, Shimon and the house.

When I tell him the story of not having the address, of Ketter, of wandering through fields and over the railway tracks, Eytan says: "We are not in a real world here." He flicks the end of his pen against the desk. "So basically, what you're saying is the state took the land away from Abu Dalo, then agreed to give it back?"

"Yes.

"What you are saying is a perfect example of the right of return."

BEFORE I LEAVE the office, I promise Eytan to take him to see the house so he can interview and record the stories of Abu Dalo and Shimon. As I'm getting up to leave, he asks me for one more favour: Am I willing to help him write a letter to the donors to Canada Park to tell them how their money was spent? He hands me a piece of paper with a list of names on it. Immediately I feel queasy, that I might black out. Out of the corner of my eye I notice a short older woman sitting on a chair behind me. She wasn't there before. I turn around to look and it's Mrs. Blintzkrieg. Her hair is dyed black. There are dark rings under her eyes.

MRS. BLINTZKRIEG: Shalom. You don't look so good.

ME: I recognize these names. They were my neighbours.

MRS. B.: Exactly. You criticize your neighbours. For what?

ME: Their money planted trees on top of a Muslim cemetery.

MRS. B.: Have you gone to the cemetery? Have you seen it for yourself?

ME: No.

MRS. B.: Don't jump to easy conclusions.

ME: Shouldn't people know where their money is going?

MRS. B.: Who are you, Cat Stevens? There was a war, and there was a losing side. Fortunately it wasn't us.

ME: They were civilians, not soldiers.

MRS. B.: You're talking like this because you're about to
meet your Palestinian friend.

ME: No.

MRS. B.: You need to impress her. Very predictable,
Garfinkel. Fine. Write the letter. Teach us the
errors of our ways. Self-hating Jew.

"I only came here to learn," I want to say to Eytan, as he busily
searches through his email to show me a rough draft of the letter. I
want to say: "Maybe you should find someone else for the job. Really,
I'm not a protester like you." I catch myself in the reflection of the
computer screen, framed in beige plastic. Think: How far am I
willing to go for a belief? And does an idea mean anything if one does
nothing with it? I can feel Mrs. Blintzkrieg's eyes on my back but
when I turn around to put on my coat, she is no longer there.

CHAPTER 36

I must've gotten lost four times on the way here. There are signs for Tiberius, Nazareth, Haifa, Akko, but not a single sign indicating where this town is until you actually reach it. By the time you see the word *Tamra* scrawled in Hebrew, you have to make a crazy move on a hairpin curve just to make the turn off without flipping into oncoming traffic.

I'm jazzed up on coffee and highway adrenalin: a necessary antidote to the hangover from Shimon's syrupy wine. It's eight at night, Shabbos eve, the first night of Chanukah, and I'm in a dilapidated gas station. I haven't seen Rana in months, kiss her formally on both cheeks. Rana's father smokes next to the pumps, hands in the pockets of his blue Milano football hoodie. He watches me attentively.

"Welcome to Tamra," he says to me in Hebrew. He shakes my hand firmly, looks me in the eye. "Follow me."

I'm nervous but tell myself this should be fine. After all, I've been to Ramallah and Qalandia refugee camp; Tamra is not the West Bank. There are no checkpoints to cross, no military inspections to worry about. And yet to set foot in Tamra is to enter another world. Here the roads are rough, the streetlights dim. From the darkness a voice bellows the call to prayer.

Nerves aside, I'm excited. I get to meet Rana and her family. I want to understand more of her perspective. What's made her the person she is today? What's life like for Palestinians living in Israel—and what hope do they have, if anything, for peace?

Things are going okay, I think. I mean, she and her father met me at the entrance to their town. That's the famous Arab hospitality one always hears about. However, I soon realize there's a more practical reason for our convergence beneath fluorescent lights and benzine. The roads of Tamra have no street signs, and there are no numbers on the houses either. Rana explains the layout of the Palestinian-Muslim town as we drive through the dilapidated streets. Things are a bit complicated due to the town planning, or rather, the impossibility of it.

She tells me that in '48 Tamra had two or three thousand people. When the Israelis destroyed many of the neighbouring villages, thousands of refugees came here. Now a third of the town comprises internal refugees; the total population is over twenty-five thousand and growing. Because of the difficulty Palestinians have in acquiring land in Israel, people are forced to build on top of and beside each other, often illegally.

The main street's barely lit so it's hard to see much. We turn right up an unmarked pitch-black road and follow the steep incline, up, up, up. At the top of the hill, Rana tells me to park. Light spills out from inside a house, and the sound of people talking comes from that light.

RANA'S FATHER SITS next to me on the U-shaped couch. He starts with a test: Can you read this piece of paper? It's written in Hebrew, and he wants to see if it's true. Does the Canadian speak and read the language of Israel? I read it out loud to members of the family, the dozen or so who are here (Rana's sister Zainab tells me they have over six thousand relatives in Tamra; Rana's clan, or *hamula*, is one of the four in town). The letter says Rana's father must pay a bill by such and such date. I feel like I'm back in Grade Three, trying to pass a reading and comprehension exam. Rana's father is dumbfounded.

"But why Hebrew?" he asks.

The question seems ridiculous to me, but from their point of view it must be a bit strange. Aren't the languages of Canada English and French? I explain I don't actually use Hebrew. This baffles him even more. Then I tell him my parents weren't hardline Zionists—they just wanted me to have a Jewish education, and they wanted it to be at a secular school. There weren't many choices and Bialik was as safe a bet as any.

I try to continue with my explanation, but I find myself more defensive than anything. Tell him that prayers were not a regular part of the daily rituals, that there was a spin on history and the teaching methods were questionable at times. I feel hot eyes on my neck. I look up and there's Mrs. Blintzkrieg in the doorway.

MRS. BLINTZKRIEG: Nice, Shalom. Way to help with the PR.
Wasn't there anything you liked about Bialik?
ME: Sure, um, you taught me how to work hard.
MRS. B.: So the only thing you learned was how to obey orders.
ME: I didn't say that.
MRS. B.: So what did you learn?

I notice that everybody's staring, listening, waiting for me to go on. I don't know what to say. Don't know how to articulate it. Bialik was incredibly intense. But it's not just the lessons in discipline that I value. It's the passion with which we studied. How a piece of theatre could be heroic. A book: Revelation. What we sang, believed and wrote meant everything. When I turned fourteen, I was dying to leave Bialik. But ever since I left, I've wanted to get back the same sense of purpose I had there.

When I don't respond, they resume their family talk. Zionist or not Zionist, believer or not, nobody seems to care. Then again, I have no idea what they're saying to each other when they shift effortlessly from Hebrew to Arabic. I've come to Tamra to get to know Rana and her family, but really, it's they who want to learn about me. I look up at the doorway. Mrs. Blintzkrieg's incredulous. She's shaking her head.

AFTER A SUMPTUOUS MEAL, Rana takes me to the highest point in Tamra. It's midnight and we park the car on a slope. A half moon rises over the Mediterranean. Haifa shimmers in the distance. The smell of wild sage and mint fill the air. For a moment I forget I'm in an over-crowded town, a ghetto in the hills; I've entered peace, an oasis on a hillside with a lovely ocean view.

Voices from a truck parked higher up: High school kids are getting high on grass and whisky. They blast Arab remix from a boom box. Rana and I sit in the car smoking thin, cheap cigarettes. In Tamra, women aren't supposed to indulge in cigarettes.

"Growing up in this town was like living in a bubble."

"What do you mean?"

She points at the city lights by the sea. "Once, when I was nine, I was in a public swimming pool in Haifa. I was playing with a Jewish boy. All of a sudden he turned to me and said, 'Get away, you dirty Arab.' I'd never heard someone say that. When I told my father, he said, forget about it. And when we came back to this town, I did. Tamra, my family, they let me forget."

"You were lucky to have so much support."

"Growing up I had no sense of who I am."

"Palestinian, you mean."

"Yeah."

"So how did you change?"

"I left."

Rana moved to Jerusalem when she was eighteen. That year she left Israel for the first time to go on vacation in the Sinai. "It was the first time I met Arabs who weren't from Israel. It was strange, they called me Palestinian. I felt uncomfortable. Why are they calling me this? Growing up I knew that Palestinians were my relatives. They lived in the West Bank, Gaza, Syria or Lebanon. But I'd never met any of them. I knew about the first intifada, but that wasn't me throwing stones. I thought, Palestinians are heroic. They're fighters. What am I?

"So I'm in Egypt, checking into a hotel, and the person behind the desk says, 'What nationality are you?' And I say, 'Palestinian.' I said it without thinking. An Israeli man standing behind me pulled me over afterwards and said, 'How dare you call yourself that. Do you know how good we are to you? You should be proud of being Israeli.'"

"What did you do?"

"I turned red in the face. Didn't know what to say. I felt guilty, like I'd betrayed him. Like you probably do when you start to question your upbringing."

Ah, the Blintzkrieg complex. I suppose what's most unsettling about her is she makes the questions I ask about Israel feel like the ultimate act of betrayal; critical thought is equal to being a Nazi or a terrorist. The Blintzkrieg-in-the-head: "What do you know, you foreigner, you Diaspora Jew? While we stay here and fight your wars—yes, every war we fight in Israel is for all Jews all over the world—you stand back and criticize us. Like a typically spoiled North American liberal."

I listen to Blintzkrieg's voice, but I also listen to what I learned in Sinai: One mustn't silence the moral conscience in order to go along with the group. More and more Israelis and Jews struggle with the "either you're with us or against us" choice. Take Eytan. He started off as an excellent soldier. But when the invasion of Lebanon happened in '82, he couldn't justify fighting. Morally it was unacceptable to him, and he went to jail for his beliefs.

Rana's journey is different from mine or Eytan's, but I'm surprised to hear how difficult it was for her to criticize the Jewish state. To call herself Palestinian presented an existential crisis. It was a form of rebellion, but she needed to figure out what it really meant, what she actually believed in. "When I couldn't answer the Israeli, I knew I needed to educate myself. Back in Jerusalem, I joined B'Tselem [an Israeli organization for human rights in the West Bank]. I went to demonstrations. I read a lot. And once I started to learn things, I saw the world in a different way. I realized I'm never going to be Israeli. It says so on my passport, but it's bullshit. To be a Palestinian in Israel you have to play a certain role in order to survive. One should never speak Arabic in Jewish places. Later on I decided I didn't want to act anymore. That's why I left."

WE SPEND THE NEXT DAY on the front porch. There's a steady stream of family and visitors—a normal day, Rana explains—and with them comes plenty of Arabic coffee and conversation. Anwar, a local town planner and Ph.D. candidate at Haifa Technion, grew up in Tamra, an internal refugee from a nearby village destroyed in '48. He wants to give me a lesson. Shows me his Tamra, as seen from the Rana family porch.

"To the north is the quarry used by Jews. To the south, there's a settlement. To the west, the highway. And to the east, forests planted by the JNF on top of a former village. Those pine trees," he says, pointing at the far-off hill, "make the land impossible to cultivate. The JNF will tell you that Israel needs the trees, they provide necessary oxygen. In reality, the trees are completely hostile to the land." He explains there's an old Ottoman law in effect that says any farmland that goes unused for a certain period of time can be taken away by the government. The JNF often monitors what land is being used or not, and will expropriate any land deemed fallow in accordance with this law.* They then lease the land to kibbutzim or moshavim, or plant trees on it. Often the land is not farmed because the Palestinian farmers lack adequate infrastructure—water, electricity and roads that

---

* This same argument is put forth in Susan Nathan, *The Other Side of Israel*, p. 157.

lead to their fields. Thus the "empty" land is "redeemed" and becomes Jewish property.

"We have become criminals, just to survive," Anwar says when describing the extensive illegal building going on in Tamra so people will have places to live. "Is it any wonder that so many people are turning to religion? When you have nothing else, you need to reach out for some kind of hope. Even if it's bullshit."

It's difficult to listen to these testimonies. One wishes they could be simply written off as propaganda. But more and more people in Tamra air their complaints to me. (Their secrets, too: One whispers that when the next intifada happens, it won't be starting in the West Bank, but right here in Israel.) Their confessions are a kind of reaching out. *Listen to me,* plead their voices. Even if only half of what they say is true, I still have to ask the question, "Why?" Why does the Israeli government deprive Tamra of a proper sewage system? Why does a town of twenty-five thousand people not have adequate garbage disposal? Why is there not a single green space or playground for children to play in? What does any of this have to do with building the Jewish nation?

Anwar says, "The people in power want to make it so we, the non-Jews, will have to struggle. So we will only have the energy to survive, and we will disappear. Then, you will keep your Jewish state." Anwar says this wearily. "You know, I was taught a lot of things about the Jews when I was a child. 'You're land stealers, you're evil, you control all the money in the world.' All that anti-Semitic propaganda. As an adult, I realized I knew nothing about you. So I read your history books. The Holocaust in all of its horrible details. And I became very sad when I realized that after all your suffering, Jews have learned nothing at all."

CHAPTER 37

"If they don't like it, they should go and live in Jaljulia [a Palestinian village in Israel], which is an Arab name ... Why should I change the name, because Jamal wants to change the name? He should change his Allah."

So said the mayor of Ramle, Yoel Lavi, in late November 2006.

He was responding to a request from Palestinian residents in his city to change the names of certain streets from Hebrew to Arabic. (Ramle is one of the few mixed cities in Israel. Of the sixty-five thousand people who live there, twenty percent are Palestinian.) The Palestinian residents felt they could not identify with the streets they lived on like "Street of Ghetto Fighters" or "Chayim Nachman Bialik"; they wanted the names to represent their own cultural background. In the end their request was denied, and the mayor's supposedly off-the-record comments to a journalist were made public. The mayor apologized, but stood by what he said. This is Israel. A Jewish country. If you don't like it, get out.

Ramle has a sensitive history in these matters. In 1948 almost all of its Palestinian population was expelled by the Israeli army—the largest forced expulsion during the war. The order was signed by Yitzhak Rabin and given by Ben-Gurion (when asked what to do with the indigenous population, Ben-Gurion famously swept his hand across the air, indicating they must be driven *away, away*). Along with those from the neighbouring city of Lydda, some forty-five thousand Palestinians were told to seek their fortunes elsewhere, thank you very much, this is now a Jewish state. And so the comments by the mayor were a kind of spark in the haystack of Ramle's memory. The very hint of population transfer touches a nerve.

Eytan and Zochrot have chosen Ramle for their latest signposting tour. The march is Zochrot's way of responding to Lavi's racist comments. The gathering is a decent size, about one hundred people. Most were bused in from Tel Aviv. I drove with Rana from Tamra. She was curious when I told her where I was heading, wanted to see for herself. When I told her about Eytan she said, "I never met Israelis like that when I lived here eight years ago."

The street we're on is crumbling and neglected. Already I'm getting a hint of the poverty in old Ramle (it has high crime and drug rates, a woman from Tel Aviv named Miri tells me, and a half-decent rap scene). The leader of the tour is Dr. Awni, a pediatrician who lives in Ramle. Dr. Awni announces the first street will be renamed Emile Habiby. I'm a fan of Habiby, having read his satirical novel *The Secret Life of Saeed the Pessoptimist.* It's about a Palestinian who flees to outer space with an extraterrestrial friend and writes a series of letters about his life as a collaborator in Israel under military occupation during the first years of the state. Habiby was a member of the Arab Communist Party, and a strong believer in coexistence between Jews and Palestinians; he was an advocate of the 1947 UN partition plan.

There's some commotion as an older man with shocked white hair and a white goatee grabs the microphone out of Dr. Awni's hand and announces that this street will be named Emile Habiby "over my dead body." I ask what's up, but Miri's as confused as I am. The white-haired man delivers an eloquent speech about the sign he will now erect; the street will be named after someone or other, a dear friend and important academic who fought for human rights and died last year. Dr. Awni and the others seemed miffed by this change of order. *Can't we at least agree on the names of the streets?* people's faces ask. In the end there's a cranky consent. As long as a new sign gets put up, what difference does it make? And so Emile Habiby is put into a bag with the other green and yellow signs, due to be posted on another street later this morning.

We follow one banged-up alleyway and turn onto another. It's Saturday-silent, much of the city shut down. We saunter leisurely through the old marketplace, one of the largest in Israel. People snap pictures. Miri tells me that Ramle was a real hot spot in '48. In February of that year, a member of the Haganah dressed as an Arab planted a bomb in this market, killing seven and injuring forty-five. One forgets that terrorists operated on both sides. As though violence is part of the landscape, the way people shout when trying to get things done.

That same year the expulsion occurred. Originally the Israeli army told the local Palestinians they could stay if they surrendered, but they soon reneged on their promise. According to Miri, Ben-Gurion came to unofficially support a policy of Palestinian population transfer in April '48 for reasons of security—to avoid a potential fifth column in the new Jewish state.* Ramle and Lydda were the fruit of this thought.

The sight on the highway that summer must've been surreal. If you were a Jew from Europe newly arrived to the country, what would you think? The gravel road shimmered from the July heat, and a river of people slowly flowed east to Ramallah and the surrounding refugee camps. Children and the elderly died of starvation, thirst and exhaustion. And there were reports of Israeli soldiers stealing jewellery from women at checkpoints along the way.

I'M THINKING ABOUT MOSES. Wondering, if he had crossed the Jordan into Canaan, would he have led the Israelites in the brutal

---

* This argument is supported in "Survival of the Fittest? An Interview with Benny Morris" by Ari Shavit, *Haaretz* (January 9, 2004). In the interview, Morris argues that Ben-Gurion didn't go far enough; if he was going to bother with expulsion, he should've done "a complete job ... [After all], you can't make an omelet without breaking eggs. You have to dirty your hands."

onslaught in Jericho? Moses knew God's plans in the desert. Still, I can't help but wonder if he might've had the balls to ask God a question or two when they'd finally reached the River Jordan. To say, "I don't know if this is such a good idea, God. I'm not against self-defence. But slaying every man, woman and child? Why so brutal, God? What happened to that justice you talked to me about on Mount Sinai? What happened to 'Thou shalt not covet thy neighbour's house?'"

Joshua the General didn't ask those questions. But let's not be too hard on Joshua. Maybe he struggled with God's command. Maybe the question, "At what price a nation?" ran through his head, but he didn't have the guts to ask. He might've thought, "Now's not a time to be an unbeliever. After all, we've wandered in the bloody desert for forty years. I'm going to disobey God *now*?"

The 1948 War is a different story from the Book of Joshua. The Jews didn't simply land in Israel and start to expel and murder the indigenous people. There were years of brewing tensions, riots and clashes between Jews and Palestinians. Both sides committed acts of brutality and terror. And there was a war—seven nations against one. Still, I can't help but wonder what went through Rabin's head when he signed the expulsion papers. Likely, he felt ambivalent. He saw the operation as necessary for Israel's security (holding onto the Tel Aviv–Jerusalem corridor). But, in an interview years after the fact, Rabin said that Ramle was "psychologically ... one of the most difficult actions we undertook."* Forced expulsion is not a neat, orderly affair. There were battles, massacres, beatings. "Like after a pogrom,"† one soldier described the way the city looked. Did Rabin ever think to challenge Ben-Gurion's authority? To say, look at the problems these generations of refugees will cause? Did he want

---

* Kurzman, Dan. *Soldier of Peace: The Life and Times of Yitzhak Rabin,* p. 141.
† Morris, Benny. *The Birth of the Palestinian Refugee Problem Revisited,* p. 433.

to argue, as Anwar argued, that the Jews have not learned anything from Europe?

I wonder if the memories of Ramle, and later Imwas and Yalu, haunted Rabin. If events in '48 and '67 inspired him to change in his final years, to reach out and make peace with the Palestinian people. When did our modern Joshua decide to put down his arms, to be a bad general, to finally ask questions? To use words instead of weapons.

THE SIX SQUAD CARS and a dozen cops in bulletproof vests with handcuffs at the ready seem excessive. Maybe they have nothing better to do on a Saturday. Or maybe these signs are just that power-ful. Regardless, here they are, right in our face.

Eytan is putting up a new sign on the main street. He uses a plastic tie to get the sign around a lamppost. The moment he's done a cop snips it off and takes the sign away. A huge commotion erupts among us. Well, most of us. I'm on the outskirts, cowardly taking pictures, talking to a man from a group called "Mennonites from India."

"The police only give us problems in Ramle," he says.

"You mean this has happened before?"

"Yes, the last time we were here."

The sign is confiscated. In the ensuing chaos, I notice Rana cross-ing the street with the white-haired guy. They're confronting the cops.

"Hey! What are you doing?" I yell. She can't hear me as she practi-cally has her head in the open window of a cop car. The white-haired man pulls her back and a giant of a cop emerges from the car. He's a cliché, right out of the movies: shaved head and mirrored sunglasses and a muscle mass that is, well, impressive. He stands directly in front of her. All I can think is: What am I going to tell her father when she gets arrested?

I'm swept up in the crowd of marchers heading left up a side street. One of the demonstrators puts the five remaining street signs on the sidewalk outside a bank as people discuss the next plan of action. Meanwhile, the police cars—all six of them—pull up beside us. They take the remaining signs away and this causes a huge uproar. After all, there's nothing illegal happening. The cops shout through a loud-speaker to get off the road. A professor in her sixties steps off the curb—I'm not sure if it's intentional or not—and is promptly arrested. Thrown into the back of a cruiser.

Others are arrested, too. Dr. Awni is taken in because he doesn't have his ID card on him—he lives around the corner and is willing to go home and get it, but that doesn't suit the police. Two others are hauled off—one Palestinian, one Israeli. Now Rana comes jogging up the street. The white-haired man is with her. When he sees our fellow demonstrators carted off, he stands on some steps and announces, "Let us all join our brothers and sisters in solidarity by marching down to the police station and waiting outside!"

"Rana, where were you?" I ask.

"The fucking cops. They wouldn't give the sign back."

"Are you okay?"

"They want to ask me some questions and see my ID."

She and I are separated in the crowd. I'm confused: She's not being arrested, is she? She walks ahead, leading the pack.

Reluctantly I follow the throng. How did I get caught up in this? A falafel-shop owner approaches and asks, "Who's your leader?" I point at Eytan. "Do you think he could make an announcement and tell everyone they should eat at my restaurant?"

"You might be better off doing delivery."

"Where you all going?" he asks.

"The cop shop," I say, and he looks at me like I'm crazy.

"I only came here to learn," I say to no one, turning down the side street that leads to the station.

THE LINEUP of Zochrot demonstrators stretches from the police gate to the street. Inside a small booth a pair of police officers man the

gate, avoiding questions from Eytan and the rest. Rana is not brought
in for questioning; she mingles with the other Zochroters and pesters
the cops from time to time.

I'm standing on the other side of the street talking to another reluctant protester. His name is Sagi, from nearby Rechovot.

"I don't belong to this group," he says. "I came to Ramle for the
tour, that's all." Nervously he adjusts the backpack on his shoulder.
"This is a sensitive issue, and I'm not saying the police acted in a nice
way. But putting up that sign on a main street was too provocative."

"Don't you think the police could've waited for us to leave before
taking it down?"

"That's not the point. People don't want to know that in 1948
over four hundred villages were destroyed by the Israeli army. The
problem is how to get this information to people's minds and
hearts."

Sagi's in his fifties. He wears wire-rimmed glasses and his shoulders
are hunched. He understands the issue is complex. "It would be much
easier to deal with the past if the present situation were calm. When
there are issues of security it becomes too sensitive. But I say it's
because of the present situation we need to look at the past. We need
to ask ourselves why these bombs are going off."

I ask Sagi if this Ramle tour would've happened thirty years ago.
"No way," he says. "In the early seventies, I had a friend who went to
jail for four years simply for talking to a member of the PLO. For
having a *conversation*." He says things are more open today, that
people are starting to talk about these things. "We need to."

He tells me about the Parents Circle Families Forum (PCFF), a
group of bereaved Israeli and Palestinian parents who've lost loved
ones in the conflict. Composed equally of Palestinians and Israelis,
the members of the group argue that we need to reach out to each
other, not to build walls and spend more money on security. Part of
their program is to go around to schools and talk to students. "I went

and listened to them speak at a high school in Rechovot. There was one Palestinian and one Israeli, and I found it very moving." Last year, PCFF visited approximately one thousand classes in Israel. "I wanted my daughter's high school to invite them, so I went and talked to the principal. 'Sorry, it's the end of the year, there's no time,' he said. So this year I came early in September and asked again. Can we have these people come and talk? He said, 'Yes, yes, after the holidays.' So I go after the holidays with all the necessary forms. Finally, last week, I got the call. 'Look, there's just no time,' they said. Come on. They have the time. They take the children on field trips to the Golan Heights to show how the Six Day War was won. They have time for someone from the army to give a seminar on what it's like to be a soldier. But to hear the personal story of a Palestinian and an Israeli, two people who lost family because of senseless violence, there's no time for this." Sagi blows his nose into a handkerchief. "In a poll last year, sixty-eight percent of Israelis said they wouldn't live in the same building as a Palestinian.* We need to have contact, to talk to each other, to see each other as human. But we have to want to." Sagi adjusts the straps of his backpack as though reconsidering his position. "I don't usually like demonstrations. But once in a while I go to one, and I see some Palestinian militants and ask myself, what am I thinking? *They* want to kick *me* out. That's not easy. But there are people on both sides who want the others to disappear. These extremists are a problem. Unfortunately, there will always be people like that."

Six hours later and I'm sitting in the back alley of Ramle in some cold, dank basement with dim lights waiting for someone from Al-Aqsa Martyrs Brigade to come leaping out of the closet. Instead the white-haired man (his name is Uri) sits directly across from Rana and me,

---

* He was quoting Eli Ashkenazi and Jack Khoury, "Poll: 68% of Jews would refuse to live in the same building as an Arab," *Haaretz*, March 22, 2006.

eyeing us suspiciously. I'm wondering how I ended up in this dark brick room with a strange man in a strange city. I'm wondering what the hell I've gotten myself into.

Uri is the first member of the PLO I've ever met. (At Bialik a teacher once wrote "PLO" on the blackboard, meaning "Please Leave On" whatever she had written that day. The next day she almost lost her job as the school admin went into hysterics about the terrorist hidden among us.) I'd been speaking to Uri the final hour or so outside the police station. He got very excited about the story of the house. He confessed, "The right of return is my religion." The statement seemed odd, but then again it shouldn't given the country I'm in. Uri exclaimed, "The Palestinians must be allowed to come back like the Jews can. Let everybody return!" This, coming from a Jew, or a Palestinian-Hebrew, as he calls himself.

"But how can that happen when people are living in their houses?" I asked.

Uri said, "Haven't you learned anything from Abu Dalo and Shimon? Respect the leases of the Israelis, but make sure the rent goes to the Palestinian owner. They own this land!"

Rana and Uri hit it off like a house on fire. They seemed to speak the same language, or at least subscribe to the same point of view. They talked the return of refugees for hours, how it worked in Bosnia, constructing all sorts of scenarios for how it should be implemented here.

Uri's the eternal shit disturber, the rebel academic. Raised by a Jewish mother and British father, he grew up in Jerusalem in the 1930s. He's one of a handful of Israeli Jews who lives in a Palestinian village; he lives in the north, a few kilometres away from Tamra. He was kicked out of Israel for ten years in the 1980s because he was a member of the PLO, and was jailed for being one of the first refuseniks in the 1960s. The guy has fought, and continues to fight, the Israeli status quo.

Rana and I sit next to each other. I think about what Sagi said to me about the extremists who show up at these events.

"You know, I'm very concerned about the future of this country." Uri rubs his hands together and looks at us both very carefully.

"So am I," I say, trying to show him I'm on his side.

"Good," he says, rubbing his goatee. "Now that that's clear, I want you two to know, I'll support your decision should you choose to get married."

Married? Who is this guy, the friar from *Romeo and Juliet*?

"It happens," he continues. "But it's very difficult."

Rana stops him dead in his tracks. "Uri, we're not getting married. Jonathan and I are just friends."

Uri shushes her, won't take no for an answer. He puts our hands in his. "It's important to break down the borders between people. In any way possible."

Rana takes her hand back. "There are no borders to break. If I get married, it'll be to a Muslim."

"What?" I say.

"He'd have to convert."

"But you're an atheist."

"I love my family. And my parents insist on it."

"Rana, give me a break." I know she married Muslim last time, but I didn't realize it was just to please the parents.

She looks at Uri. "He'd only have to convert for the wedding. After that, he could do whatever he wants."

Uri asks, "And if the man was a Jew and wanted to keep his faith?"

"I'd convert for his wedding too."

"You're crazy," I say. "You can't just convert to Judaism for the hell of it. They won't let you."

"Then I won't marry a Jew," she says.

I'm incredulous. After all her talk about human rights and universal whatever, she's no different from anyone else: Baba Jesse, Rabbi Spero, Israel. Intermarriage is wrong.

Uri says, "Jonathan, it's not as ridiculous as you think. In this country, the tribal is still more powerful than the civil."

"So how is there ever going to be peace?"

"That," he says, "is a very good question. One that depends on one's objectives."

"What do you mean?"

"My objective is to separate Church from State."

"You mean the end of the Jewish state," I say.

"I mean the end of the Jewish ethnocratic regime. I could believe in a Jewish state that was decoratively Jewish. The way Norway has a cross on its flag, Israel could have a Star of David on its own. But I can't support a Jewish state that has democracy for some and not others. There has to be equality for everyone."

"All right. How do you propose we achieve that?" I ask.

"Through protests. Sanctions. Dialogue."

"And violence?"

Uri looks around the room, as though checking to see if it's bugged. "An occupied people have the right to resistance. But I am strongly opposed to acts of terror. I won't support suicide bombing." I'm relieved when he says this. Then Uri turns to Rana and asks the question: "Rana, how do you feel about suicide bombs?"

She says, "I think they're a legitimate form of resistance."

I can barely catch my breath. It's the question I've been avoiding, the elephant in the room.

"It's not the only way," she says. "But we've seen what negotiation has done in the past. Nothing."

Uri says, "You see the problems that would arise should you two get married."

I'm too pissed off to respond.

Uri talks on my behalf: "According to the Geneva Convention, armed resistance is allowed when you're an occupied people. However, terrorism is explicitly banned."

"Define terrorism," says Rana.

"I will define terrorism as the killing of innocent civilians. I will venture to say that a Palestinian suicide bomber is a terrorist as George W. Bush and Ariel Sharon are terrorists. And I say that terrorism does not in any way help to achieve the goals of democracy. That it is contrary to the Geneva Convention and the United Nations Declaration of Human Rights."

Rana's getting impatient. "Uri, give me a break. Those don't mean anything."

"They were written after one of the most barbaric episodes in human history. They mean a lot."

"Nobody follows them."

"It's not about that. It's about taking the higher moral ground. Armed resistance is okay—if it's against the occupying army. Other methods must be employed too. But not terror."

"I disagree with you. I think the suicide bomber has helped the Palestinian cause."

"How?"

"We have the world's attention."

"For all the wrong reasons."

"Nobody is innocent, do you understand?" Rana says.

"Is a baby guilty for being born?"

"That's not the point."

Uri asks, "So what is?"

They talk and shout and the arguments go on forever. The lights in the room seem to grow dimmer. It's getting late, near midnight. Who is this person I came here with? I look at her black eyes, her high cheekbones. Her face is harder than when I first met her all those years ago, like granite. Calmly and logically she puts forth the argument for why it's okay to blow other people to smithereens. She's thought this through very carefully, as though this is her area of specialty, and she's presenting her paper to a panel of experts.

I can't talk. Uri holds his course. He's been doing this for years. I can see him with Arafat in the Muqata over cups of coffee and stale cigarettes, seated behind rows of armed guards. The idealist rants to the warrior, the rebel academic to the rebel leader, until Uri too finally admits defeat. He says to Rana, "I cannot convince you. But I would like you to try to see my point. Try the higher moral ground. Please. Be sensible."

I turn to my right and there's Mrs. Blintzkrieg standing under the light. She seems to have grown a few feet in height. She towers above me, laughing, pointing her finger at me. "This is your great gift, your thank-you note to Bialik. Death to the Jewish people. Death to Israel. Yes, Shalom. This is your beautiful peace."

CHAPTER 38

I haven't taken the suicide bombing discussion very well. I'm not an Israeli who's lost a child to a bus bomb, and Rana's not strapping explosives to her body. But I can't accept her position; it's completely illogical. She doesn't hate Jews or Israelis. In fact, we're sitting in an Arabic café in Jerusalem, and she's on the phone making plans to meet a friend who lives on a Jewish settlement near Ramallah. How can suicide bombings make sense to her?

In the past week Rana's helped me search for the official records in the Jerusalem archives that will give us clues to the who's, where's and when's of the house's ownership. I'm trying to confirm the story of the house, clues to which version is most accurate. The search hasn't turned anything up yet, but to be honest, I don't really give a shit about the documents.

Before Rana leaves she says, "Do you think I'm an extremist?" She asks the question seriously.

"I don't know what I think."

"Look, I'm not saying all Jews should die. I'm saying the bombs might help the Palestinian situation."

I'd consider strangling her, but that might put a dent in my argument for non-violent resistance. Rana wants the world to understand how desperate Palestinians are and how inhumane the conditions are that they live in. A world of refugee camps, bulldozed homes and second-class people. I don't dispute that reality. But to kill innocent civilians for some lousy PR?

I say, "What if I was on the bus? Or Uri? Or your sister, on her way to pick up socks in Tel Aviv for her store? What if your mother was there, on her way to visit relatives in Yaffo?"

She shakes her head. Won't change her mind.

"What do you hope to achieve by this?" I ask.

"What Uri said. Separate Church from State. No religion and a real democracy."

"Bombing people won't help achieve democracy. We've seen that."

"Look, I'm not about to join Islamic Jihad. I'm just saying it's a viable option. Look at the size of Israel's army. How else can we fight back? You want us to keep using stones?"

"I'm sorry. I can't support terrorism."

"Rather than labelling it as 'terrorism,' ask yourself what it is people are doing. And why."

Rana's late. Her cellphone's telling her so, ringing away stupidly in her bag. She rushes off and I'm left in this café near Dung Gate. The men are playing shesh besh or cards with their buddies, shooting the shit, passing the day. I order a coffee, pull out a blue folder I've been using to carry articles of interest from the past few weeks. One of them is about a sixty-four-year-old Palestinian woman named Fatma who blew herself up at a military checkpoint in Gaza. Her daughter explained her mother's motives in carrying out the attack: "They [Israelis] destroyed her house, they killed her grandson—my son. Another grandson is in a wheelchair with an amputated leg."* Her mother had been sent in by Hamas's military wing.

When I read about it I was shocked, as many people were. But I've kept the article, mostly because it's difficult to imagine a woman of that age wanting to. When I hear suicide bomber, I automatically

---

* Associated Press. *The International Herald Tribune*. November 23, 2006.

imagine a twenty-something man, bearded and chanting *death to Israel* (sort of like the kind man who brings me my coffee. He kindly offers me a cigarette). But a grandmother isn't supposed to blow herself up. She's supposed to be enjoying the twilight of her life. I pull the article out now because I want to ask the woman in the photograph, why?

Fatma reminds me of my grandmother in the way her eyes are slanted. But I can't imagine Baba Jesse carrying a Kalashnikov. Can't imagine her making the speech before a camera: *Look what you've done to my family. My neighbours. My streets. This isn't about virgins or heaven. It's vengeance. Pure as the blood in my veins.*

When someone chooses to commit suicide it's the last resort. The other exits are sealed off; the detours no longer possible; no choice but this. To take one's own life is to say, "Enough. Give me a fucking break already."

But this woman, Fatma, is not saying that. I can't buy the argument there's no alternative. She's chosen to be the weapon, to turn body into bomb. It's a sign of how cheap life has become, says one newspaper writer. And there's truth to that. But the suicide bomber is also the bottom line. She takes her own life, but she also stares at the future, sees the bodies she will execute lying scattered on the earth. She envisions an entire country shaking in blood, soaked in fear. Her final plea to the world.

I stare at the photograph. *Too much*, her eyes say. That is the price of this war.

CHAPTER 39

Finally a stroke of luck. A friend of Rana's helps me get access to documents about the house from the Jerusalem land registry (*tabu*) office. The papers confirm Abu Dalo and Shimon's story; the state returned the land to Ibrahim in 1959. What the papers don't tell me is why. Rana and I speak to a number of legal experts over the course of the week. No one has ever heard of such a case, and yet nobody seems too concerned about it. I suppose it's because this one incident isn't going to shake up the entire legal system. Still, the piece of paper from the tabu does raise some eyebrows. Theories are advanced. One legal expert suggests that Ibrahim Abu Dalo was a collaborator with the Israeli military. Perhaps the land was returned as a gift, a thank-you note for letting the military use the house for a certain period of time or for information supplied about the enemy. Another possibility raised is that the Abu Dalo family never owned the house; this was given to them as compensation for losing another one (given the fact that both Shimon and Hassan Abu Dalo say otherwise, it seems rather unlikely). Another lawyer argues that Ibrahim got the land back simply because he was stubborn. This lawyer does not want me to think the Israeli system treats Palestinians fairly; rather, he says, Ibrahim succeeded because of determination, pride and luck. No Jew would have to go through what the Abu Dalos did to get a piece of land.

The why of the house is interesting, but that's not what I struggle with. It's why I want to be friends with Rana. I don't *need* to find out the legal ramifications of the house, and she doesn't either. She could be with her parents, who are calling her daily, wondering what she's doing in Jerusalem.

And yet here we are in the famous law firm of Yigal Arnon, with its schmancy cream-coloured walls, its lukewarm beige Venetian blinds and delicate, angled ceiling lights. We've arranged to meet with Chagi Shmueli, the lawyer who represented Abu Dalo in the case against Azulay's daughter some fifteen years ago, when she occupied the part of the house that Rana lived in. Chagi won Abu Dalo the case, securing his ownership of the house in 1993.

Chagi has saucer-blue eyes. His tone is firm but gentle, so you don't even realize you're being convinced by his argument until you're nodding in agreement—a good lawyer. I figure he might know something of the history of the house. But when I show him the piece of paper indicating the 1959 land exchange, Chagi does a double take.

"What is this?" he says, taking a pair of bifocals out of his desk drawer. "It's very unusual."

Rana says, "It's the right of return."

Chagi says, "Yes, it really is." He scratches his head, examines the paper closely, then looks at us. "It's crazy. Do you realize how many Palestinians come into my office and say, 'Chagi, this is my land.' And I say, 'Sir, I feel for you. Really I do. Because you're a good person and the just thing would be for you to get your land back. But according to the laws of this country, you own nothing, do you understand?'" He looks at the paper again, bifocals resting on the edge of his nose. "So, other than to show me this interesting piece of paper, why are you in my office?"

I want to ask Chagi if he'll help us get into the legal records that might reveal something more about the case—the reason the courts gave for returning the land to Abu Dalo. But before I can say anything, Rana jumps in. "So you believe in the right of return, right?"

I turn to look at her. Chagi, like everybody else in this country, responds like this is a normal "How are you?" sort of question. "Look. Some terrible things happened in 1948. There was a war, people were hurt and many people lost their homes. It was a terrible injustice. I'm sorry, my father's sorry and my grandfather's sorry. So can we please get over it?"

Rana doesn't like this response. "Don't you think Palestinians should get their land back?"

"It's an impossible situation. Okay, we should apologize and give you compensation. At least acknowledge that wrong was done. But we're living in the houses now. What do you want us to do? My mother was from Syria. She was kicked out of her country. Are we supposed to go back there?" Chagi leans forward onto the desk. "Look, it's not only our fault. The Arab nations didn't let the Palestinians integrate into their countries. They love having them in the camps, fanning the nationalist flames."

Rana's phone starts to ring, extra loud, coming from her purse. She ignores it and says, "Are you suggesting Israel bears no responsibility?"

"I'm saying the Palestinians got screwed by everybody. The Arabs and the Israelis." Chagi sits back in his chair and rests his head in his arms. "In the end, I think we need to let history go. Forget about it. We say we're sorry, you say you're sorry and that's that."

On the anger scale, Rana is starting to register slightly red-hot on the way to burning. "*We* say we're sorry? For what?"

"Look," Chagi says. "I have friends who are Palestinian. You're good people. Some of the brightest and the best. Give you the opportunity to flourish, you'll do it all: doctors, lawyers, judges."

Rana: "But what about these mistakes you're talking about?"

"Everyone makes mistakes. I'm saying, forgive and forget."

Rana turns livid. She starts to spout off years and numbers, details that don't make sense. She talks about her cousins who live in Sabra and Shatila, her uncle in Gaza, so-and-so stuck in Syria. But the argument isn't coherent, and she doesn't stand a chance against the lawyer.

"It's terrible," Chagi says. "I completely agree."

Rana talks about Haifa—says that in 1948 the Palestinians were kicked out, sent to Nazareth and their homes taken away under the pretext of being the enemy. "But Haifa wasn't even invaded by the so-called enemy. And we weren't fighting at all," she says. "How can Israel get away with taking our land away? Meanwhile the world stands, watches and does nothing."

"What should we do?"

"Give the land back."

"And where do we go?"

"You stay here, too. It'll be a democracy. For everyone."

"Look, I believe the Palestinians should have a state. But we need a country of our own."

"Why can't we share it?"

"We offered you that in '47. You didn't want it."

"Circumstances were different then. We weren't organized like you were. And besides, you grabbed another twenty-five percent in '48."

"There was a war," Chagi says.

"It's called ethnic cleansing and colonialism," Rana says.

"Please."

It's as though my skin is leading me. My right hand lifts itself through the air, reaches Rana's left thigh and rests there—barely—for a moment. Rana does not look at me. Her face changes ever so slightly. She smiles, but it's a forced smile, and it's there to cover the anger wanting out. I take my hand away. Her phone rings again. This time she answers it on the second ring and leaves the room.

Chagi continues with his argument like the good lawyer he is. He tells me he's sympathetic to the Palestinian situation. After all, he grew up with the Abu Dalos—that's why he represented him. They went to the same Jewish high school. Seeing this document, it makes him happy to know that Abu Dalo has justice on his side. As for the others who come to him for advice, he's sorry about the loss of land and homes. If there was something he could do, he would.

I'm listening to Chagi but I've lost the line of his argument. I'm thinking about my hand on Rana's left thigh. I put it there because I wanted to send a message: Please stop. My hand was saying what my mouth won't. I'm tired of these arguments, the endless debate about who is right and wrong. At a certain point the words of Chagi and Rana lose meaning, the dialogue becomes vitriol, a sailboat without a rudder. I wanted to hear Chagi's story, not because I agree or disagree with him, but because I need to hear the right and the wrong of what he thinks. To enter it into the narrative.

Rana returns to the office and Chagi stops talking. Silence invades the room. I haven't asked the questions I wanted to ask, the ones I scribbled down this morning. I think about my hand on Rana's thigh instead. Think, perhaps there is something in Chagi's argument that appeals to me. Beneath his smarmy lawyer arguments, his condescending "I'm so good I like Palestinians" speak, part of me believes Chagi is right. *Admit the wrongs we've done. Give them compensation. Forget history and move on.* In spite of everything I've seen, heard and read about, I'm not willing to concede the land. I cannot abandon the idea of a Jewish state.

CHAPTER 40

Rana and I stand in front of a café on Hillel Street. She's pissed at me, and I'm pissed at her. But we don't talk about what is bothering us. Instead I ask, "Who called?"

"My father," she says. "I have to head for Tamra."

"When are you coming back?"

"In a few days."

Rana puts on her backpack and does up the chest strap as though to say, "Time to get going." But she doesn't leave. She rocks back and forth on her feet. I don't know what to say. So I tell her I made arrangements to visit the Oasis of Peace on Monday—the only community in Israel where Palestinians and Israelis choose to live together.

"Do you want to come with me?" I ask, half-hoping she'll say no.

Rana tells me she isn't sure, has to see what her family wants. Her phone rings again and she answers it. When she hangs up she says, "Look, I have to go. I'll call you."

I walk back to my hotel in the Christian Quarter of the old city. I'm exhausted from the week. I don't know what I think about anything anymore. I go over the arguments in my head. How can Rana want peace if she also thinks it's okay to blow up other people? I feel cheated. I've been willing to criticize my culture. Why isn't Rana willing to criticize hers?

I pass the weekend alone in Jerusalem. It's late December, and the

319

weather's grown cold. The air in Jerusalem is heavy, thick and unpleasant. There's too much history on every corner. Too much meaning beneath the rock, rubble and road. On Ben Yehuda Street and on Salakh-al-Din, in the west and in the east, Jews and Palestinians gather in groups, their presence asking the question, *To whom do you belong? Are you with us, or them?* Israel and Palestine: The place shoves you toward a position.

IT'S LATE SUNDAY NIGHT and I'm in my hotel. There's a knock at the door. I open it and there is Rana. She says she wants to talk, stands at the threshold and does not come in.

"I didn't expect to see you again," I say, anxiously twisting the door handle.

"I wasn't going to come back. I thought maybe you believed in what Chagi was saying."

I don't say I thought Chagi had a valid point, and that part of me still clings to the idea of a Jewish state. Though what a Jewish state is, I'm not sure anymore. Whatever it is, I wish it were more fair, democratic and equal.

Instead I say, "Rana, I didn't even get to hear what he was saying."

"Yeah, well it bothers me sometimes. You're so passive. You just don't say anything."

She's wearing her backpack and not taking it off.

"Look, this guy was taking an hour out of his time to talk to us. I didn't think it was the right moment to get into a fight over history. And besides, I know where the argument goes. Nowhere."

"I always say what I believe in. I try to open people's minds."

"I'm all for that. But when two people are just yelling at each other, nobody's mind is open."

"You know what your problem is? You listen to everybody. Can't you understand that sometimes people are just wrong?"

I don't know what to say to that.

"Look, we're different," she says, and I don't disagree.

It's mutual. I'm tired of her fight-everything-attitude, and she's sick of my so-called passivity. I'm ready to let this friendship go. Instead Rana rolls her knapsack down off her back. The sound of her luggage hitting the stone floor surprises me.

"Can I crash on the spare bed tonight?"

Incredulous, I look at her bag.

"My friends aren't home," she says.

"Okay," I say. "It's fine."

CHAPTER 41

"If you ask a Palestinian or Jew on the street, they'll say people prefer to live separately," Ahmed, the development director of the Oasis of Peace, says. "I have no problem with people wanting to live in their own community. But in Israel, it is not a simple matter of preference. There is a policy of segregation here. You're either a Jew or non-Jew. The education and health system, employment opportunities, all services provided by the state make this distinction. At the Oasis of Peace, we're saying we don't accept this policy. This community is a way of protesting. But we're not just saying what we don't like. We're doing something about it. We're suggesting an alternative."

Ahmed's words are strong, but his tone is soothing. He leads Rana and me through the gated community of the Oasis of Peace, which began in 1978 with five families. Now there are fifty Palestinian and Israeli families living in lush surroundings south of Latrun, on land given to them by a Trappist monastery. A security guard searches us as we enter the children's playground. Ahmed points to a single-storey building: the elementary school and kindergarten. "It was the early 1980s, and we weren't going to have two nursery schools when there are only two Arab students and three Jews. And that's how we started the first binational and bilingual school in this country." Ahmed smiles as we approach the school. "When we started the primary school, people from all over started to come here and watch: 'Look! Jews and Arabs in the same school!' It became a kind of zoo here.

In 1992, the school opened its doors to surrounding communities. Now ninety percent of the students come from more than twenty neighbouring communities in a thirty-kilometre radius. This is a big deal and requires a lot of effort. When a child comes here, it's not simply the child: A whole family becomes involved."

Inside the main hallway there's a bulletin board with the words in Hebrew: "Man of Peace." A picture of Yitzhak Rabin. Children have written poems praising him. An excerpt from Rabin's final speech: "I fought so long as there was no chance for peace. I believe that there is now a chance for peace, a great chance. We must take advantage of it."

I ask Ahmed what the children learn about 1948.

"The school only goes up to Grade Six. Because of the ages of the children, it's too young to teach everything. So we teach a bit about the war, but more about what went on before '48. The bigger problem is when national holidays come up. How do you celebrate the Day of Independence *and* the Nakba? It's difficult. In the beginning the Oasis of Peace was like a co-dependent marriage: We thought everything had to be together. It took us many years to realize we can do things separately. If the parents of certain children want to celebrate the Day of Independence, we let them do something on their own. Same with Nakba day. Other events, like Christmas, Ein-ad-Hadda and Chanukah, we celebrate together."

There are other challenges. The primary school was given official status in 2000 by then–education minister Yossi Sarid. Recently the school decided to withdraw from its official status. Ahmed comments, "The government was meddling too much with how we wanted to teach. They were not letting us follow our mandate, which is to promote each other's religions and cultures. People in Israel grow up ignorant of the people next door to them. I can say for myself, even though I had an Israeli education, I had no interaction with Jews. I didn't know them as people. We are anti-separation here, even if it means getting less state funding."

I met a resident from the Oasis of Peace at the Zochrot office. I told him I was curious, wanted to hear more about the community. He was reluctant to talk, seemed tired of it. *Enough of the hype*, his tone suggested, *I just want to live.* Maybe it's not all it's cracked up to be. I mean, how do people live a normal life here under the constant scrutiny of the media, state inspectors and foreign visitors? Even the name sets itself up with pretty high expectations. Why not call it "Garden of Eden"?

Ahmed says it hasn't been easy, that there have been times when the community has barely held itself together. One such incident was in the mid-1990s when an IDF helicopter en route to a mission in Lebanon crashed and seventy-two soldiers were killed. One of the soldiers happened to be from the community. The Jews here knew the boy was fighting in Lebanon; the Palestinians didn't. "When we found out, we were upset. The crash happened a few days before an important Muslim holiday. Since the '82 invasion of Lebanon, Israeli forces tend to attack three or four days before Muslim holidays. It's a bit of a sore spot. Also, some Palestinians here have family living in the Lebanese refugee camps where these helicopters were heading. So, on the one hand, people were relieved the helicopter didn't make it to its final destination. On the other hand, the boy was from this community. We all knew him. Of course we were devastated, there was mourning. But the question was, how do we remember him? Do we make a ceremony for him as a soldier? As a member of the community? Does the family make a private ceremony? In the end, it was like everything here: We made a compromise. He was remembered as a boy in the community, but not a soldier."

Rana listens closely to Ahmed. She's intrigued, as I am. Unlike the peace of Abu Dalo and Shimon, the Oasis of Peace is fabricated, a wilful social experiment. Would Rana want to live in such a place? Would I? I think about what Ahmed says about compromise. Would living here make Rana change her belief in violence? If it didn't, how would I, her neighbour, live next door to that?

It makes me think about the second intifada. After the breakdown in talks between Barak and Arafat in 2000, after the dozens of suicide bombs, Qassam attacks, IDF incursions, missile assassinations and checkpoints, how many people actually want to live in the Oasis of Peace? I cite Sagi's statistic that sixty-eight percent of Israelis don't want to live in the same building as Palestinians.

Ahmed says, "What's incredible is that since October 2000 more people want to live here than ever before. We have a waiting list of over two hundred families, both Palestinians and Israelis. The way I explain it is 2000 made you choose what side you're on. There's no more sitting on the fence. Either you actively believe in coexistence or you don't."

"So are things getting better in Israel and Palestine?" I ask.

Ahmed replies, "I like to say, things are getting both better and worse. The worse we know about: more extremists, more killing, more fear and racism. The better is more people wanting to live at the Oasis of Peace. More binational schools opening up across the country. More Jews refusing to serve in the army. More Palestinians speaking out against violence."

Ahmed opens the door to the classroom. Ten children, aged five, run around screaming and yelling while the teacher tries to keep things somewhat in order. "Look, I'm not going to pretend. We are a very small minority; 250 people in a country of seven million. Are we making a difference? I don't know. My problem is, I have faith in people. I like to watch and listen to them. If you go around this country today, you'll see that people are tired. I've never seen them so tired before. If anyone were to give a real, concrete suggestion for how peace can happen, it would be like water. We're thirsty here. We're willing to compromise like never before."

A small boy runs and leaps into the arms of Ahmed. It's his son. On the walls are writings in Arabic and Hebrew, drawings of menorahs, Mecca and the Holy Trinity. Fingerpaintings. Songs. Made-up worlds. A thin and wiry girl grabs a toy out of a boy's hands. He starts to scream. How do you teach cooperation? What is the lesson, the right phrase? What would I say? *Hey kids, learn to get along!* Ahmed swings his boy lovingly in his arms. Outside, a black chain-link fence separates the gardens of the village from the road below.

IT'S GETTING COLDER in Jerusalem. The street is busy with traffic and we're standing outside a crowded café. Rana's waiting for the bus to take her to the station, and from there, to Tel Aviv, Haifa, then Tamra. She buttons up her corduroy coat. On the lapels of her jacket are two pins: One is of a woman wearing a headscarf made of the flag of Palestine. The other is a map of this country draped in the Palestinian flag.

"Thank you," she says.

"For what?"

"For letting me be part of this."

I don't say anything. We move to hug each other. I want this embrace to be real. I want to say, "Thank you for setting me on this path, for leading me to this unexpected place." Instead I think about Judith. I haven't talked to her in two years now. This Jerusalem is so different from the one I first imagined with her all those years ago. The clamour of rush hour, eighteen-wheel trucks wheezing exhaust, and me embracing Rana, half-heartedly. We let go of each other. Rana turns up the crowded street and disappears into the throng of people hurrying to their homes.

CHAPTER 42

The wall stands before us. Spotlight on cement. I think there's graffiti sprayed on, can't quite make out what it says, perhaps the word *ghetto* or *I am not a terrorist*. We see the wall in all its immensity; it takes us over, makes us small. After all, it is four times our size. Suddenly the wall comes apart. It opens up onto the space of our lives. Becomes the frame of a house. The screen we watch TV on. The walls are a painting, a landscape, our dreams—whatever we carry within us. They're dividers, items of conversation, the background music we forget at a dinner table. The walls have wheels, and the actors push them around as set pieces for the play. Become the next scene.

The play's called *Plonter*, Hebrew slang for mess. It's been created collectively by a cast that's half Palestinian and half Israeli. It took them seven months to finish it using a process that involved bringing in real stories about the effects of the occupation on Israeli and Palestinian society. The scenes are done in both Arabic and Hebrew, with the actors playing both Palestinians and Israelis. The play is on stage at the Cameri, the biggest theatre in Israel: This is for a mainstream, urban audience. Impressive. But what is even more remarkable is the audience I'm sitting with is made up of high school students. It's a Tuesday matinee performance, and the fifteen and sixteen year olds have been bused in. They're playing with their cellphones, trying to sit next to each other, loving the fact they're away from their desks for an afternoon. When the lights go down, they shut up.

The first scene: A Tel Aviv Jewish couple has invited an Arab pair for dinner as a way of showing how liberal and open-minded they are. Instead of talking to the Arabs, the Jewish woman delivers a long, rambling monologue about shopping, the art of good hummus and, well, anything to avoid conversation.

There is pain on both sides of the wall—a Jew dies in a suicide bombing, a young Palestinian is shot by the IDF. Three Palestinian children play "Who will be the martyr?" There is humour as well. A Palestinian on a Tel Aviv bus is in a bad mood and his anger makes him suspect. He's asked to get off by the driver. His reaction: "Do you want me to undress and show you I don't have a bomb?" (This is based on the actor's own experience.) The people on the bus collectively say, "Yes." He climbs onto his seat and does a slow burlesque number, proving he doesn't have explosives attached to his body.

In another scene, a soldier kills a child because the child was holding a plastic toy machine gun. He's asked to file a report. The captain changes the wording from "child" to "young adult." "But he was a child," says the soldier. "That word is too sympathetic," says the captain. "It demands too much emotion."

The most powerful scene takes place in the West Bank, where three Israeli soldiers tie an eleven-year-old boy to a pole for throwing stones. They blindfold him, say they're going to shoot. The boy is terrified, the soldiers count to three, they shoot at the air and the boy shits his pants. The soldiers laugh their heads off and take him home to his father. When they tell the boy's dad that he threw stones, the father reaches over to the kid's shoulder. He makes like he's going to hug him. Instead he throws him to the floor and kicks the shit out of his kid. The soldiers leave appalled. End of scene.

I turn to my right and see Mrs. Blintzkrieg sitting in the row in front of me. She's completely engrossed in the play, but I tap her on the shoulder anyway.

ME: Did you ever do anything like what these soldiers are
      doing?

MRS. B.: Of course not.

ME: Did you ever lose somebody in battle?

MRS. B.: Who hasn't lost? Who hasn't paid in blood?

ME: If you love Israel so much, why did you move to Canada?

MRS. B.: Life is hard here. Nobody wants to live with war all the
      time.

We both look at the stage.

MRS. B.: What do you want me to say, Shalom? I was a bad
      teacher? That Bialik was an evil place?

ME: I'd like you to say, we can do better.

MRS. B.: We can always do better.

CHAPTER 43

It's Shabbat, a quiet day, so there's not much traffic on the roads. We whiz around a large roundabout. Heidi, the war photographer I was put in touch with by a Canadian magazine, is driving. We're going to see Samer. She pulls the car over to the side of the road onto a pile of gravel.

"Where are we?" I ask.

"Qalandia checkpoint."

I don't recognize a thing. The hill where the soldiers in the jeep shot at Crazy Boy is gone. They've levelled the landscape so it's easier to see everything.

The new checkpoint's a large white complex with a fair-sized booth for a soldier to sit in and collect ID cards. The booth is several metres from the cars, has bulletproof glass, and a speaker on the outside so the soldier can talk at the passengers through a microphone. It's eerily sterile. My first thought is it seems much improved; things are not as chaotic as they were the last time I was here. There are no vendors, no buses, no eternity of lineups. There's none of the humiliation of waiting. I wonder if people are simply not crossing anymore. Or has the system become more efficient? I walk to the white building. Instead of a walkway covered in camouflage, there's a turnstile for foot passengers. An electronic red sign reads, "Welcome to Atarot Terminal" and can be seen from the large waiting room. There's enough space for several hundred people, I figure. Only now there are three or four people waiting. For what?

Back outside, the soldier behind the glass screams through the mic at the people in their cars: "Get out! Out of the car! I want you to walk! WALK! Show me your ID! Your ID! SHOW IT TO ME!" I look for the barbed wire fence that Sam burnt his trash next to, but it's been replaced by the eight-metre-high wall. Huge slabs of concrete make my memory of the field he'd pointed to just that—a memory.

IT'S GOOD TO SEE Samer again. The big news is he's quit smoking. He's also allowed to enter Israel and Gaza from the hours of seven in the morning until seven at night for work purposes. I guess that's an improvement.

"So how are things?" I ask.

Samer dips his pita into hummus. "You want the honest answer, the situation is total shit. And it'll only get worse."

"How so?"

"My friend, Fatah is shit, and Hamas is in power. Even the Christians support Hamas. You think *they* want a fundamentalist Islamic country? People are tired of corruption. They want basic services and Hamas will actually provide that. And then what happens? The world says, *You picked the wrong people.* Fucking shit, man. Did you know that Israel encouraged the creation of Hamas in the 1980s?"

No, I didn't know that.

"So we're a democracy. Great! Abbas is a coward, and Israel keeps us locked in cages. It won't be long before there's civil war. We'll be fighting over the scraps."

"What's wrong with Abbas?" I ask.

"Look at this country he's fighting to give us, this Palestine. Would you want to live in it?"

I think about the wall, the terminal and the woman screaming behind the window. It's not very appealing.

"Look, Arafat was a corrupt asshole. But one thing I will always respect was he said no to Barak."

"What was wrong with the offer?"

"In the 1990s, when Rabin was talking peace, he continued to build settlements at a ridiculous rate. Barak was even worse— he built them ten times faster than Netanyahu.* So where is this Palestinian state going to be? How are we going to get to Gaza, by magic carpet? Here in the West Bank, every village is cut off from the other because of the settlements. You saw the checkpoint. It's a border. They've already decided what land they're taking. We're getting the shit of the shit. Don't even get me started on the refugees or Jerusalem." Samer talks about the highways built for only settlers and soldiers to travel on, and a new law proposed by the IDF to make it illegal for Israelis to drive Palestinians from the West Bank.

Samer asks me what I've been doing since I've been back in Israel. I tell him about Eytan and Zochrot. He's surprised.

"Really? You mean an Israeli is talking like this?" For a moment there is almost hope in his voice.

"They're in the minority, but it's a kind of crack in the wall, as Eytan puts it."

"This is huge, my friend. A station like Al Jazeera would be very interested in this story. If the government lets me go to Tel Aviv, I will. This is unexpected. And for once, the unexpected is a good thing," he says, writing Eytan's information down in a notebook.

"Samer, if there was a way to fix things, what would you do?"

He stops writing and puts his hands on the table. He breathes, it seems, for the first time since I've seen him.

"Separate Church from State. Throw this religion out. Forget about it! No more Jews can do this, Palestinians can't. Make it one equal state, and we'll turn this into a great country."

---

* For a more detailed account on the failure of Oslo and the Barak–Arafat talks, see Robert Fisk's *The Great War for Civilisation*, pp. 500–56.

I tell Samer I don't think too many Jews are going to go for a one-state solution any time soon.

"My friend, you waited two thousand years. We'll wait that long too."

CHAPTER 44

I go to the wall. Head down to the East Jerusalem bus station, hop on the local bus to Abu Dis. Rows of dark clouds march threateningly toward Jerusalem from the north. The day is cold. When I get off with the piles of Palestinians, I find myself face to face with the wall. Children chase each other, play tag where the road ends and turns into rubble. Their grandmothers call out, point at the sky, warn the children of the imminent storm.

Nothing is new here. So proclaimeth the history books. War alters geography, divides and conquers, swallows civilizations whole. Over time: ruins that become museum exhibits. This wall raises the question, what will its legacy be? In three hundred years, will people line up like they do for the Great Wall of China? Pay to get in for the tour and photo op? How will this structure be presented? "This fence was used to keep out Arab terrorist marauders." Or: "This wall was used to confine a refugee people." Will it be pieces in a museum, saying, "Now that we live in peace, see the example that war once brought?" The answer depends on how history sides with these current events. How this "situation" will be resolved.

I've come here because I don't have any answers, only more questions. The wall stands to divide this house, constantly at war. With its enemies, and itself.

If I were a teacher at Bialik, what would I teach? Which side of Israel would I show my children? I turn my back and walk out a few dozen metres toward Jerusalem. Beyond those hills to the north sits the Hebrew University. I think, that's what I'd like to teach the children of Bialik: the Israel of great thinkers and dazzling writers, of universities and doctors, of pioneers who braved the elements and poets who reveal the soul—the Jewish soul, the human soul too.

But if I returned to the wall, to Abu Dis, what would I tell the children about this? Would I describe this village split in two by a wall three times the size of the one that divided Berlin? How would I explain that families are separated in the name of security, and olive groves taken from their farmers for the survival of the Jewish nation? Would I show the children of Bialik pictures of the graffiti "Abu Dis Ghetto = Warsaw Ghetto"? Would I teach what's on the other side of this fence—the refugee camps where the only Jews those children know are the ones with a gun?

Likely I'd have to stay on this side of the wall. The territories are a sensitive issue. I'd pass around the Keren Kayemet box, the children would put in their money, and this time I'd have to talk. I'd tell them about the problems on this side, the dozens of unrecognized villages of internal refugees, filled with people who want to become part of the State of Israel but whom the government refuses to support.* I wouldn't remain silent, but I also wouldn't be able to explain why one man will say to another, "Get out, this is not your country. You are not wanted."

WHEN I REST my head against cold concrete, I'm asking God, "Please, help us find a way out."

I'm thinking about Moses again. What's God been doing with him all these years? Surely He didn't just get rid of the guy. The Holy One must've kept his favourite prophet around at least for conversation.

---

* For a fuller account of the unrecognized villages, see David Grossman's *Sleeping on a Wire*, pp. 80–100.

Some intelligent debate from time to time, a drinking buddy. What if God suddenly had a change of heart? What if he decided to give Moses the surprise of his life?

"Moses," God says. "You've been a good and patient man. I've decided it's time. I'm taking you to the Holy Land."

"Are you serious?" Moses says.

"Of course," God says.

God lifts Moses out of heaven and guides him through the air. Moses is beside himself with joy. He's waited over four thousand years for this day. Flying through the sky, Moses finally sees the Negev desert. He sees the stunning turquoise of malachite, the cold grey gypsum and the pink halite stone. But the desert isn't completely empty, as Moses expected. He sees the miracles of kibbutzim with date trees and irrigation tracts, Ben-Gurion's dream to make the desert bloom. "Farms in the desert. Impressive. And we had to eat manna?" Then he sees the Dead Sea, which is not looking too good these days, but Moses doesn't know the difference. God scoops up some clay so he can feel the rich nutrients in the soil. "Fantastic," Moses says, rubbing the clay in his hands. "The earth is wonderfully rich." Then God shows Moses Tel Aviv and he says, "Interesting," because what does Moses know of cities? But he likes the sea, and he can hear writers arguing in cafés, and there is art in the galleries and plays in the theatres and scantily clad women on the beaches. God leads Moses to the Galilee and its farms, the villages tucked into hills, the Golan Heights and its ragged cliffs, Mount Hermon with all its snow. "Impressive," says Moses. "Not at all like I imagined." He sees it from above: the lemon trees and their lemons, the shepherds and their sheep, the ruins of Caesarea, the cargo ships in the port of Haifa, the smokestacks of Hadera. And where there is industry there are cities, and in the cities there are people— Ethiopians and Russians, Moroccans and Lithuanians, Chinese and Americans, Thais and Kurds, rushing, sleeping, thieving, working, praying, birthing, singing.

"Who are all these people?" Moses asks. "And what are they doing?"

"It's a nation. Just like I promised," says God.

"These are my people?"

"For the most part, yes," says God, proudly.

Moses is amazed. He feels tears welling up in his eyes. He can't believe the Promise is fulfilled. "Can we see Mount Moriah?" he whispers.

God says, "Unfortunately Moriah's a little complicated. But I have something I'd like to show you instead."

And God takes Moses toward Jerusalem. Moses sees the hills rising past Latrun. He sees the Dome of the Rock, which covers Mount Moriah, and he sees the Wailing Wall and the Tower of David, the old city carved out of old stone. It's beautiful, Moses thinks. Then God takes Moses away from Jerusalem, past the Mount of Olives with the graves of famous Jews, toward Abu Dis. Moses sees what looks like a giant scar in the land.

"What's that?" Moses asks.

God says, "It's what I wanted to show you. A fence."

"What's it for?"

"Keeping their enemies out," God answers.

"Why do they need to build it?"

"Remember your Bible, Moses: 'You shall make no covenant with them and their gods. They shall not remain in your land.'"

"I didn't realize you were being so literal," says Moses, his eyes following the long route of the wall.

God says, "You know how it is. There are always sinners and evil-doers. The ones who don't pray to me."

"Couldn't you just keep them out yourself?"

"No," says God. "This wall is a sign of their devotion to me."

"Hmm." Moses doesn't know what to say. "Let me get this straight. For six thousand years, you've commanded your people to live here.

They suffer through one period of history after another, hoping to return. Now they do, and build a wall as an homage to Your will?"

"That's one way of looking at it."

"I don't like it."

"What do you mean?"

"It's ugly, for starters."

"It's *effective*," says God. "This wall is peace."

"Peace," says Moses, looking at the tanks and rocket launchers below. "How so?"

"They have their side, and we have ours."

"That's not peace," Moses says. "That's a cage."

God is taken aback. He thought Moses would be excited.

Moses says, "Don't take this the wrong way, God. You're an artist, a pretty good one. But reality is a hell of a lot messier than good on one side, bad on the other. When I was in the desert, I thought there wasn't a Promised Land. That is, it existed, but it wasn't a place we'd ever reach. I liked that idea. I thought it was yours."

God doesn't say anything, and Moses isn't sure if he's offended the Holy One or not. Moses and God look down at the mess of concrete below. Moses entertains another thought: Maybe in the world of humans, Israel is the Promise fulfilled. It's the most real of all places. God likes the wall because its ugliness is honest; it holds up a mirror to His people.

Moses wonders if God is listening, like he is listening, to the ones on the other side, wanting to get in. They're His people too. These children of Abraham, Isaac and Ishmael.

God starts to cry.

"God?" Moses says. "Are you okay?"

No, God thinks, but doesn't say. God doesn't utter a word. His tears turn into a storm over Tel Aviv (giant gales, torrential downpour). His weeping turns into large stones of hail over Galilee. And over Jerusalem it starts to snow. Flakes so big you can taste them on

your tongue and think you can follow them. Which I do, all the way
back to Jerusalem, as though God's tears were guiding me, as though
His cold tears could lead me through this mess.

I GO BACK to the house one last time, but Shimon isn't there. So I
go to the house of Mary, the one in between, and knock on the door.
A man opens the door and greets me.

"Where's Mary?" I ask.

"Doesn't live here," he says in Hebrew. "Didn't pay the rent, so Abu
Dalo kicked her out." Roy's his name; he's a painter and he invites me
in for a cup of tea. There are no lights on. A few streaks of sky from
the snowy Jerusalem day filter in through the windows.

Roy's back is turned while he fills the kettle with water. He says,
"You know, I get a good feeling living in this house. I like to know
there's this history behind it."

"You mean the fact a Palestinian owns it?"

"That's part of it. But I also feel like I'm living in between an
argument. I like that."

"Why?"

"I grew up in the old city. And you know, there's nowhere else in
Jerusalem like this place. It's quiet here, but not completely. If it were
totally peaceful I'd go out of my mind. It's like I need to hear
both sides of the debate in order to feel alive. I don't know how else
to say it."

Roy asks why I'm so interested in this place. I explain.

Then he says, "Hey, I should tell you. There's been a land surveyor
from the city coming by lately."

"Really? What does he want?"

"They want to widen the road in front of this house. So more
people can get to the shopping mall from this side of town."

"What does that mean?"

"They'll tear down this house. And the one Shimon lives in."

"Is that for sure?"

"Look, nothing's for sure in this country. But I just thought you should know. They've been by."

We drink our tea in silence. Roy shows me a series of paintings he's working on, landscapes of the area outside the house. I look at the clock. My plane's leaving tonight. With the snow I'd better get my stuff together and head to the airport before the roads close.

When I leave, it's snowing even harder. I pass the house one last time, think I see a figure on the other side of the living room window. He's staring back at me, won't avert his gaze. It's me I'm seeing. I turn left at the train tracks. The skies are dark and heavy over Jerusalem. Either God is still weeping or there's a hell of a cold front moving in from the north. The tracks, the stones, memory—everything is quickly coated in white. The children, the cars, the trees, the falafel man; the whole world screams in wonder and fear. Nobody knows what to do with God's cold and heavy tears. And there's something free in this, to be crossing into the storm.

A Note from the Author

I have taken several liberties in the writing of this book. In the interests of maintaining dramatic tension, I compressed time. Certain events and conversations that took place over many months or in several instances now occur in a shorter time frame. For example, my first conversation with Rana at the café, and what I learn, combine many conversations into one. The childhood memories were also approached in this manner; often I merged various memories into a single scene. For the Bialik sequences I chose a style that mimics a child's perspective on the world: exaggeration tinged with magic realism.

This book is not meant to reflect what Bialik is like today; it is my memory and opinion of how things were some twenty-five years ago. Times have changed, as have political awareness and teaching methods. And the facilities have expanded to include a really nice playground.

The "Dunam after Dunam" song was written by Yehoshua Friedman and the music was composed by Menashe Ravina. While we sang many songs on those Friday afternoons when the Keren Kayemet box was passed around, I chose this one because I believe it represents the sentiments of those days.

In the Toronto sections, I have re-created dialogue according to memory. In the Israel parts of the book, I based some of my writing on notes taken during interviews. Occasionally I used a voice recorder. Other events in Israel are reconstructed from memory.

For reasons of privacy, G. is a composite character, as are the Engineer, Yankl, Max, Ruthie, Rainbow and Yosef. Mrs. Blintzkrieg is a fictional character based on some of my childhood memories. While Jacob is based on a real friend, certain details encompass other friendships.

I have changed many of the names in this book.

Glossary

Aliyah (aliyot, plural): Literally means "ascent" or "going up." It refers to a Jew who immigrates to Israel from the Diaspora. [Hebrew]

Baruch Hashem: Blessed is the Name, i.e., God. [Hebrew]

Bimah: The elevated area in a synagogue, much like a stage, where the kantor or rabbi leads the congregation in prayer. The Torah is also read on the bimah. [Hebrew]

Bubele: A term of endearment meaning honey, darling, sweetheart. [Yiddish]

Chametz: Leavened bread. [Hebrew]

Charoset: A very tasty garnish on the Seder plate that represents the mortar the Israelite slaves used in Egypt to make bricks. It's made of walnuts, cinnamon, apples and sugar. It is recommended that you do not try to build houses with charoset. [Hebrew]

Chazzan: A trained professional who leads the congregants of a shul in song. [Hebrew]

Chumash: The Torah or Five Books of Moses. [Hebrew]

Chuppah: A canopy used at Jewish weddings. It usually consists of a sheet held by four poles above the bride and groom. The chuppah is meant to represent the home the husband and wife will build together. [Hebrew]

Davening: Praying. [Yinglish]

Dunam: A unit of area that originated in the Ottoman Empire. Its standard was forty paces in length and breadth. This would fluctuate, of course, depending on your shoe size. Likely for this reason (and due to the small size of British feet), British Mandate Palestine developed a standard of one thousand metres squared. This measurement is still in use in Israel today. [Turkish]

Frum: An Orthodox Jew. [Yiddish]

Gonif: A thief, a crook or a clever person. [Yiddish]

Ha-aravi: The Arab. [Hebrew]

Haganah: From 1920 to 1948, a Jewish paramilitary organization in British Mandate Palestine that served to protect Jewish settlers from Arab attack (the right-wing groups Irgun and Lehi splintered off from the Haganah and were more radicalized). After May 1948, the Israel Defence Forces succeeded the Haganah. [Hebrew]

Halachma: An ancient Aramaic prayer sung at the Passover Seder, where all those who are hungry are invited to join the Seder table.

Halakah: *See* Laws of Halakah.

Halutzim: Literally "pioneers." Mostly coming from Eastern Europe, they were the original Jewish settlers of Ottoman and British Palestine who believed in the virtues of collective labour to liberate the land of Israel for the Jewish people. Their somewhat ridiculous-looking hats were designed to protect them from the sun, wind and rain. [Hebrew]

Hatikva: Literally "the hope." Hatikva is the name of the Israeli national anthem, which Naftali Herz Imber wrote as a poem in 1878. Its last lines are:

> Our hope is not yet lost / the Hope of two thousand years / to be a free nation in our own land / the land of Zion and Jerusalem. [Hebrew]

Irgun (IZL): A clandestine militant Zionist group that operated in British Mandate Palestine from 1931 to 1948.

Keren Kayemet L'Yisrael: Jewish National Fund. [Hebrew]

Ketuvah: Marriage certificate. [Hebrew]

Kippah: A skullcap worn by observant Jewish males. [Hebrew]

Kittel: A white robe worn by religious Jews during the High Holy Days and other major festivals. A groom will wear a kittel at his wedding, and the dead are also buried in them. The robe signifies purity and simplicity. [Yiddish]

Kol Nidre: One of the holiest prayers in Judaism chanted in synagogues on the eve of Yom Kippur. Also denotes that entire evening of prayer. [Hebrew]

Kugel: A tasty, though sometimes overly dry, potato pie. [Yiddish]

Lamed: The twelfth letter of the Hebrew alphabet.

Laws of Halakah: Known as "Jewish Law," these involve the practical application of the 613 commandments of the Torah, plus the laws of the Talmud and later rabbinical interpretations.

Lokshn: A noodle or a very thin person. The former is often used in chicken soup. The latter doesn't eat enough chicken soup. [Yiddish]

Mem-sofit: Mem is the thirteenth letter of the Hebrew alphabet. When Mem put at the end of a word, the letter is called "Mem-sofit."

Midrash: Literally "commentary" or "interpretation." Midrash usually refers to the analysis and exegesis of the Tanakh (see "Tanakh" below). [Hebrew]

Mishnah: One of the two parts of the Talmud (the other is the Gemara). There are six books of the Mishnah, and it is the first written account of the oral law.

Mit chayim: "With life." [Yiddish]

Mohel: The Great Circumciser. [Yiddish]

Nisan: The seventh month of the Hebrew lunar calendar. Pesach falls in Nisan.

The Pale of Settlement: An area from western Russia to Eastern Europe where Jews were allowed to live from the eighteenth to the early twentieth centuries. Catherine the Great first established The Pale in 1791.

Peyes: The long sideburn curls worn by Orthodox Jewish males. [Yiddish]

Shesh besh: Backgammon. [Hebrew]

Sheva Brachot: Literally "the seven blessings." These are the blessings recited for the bride and groom at a traditional Jewish wedding. These blessings are also recited for the week following the wedding at nightly festive meals in honour of the newlyweds. [Hebrew]

Shin: The twenty-first letter of the Hebrew alphabet.

Shmendrik: A foolish, clueless person. While there are many variations on the word idiot in Yiddish (like schlemiel, schlemazel, shmegegge), a shmendrik denotes the type of idiot who is a mama's boy. "I hope one day, shmendrik, that you grow up and finally become a mentsch." [Yiddish]

Shmutsik: Really, really dirty. [Yiddish]

Shukran: Thank you. [Arabic]

Siddur: Prayer book. [Hebrew]

Simcha: Comes from the Hebrew "rejoicing." A simcha is a happy occasion, a party. [Yiddish]

Tanakh: An acronym for the Hebrew Bible derived from the initial Hebrew letters of the names of the three parts: Torah (the Five Books of Moses), Nevi'im (Prophets) and Ketuvim (Writings).

Treyf: Unkosher food, as in, "I love lobster, even though it's treyf." [Yiddish]

Tsitses: The fringes on the corners of the prayer shawl. [Yiddish]

Ulpan: A school for the intensive study of Hebrew. [Hebrew]

Vav: Sixth letter of the Hebrew alphabet.

Zaatar: An Arabic spice mixture containing thyme, toasted sesame seeds, salt and oregano. [Arabic]

Sources and Selected Readings

Books

Amichai, Yehuda. *Open Closed Open*. Translated by Chana Bloch and Chana Kronfeld. Harcourt, New York (2000).

Barghouti, Mourid. *I Saw Ramallah*. Translated by Ahdaf Soueif. Anchor Books, New York (2003).

Bialik, C.N. *Selected Poems*. Edited and translated by David Aberbach. Overlook Duckworth, New York (2004).

Buber, Martin. *On Judaism*. Edited by Nahum N. Glatzer. Schocken Books, New York (1967).

Daniel, Jean. *The Jewish Prison: A Rebellious Meditation on the State of Judaism*. Translated by Charlotte Mandell. Melville House, Hoboken, New Jersey (2005).

Darwish, Mahmoud. *Unfortunately, It Was Paradise*. Translated by Munir Akash, Carolyn Forché, Sinan Antoon and Amira El-Zein. University of California Press, Berkeley, California (2003).

Fisk, Robert. *The Great War for Civilisation: The Conquest of the Middle East*. Harper Perennial, London (2006).

Grossman, David. *The Yellow Wind*. Translated by Haim Watzman. FSG, New York (1988).

———. *Sleeping on a Wire: Conversations with Palestinians in Israel*. Translated from the Hebrew by Haim Watzman. Farrar, Straus and Giroux, New York (1993).

Habiby, Emile. *The Secret Life of Saeed, the Ill-Fated Pessoptimist: A Palestinian Who Became a Citizen of Israel*. Translated by Salma Khadra Jayussi and Trevor Le Gassick. Vantage Press, New York (1982).

Hass, Amira. *Reporting from Ramallah*. Edited and translated by Leah Jones. Semiotext(e), Cambridge, Massachusetts. (2003).

Hussein, Hussein Abu, and Fiona McKay. *Access Denied: Palestinian Land Rights in Israel*. Zed Books, London (2003).

Kurzman, Dan. *Soldier of Peace: The Life and Times of Yitzhak Rabin*. HarperCollins, New York (1998).

Masalha, Nur. *The Politics of Denial: Israel and the Palestinian Refugee Problem*. Pluto Press, London (2003).

347

Morris, Benny. *Righteous Victims: A History of the Zionist–Arab Conflict, 1881–2001.* Vintage, New York (2001).

———. *The Birth of the Palestinian Refugee Problem Revisited.* Cambridge University Press, Cambridge, U.K. (2004).

Nathan, Susan. *The Other Side of Israel: My Journey across the Jewish/Arab Divide.* Doubleday, New York (2005).

Oz, Amos. *A Tale of Love and Darkness.* Translated by Nicholas de Lange. Harcourt, Orlando, Florida (2004).

———. *How to Cure a Fanatic.* Princeton University Press, Princeton, New Jersey (2006).

Segev, Tom. *1949: The First Israelis.* Henry Holt and Company, New York (1998).

———. *Elvis in Jerusalem: Post-Zionism and the Americanization of Israel.* Translated by Haim Watzman. Metropolitan Books, New York (2002).

Articles

Ashkenazi, Eli, and Jack Khoury. "Poll: 68% of Jews Would Refuse to Live in the Same Building as an Arab." *Haaretz.* March 22, 2006. http://www.haaretz.com/hasen/pages/ShArt.jhtml?itemNo=697458&contrassID=1&subContrassID=7.

Associated Press. "Matriarch Who Lost Grandson in Conflict Turns into Suicide Bomber." *The International Herald Tribune.* November 23, 2006. http://www.iht.com/articles/ap/2006/11/23/africa/ME_GEN_Grandmother_Bomber.php.

Eckstein, Rabbi. "The Bible on Jewish Links to the Holy Land." 2007. http://www.jewishvirtuallibrary.org/jsource/Judaism/biblejew.html.

Ettinger, Yair. "IDF Told Villagers They'd Be Home in Two Weeks" [about Ikrit and Biram]. *Haaretz.* June 27, 2003. http://www.haaretz.com/hasen/pages/ShArt.jhtml?itemNo=312084.

Shatz, Adam. "A Poet's Palestine as Metaphor." December 21, 2001. http://www.mahmouddarwish.com/english/articles.htm.

Shavit, Ari. "Survival of the Fittest? An Interview with Benny Morris." *Haaretz.* January 9, 2004. http://www.counterpunch.org/shavit01162004.html.

United Nations Relief and Works Agency website. http://www.un.org/unrwa/publications/index.html.

Other

All Bible quotes are from the JPS Hebrew-English Tanakh.

The "Dunam after Dunam" song translation is from an article by Uri Avnery called "Dunam after Dunam." http://www.vopj.org/issues71.htm.

The excerpt from the C.N. Bialik poem "To the Bird" is translated by Jonathan Garfinkel.

The Jewish prayers are from *The Complete ArtScroll Siddur.*

Acknowledgments

I am grateful to the many people I talked to during the past five years who made me question the way I think about Israel and Palestine and were patient with my ignorance on the subject. Their opinions drove me to read in the hopes of untangling some truths. In addition to sources, I have included a selected bibliography of books that educated, inspired and challenged me along the way.

I am indebted to some of the ideas of French intellectual and journalist Jean Daniel, who wrote the book *The Jewish Prison*. It is a profound meditation on religion, nationalism and history.

I had immense help from Samer Shalabi beyond these pages. On the return trip, Heidi Levine also helped greatly; unfortunately, the dramatic needs of the book made it impossible for me to make this evident in the narrative. Max's patience, Torah and hospitality were greatly appreciated, and Rabbi Spero was always welcoming and encouraged my questions. Barak reminded me to avoid the cliché. Eytan Bronstein sat with me for many an hour and was an inspiration. Susan Nathan welcomed me into her home, and the Diab clan was warm and generous. Thanks to Ahmed and Omar at the Oasis of Peace for their time, and to the lawyer Usama Halabi, who sat and talked about his passion. David Fingrut, co-Bialiknik, voiced his support and criticisms of the book. Judith, thank you for your support of this endeavour. And thanks to Rana, for setting me out on this journey and remaining a friend throughout.

I began *Ambivalence* thanks to the prodding of Rosemary Sullivan and Ian Pearson. I'm grateful to John Pearce, my agent, who took this on at an early stage. Goldberry Long, Paul Quarrington,

Greg Hollingshead and André Alexis offered encouragement and thoughts along the way. Paul Thompson and Anne Anglin rooted from the sidelines. The Vodka Poets Society saw early versions of this book and knew I could do better. Big thanks to Barbara Berson, editor extraordinaire, for believing in me and asking the hard questions. Thanks to David Davidar and Penguin Canada for taking the risk.

Thanks to the arts councils—Toronto, Ontario and Canada. Without their generous support this book would not have been possible to complete. Thanks to *The Walrus* for publishing "A House Divided," and to Marni Jackson for her fine editing. And thanks to the Banff Centre Writing Studio and Gibraltar Point Centre for the Arts for providing me with time and space to work.

Medeine Tribinevicius, your patience, love and insight from beginning to end were invaluable.

Finally, I'd like to thank all the friends, teachers and family who appear in this book. You have made me who I am.

TORONTO–BANFF–VILNIUS–JERUSALEM (2005–2007)